WRITERS AND THEIR WORK: NO. 118

Trollope

by

HUGH SYKES DAVIES

Published for the British Council
and the National Book League
by Longmans, Green & Co

Three shillings and sixpence net

'To be known as somebody... is to me much', wrote Anthony Trollope when in middle age he had achieved respect and worldly success as one of the most popular of Victorian novelists. In childhood he had suffered from his father's financial troubles, and his craving for recognition and friendship was a reaction to what Trollope described in his *Autobiography* as the 'absolute isolation of my school position' as an impoverished dayboy at Harrow.

Trollope started his career as a junior clerk in the Post Office in London but, after seven years, he was given a job in Ireland and it was here that he started his first novel. He believed that his object in writing was to make money yet, as Mr Sykes Davies shows, his writing satisfied deeper needs. Trollope 'became exactly what he wished, the moral historian of men and women in the middle range' so that, as Trollope wrote in his *Autobiography*, 'my readers might recognize human beings like to themselves and not feel themselves to be carried away among gods or demons'. As Henry James remarked, 'His great, his incontestable merit, was a complete appreciation of the usual'. In the Barsetshire novels, as in the later political series, there are a vast number of characters, many of them set in motion by the conflict between love and the Victorian sense of property. This conflict saved Trollope from the trouble of making plots for, as Trollope observed, 'When I sit down to write a novel, I do not at all know... and I do not very much care how it is to end.' A few years after Trollope's death, Henry James paid him a remarkable tribute: 'Trollope will remain one of the most trustworthy, though not one of the most eloquent of writers who have helped the heart of man to know itself... A race is fortunate when it has a good deal of the sort of imagination—of imaginative feeling—that had fallen to the share of Anthony Trollope; and in this possession our English race is not poor.'

Mr Hugh Sykes Davies is a Fellow of St John's College, Cambridge.

Bibliographical Series
of Supplements to 'British Book News'
on Writers and Their Work

★

GENERAL EDITOR
Geoffrey Bullough

¶ ANTHONY TROLLOPE was born on 24 April 1815 in London. He died on 6 December 1882 at Harting, Sussex.

TROLLOPE
from a drawing by 'Sem'

TROLLOPE

by

HUGH SYKES DAVIES

PUBLISHED FOR
THE BRITISH COUNCIL
AND THE NATIONAL BOOK LEAGUE
BY LONGMANS, GREEN & CO

LONGMANS, GREEN & CO. LTD.
48 Grosvenor Street, London, W.1

*Associated companies, branches and
representatives throughout the world*

*First published 1960
Reprinted 1967*
© Hugh Sykes Davies 1960

*Printed in Great Britain by
F. Mildner & Sons, London, E.C.1*

TROLLOPE

I

ANTHONY TROLLOPE was born in 1815. His father was a barrister, learned in law, but of difficult temper and unpractical in the management of his affairs. The first twenty years of his son's life were overshadowed by the gradual failure of the legal practice, and by a series of ill planned and worse executed manoeuvres to make money in other ways.

The ruin of the family was delayed, and at the last made less ruinous, by Anthony's mother, Frances Trollope. One of her husband's weirdest schemes was to set up a great bazaar in Cincinnati, and he despatched his wife to America to supervise its building, in a striking medley of classical and oriental styles. Funds were exhausted before it could be stocked with goods, and Mrs Trollope found herself in penury. She learned from this crisis not only that she must herself take on a great part of the task of supporting her family, but also a possible means of performing it. On her return to England, she wrote her first book, a racy and rather acid study of the American way of life. It was successful, and she went on at once to write novels and other travelogues. When her husband finally became bankrupt in 1834, she took the family to Belgium, and supported them by her pen, never laying it aside for long, even while she saw to the housekeeping, and tended the deathbeds of her favourite son, her husband, and her youngest daughter. Her later days were happier and more prosperous, but she went on writing indefatigably when the financial need had passed. When she died, at the age of eighty-three, she had written forty-one books, and her annual rate of production had not been far below that achieved by Anthony himself. They were both late starters in literature: he was forty when his first book was published, and she fifty-two. For both of them, the first conscious aim in writing was to make money; but once started, they both found that it satisfied in them needs much deeper than that of money.

Possibly Trollope inherited from his mother some qualities of mind and spirit that favoured quick and copious writing, and certainly he had before him her example of what might be made of these qualities. But the deeper needs which writing came to satisfy were the unhappy by-product of his father's misfortunes. When he was seven, he went to Harrow as a day-boy. At twelve, he was moved to his father's old school, Winchester, but taken away three years later because the bills had not been paid, and could not be paid. Long before his departure, the other boys had known of the unpaid bills, and had made use of their knowledge. 'It is the nature of boys to be cruel,' he mildly observed of their doings when he wrote of them in later life. But worse was to follow, for he went back to Harrow again as a day-boy. By this time, his mother was in America, and he was living with his father, unkempt and uncouth, in a gloomy tumbledown farm-house, from which he tramped twice a day through muddy lanes to sit among the well fed and smartly dressed boarders. 'The indignities I endured are not to be described,' he wrote later. 'I was never able to overcome—or even attempt to overcome—the absolute isolation of my school position. Of the cricket-ground or racket-court I was allowed to know nothing. And yet I longed for these things with an exceeding great longing. I coveted popularity with a coveting which was almost mean. It seemed to me that there would be an Elysium in the intimacy of those very boys I was bound to hate because they hated me. Something of the disgrace of my school-days has clung to me all through life.'

He was removed from Harrow at last by the bankruptcy of his father, and went with the rest of the family to Belgium, a useless and aimless witness of their successive deaths. At the age of nineteen, however, he was wangled by family friends into the Post Office as a junior clerk; competitive examinations to the Civil Service being still to come. In later life, he wrote and spoke vehemently against that mode of recruitment, on the ground that it would certainly have excluded him, and that the Service would have lost a good official by his exclusion. Probably he was right on both points, yet it would not have been easy for any department to function with more than one or two Anthony Trollopes on its strength. He was unpunctual and insubordinate, and he got into 'scrapes'. Once, in an argument with the secretary, he banged a table so hard that it catapulted an inkwell into his chief's face: since the Post Office was at that time ruled by a retired Colonel, he was lucky to have escaped dismissal or something worse. And one day the office was invaded by a lady under a vast bonnet, with a basket on her arm, crying loudly, 'Anthony Trollope, when are you going to marry my daughter?' He did not have to marry the young lady, but he admitted that 'these little incidents were all against me in the office'.

This period of his life lasted for seven years, and it is the one period of which he has told us very little. He lived in poor lodgings, spent much time in bars, got into debt and made his one and only acquaintance with a money-lender. He began, however, to make friends and, after the disgrace of his schooldays, it was much to him that men of his own age were willing to like him, to talk with him, and to spend their week-ends walking with him. In the office, he kept his place, largely because he turned out to be very good at writing letters, and in the end even his 'scrapes' did him a backhanded service, for the ink-stained Colonel recommended him for a job in Ireland, as the best way to be rid of him.

It was a very great service, however backhanded. Ireland accomplished a transformation in him hardly less dramatic than that which characterizes the life-cycles of insects. Hitherto, his state had been dark and larval, or chrysalid at best, and his days had been spent in obscurity and lonely poverty. 'From the day on which I set foot in Ireland,' he wrote, 'all these evils fell away from me. Since that time who has had a happier life than mine?' The essence of the Irish magic was that for the first time he found himself among people who liked him, who did not regard him as a shameful and useless encumbrance. The work was not in an office under superiors, but in the open air on his own, riding up and down, making arrangements or putting disarrangements to rights. He became good at the work itself, and passionately fond of riding. He took to hunting, and found a hobby that was his only major addiction to the end of his life. After three years of this new life, he married, was promoted, and soon began to write his first novel.

He spent most of his time in Ireland until 1859, and remained in the Post Office until 1867. He rose from being an ill-reputed and difficult clerk to being an efficient but still rather difficult public servant, with a flair for negotiating with all kinds of people, of many nations. He had a fine eye for the practical—he was the inventor of the English pillar-box. Above all, he made himself useful to his department in ways which meant that he was kept on his travels, rather than in an office. He came to know many parts of Britain itself, and visited Egypt, America and the West Indies on postal business. He hunted two days a week, and became a haunter of London clubs, partly for the sake of whist, partly because his acquaintance was now reaching up into higher circles of society and letters. And on top of all this, he wrote books at the average rate of 1·7 per annum, and made money by them.

So, in middle life, he found all that he had missed as a boy—respect, friendship and worldly success. And he enjoyed it all, hugely and noisily. He banged about the world, rode about Essex and other hunting counties, fell off his horse and lost his spectacles and laughed: dined at the club and laughed: dined at home or with his friends and laughed. In 1882, he was laughing at a comic book read aloud with his family after dinner when he had a stroke, from which he died a month later.

He had been successful, and had valued his success all the more because of his early failures. 'To be known as somebody,' he wrote, 'to be Anthony Trollope—if it be no more —is to me much.' But to understand both the man and his work, it is needful to set this beside that other verdict: 'Something of the disgrace of my schooldays has clung to me all through life.'

II

The above quotations are all from Trollope's *Autobiography*, written in 1875-6, but not published until 1883, a year after his death. Its reputation has kept pace with the recent revival of respect for his novels, and it is now probably one of the most widely read of English autobiographies. This modest popularity it well deserves. As an account of his life, it is so complete and so just that his biographers have added little to its detail, and less to its broad outline. It is in no sense a work of intimate self-revelation, and was not intended to be. It is rather a *tour de force* of self-description by a man who, sitting for his own portrait, brought to it precisely the same technique of direct solidity which he had developed in painting scores of portraits in his novels. He did not even spare himself the slightly ironic distance from which he usually observed his male characters. And what it describes is not merely an attitude taken up for the occasion, but one which served him constantly for the more serious purposes of self-regard.

Yet the self-portrait is a little uneven, clearly delineated where his habitual perceptions were strong, but fainter and more confused where they were weak. His strength lay in describing the manners and morals of the world in which he was so anxious to bear—and even more anxious to deserve—a good name; and in his account of his dealings with this world, he has a natural rightness and honesty which enabled him to behave well, and to describe clearly. His moral standards were not, perhaps, very profound or very subtle, but they were worthy and workable, and they made his conduct better than that of many men who were his superiors in moral perception. His weakness lay rather in his attitude to his own writing, and to literature in general. Here he fell into confusions and distortions which have harmed his reputation and—what is worse—damaged his work.

The problem for him lay in a simple contradiction. On the one hand, he was trying to rise in the world by writing novels; on the other hand, the world into which he wished to rise did not have a high regard for novels, or for those who wrote them. 'Thinking much', he said, 'of my own daily labour and of its nature, I felt myself at first to be much afflicted and then to be deeply grieved by the opinion expressed by wise and thinking men as to the work done by novelists.' To this problem, he found two possible answers. Very early in his career as a novelist he proposed to write a history of English prose fiction, which was to have 'vindicated my own profession as a novelist' by demonstrating in the work of his predecessors and contemporaries 'that high character which they may claim to have earned by their grace, their honesty, and good teaching'. But this history was never written, though a few of its leading ideas are suggested briefly in Chapters 12 and 13 of the *Autobiography*. The other possible answer, on the contrary, was made fully, loudly and insistently, throughout the book. It was that novel-writing should be regarded as a profession like any other, and that the object of the novelist, like that of every other professional man, was to make money for himself and his dependants. Nor was this object an unworthy or base one. 'It is a mistake,' he wrote, 'to suppose that a man is a better man because he despises money. Few do so, and those few in doing so suffer a defect. Who does not desire to be hospitable to his friends, generous to the poor, liberal to all, munificent to his children, and to be himself free from the carking fears which poverty creates?' This was the answer to which he committed himself, and it was elaborated in almost every account he gave of his dealings with publishers, up to the last page of the *Autobiography*, with its detailed financial statement of his earnings from each of his books, meticulously totalled to £68,939 17s. 5d.

It was, perhaps, the answer most likely to impress the world which he sought to impress. The men he met in the hunting field, or over the card table at his club, were more likely to accept it than that other argument about the good done by novelists in the moral education of their readers; and they were more likely to welcome among them a professional man just such as they were themselves—barristers, clergymen, engineers—who made no claim to be doing more than earn a good living. But though it was perhaps well fitted for this purpose, it was wrong, even perversely wrong. The novelist is not, of course, exempt from the common necessity of earning a living. But he earns it as a novelist, rather than as a barrister, a clergyman, an engineer, a politician or a confidence-trickster, because his tastes and abilities carry him to the novel rather than to any of these other lucrative activities. Yet although Trollope could not, or would not see this, it is typical of him that he gave a faithful report of the manner in which his own tastes and abilities were turned in this direction. Writing of those disgraced schooldays, and of the hardly less disgraced years as a clerk in the Post Office, he said this:

> I was always going about with some castles in the air firmly built within my mind. Nor were these efforts at architecture spasmodic or subject to constant change from day to day. For weeks, for months, if I remember rightly, from year to year, I would carry on the same tale, binding myself down to certain laws, to certain proportions. Nothing impossible was ever introduced,—nor anything which, from outward circumstances, would seem to be violently improbable. This had been the occupation of my life for six or seven years before I went to the Post

Office, and was by no means abandoned when I commenced my work. There can, I imagine, hardly be a more dangerous mental practice; but I have often doubted whether, had it not been my practice, I should ever have written a novel. I learned in this way to maintain an interest in a fictitious story, to dwell on a work created by my own imagination, and to live in a world altogether outside the world of my own material life.

It is here, and not in the passages on money-making, that Trollope describes his real impulse to write novels. He became a writer, not because of his need for money, but because of his talent for imaginative day-dreams. It was natural that he should have confused the need with the talent, for both drew their strength from the same source. The former was a conscious passion, almost an obsession, because it was the outward symbol of his desire to rise above those early outward troubles, and the latter also was passionate, but more obscurely, because it had been his hidden inner resource against them. The confusion was natural, but none the less unfortunate. At first it prevented him from discovering where his true gift lay, and even after this discovery, he under-rated its value in himself. In deference to the standards of the hunting-field and the club, he abused and exploited it by writing too much and too quickly, without waiting for his imagination to gather weight and depth. Like some of the more enterprising bankers of his time, he possessed genuine gold, but made it serve to support a recklessly diffuse paper circulation.

III

Misconceiving both his own powers and the nature of fiction, Trollope fell an easy prey to the shallower notions of his age about the way novels should be written. It was his job, he supposed, as an honest professional man, to provide his customers with the commodity they expected; and what they expected, he was taught to believe, was 'realism', slices of life faithfully observed and entertainingly told, with a few touches of wholesome morality. When he first resolved to write a novel, the life that lay under his eyes was that of Ireland, so he cut a few slices from it, observed them industriously, and wrote them down as best he could. His two Irish novels were failures, as they deserved to be. An historical novel followed, as dismally cluttered up with book-learning as the Irish novels had been by unimaginative reporting. Then he tried his hand at a guide-book, but the publishers to whom specimens were sent omitted to read them, and the project was dropped.

He was turned from these false starts, from his conception of the novel as a mere animated guide-book, not by any growth of literary perception on his own part, but by a lucky accident of his official career. In 1851 he was given the task of organizing country posts in South West England, and for two happy years he rode up and down and about in six or seven counties, visiting many places, meeting many people, but always in a hurry. It was his first experience of England outside London, and its combination of variety and hurry was exactly what his imagination needed to work upon; the materials offered to it were extensive, but he moved too quickly to become bogged down anywhere. From these wanderings, he got, not another careful slice of life, but a hazy, rich impression of towns and villages, of churches and country houses, of clergy and laity, and of the quietly intricate patterns of their manners and social life. It was upon this impression that he based his first truly imaginative novel, *The Warden*, the first of that Barsetshire series which has come to be regarded as his highest achievement. The book was conceived one summer evening in Salisbury, but the Barchester of the novels was never merely Salisbury, nor was the county round it any one of the counties through which he had travelled. It was pieced together from memories of them all, and though it grew to be so clear in his head that he once drew a very detailed map of it, its solidity was imaginative, not geographical. In the same way, the clergy who were its main characters were not of his acquaintance. 'I never,' he tells us in the *Autobiography*, 'lived in any cathedral city,—except London, never knew anything of any Close, and at that time had enjoyed no peculiar intimacy with any clergyman. My archdeacon, who has been said to be life-like, and for whom I confess I have all a parent's fond affection, was, I think, the simple result of an effort of my moral consciousness. . . . I had not then ever spoken to an archdeacon.' Similarly, the great journalist Tom Towers was thought to be very like an eminent man on the staff of *The Times*, and *The Times* itself, in its review of *The Warden*, mildly rebuked the author for indulging in personalities. But at that time, Trollope protests, 'living in Ireland, I had not even heard the name of any gentleman connected with *The Times* newspaper, and could not have intended to represent any individual by Tom Towers. As I had created an archdeacon, so I had created a journalist . . . my moral consciousness must again have been very powerful.'

This gift for the creation of character by the use of his moral imagination was revealed for the first time in *The Warden*, but it had been developed through those long years of day-dreaming, and in its own rather unusual direction. His private fantasies had not been adventurous, nor had they conferred upon him glittering social status. 'I never became a king,' he tells us, 'or a duke . . . a learned man, nor even a philosopher. But I was a very clever person, and beautiful young women used to be fond of me. And I strove to be kind of heart, and open of hand, and noble in thought, despising mean things; and altogether I was a very much better fellow than I have ever succeeded in being since.' This passionate and genuinely imaginative concern with moral existence was the essence of his approach to the novel, from *The Warden* onwards. Above all, it was his chief means of insight into character and its depiction. The physical characteristics of his personages are rarely made clearly visible, though they are often conscientiously described. It is their moral physiognomies that are sharply drawn, through what they do and say, what they are said to think and feel, and not seldom by direct comments upon them from their maker.

In the type of moral character chosen for portrayal, *The Warden* set the pattern to which he kept in nearly all his later novels. There was no villain, indeed no character much below the middle range of the moral scale, nor was there anyone conspicuously above it, save the Warden himself. Trollope became exactly what he wished, the moral historian of men and women in the middle range, the usual run of humanity—'with no more of excellence, nor with exaggerated baseness—so that my readers might recognize human beings like to themselves, and not feel themselves to be carried away among gods or demons'.

Finally, *The Warden* was typical of all the novels that were to follow in its disregard for plot. It would, indeed, have been incompatible with his choice of the middle range of characters to have involved them in sensational and complicated situations: ordinary people commonly lead ordinary lives. But apart from this, the elaboration of remarkable incident was quite irrelevant to his main purpose—the depiction of moral character. It mattered little to him how his creatures were set in motion, for once they were on the move they had so great a capacity for living their own lives. In *The Warden* itself, he posed them a problem about the proper use of church endowments, a contemporary, if not a burning issue: just such a case had arisen in Winchester when he was at school there, and was still before the courts many years after he had written this book. But he himself had no clear view of its rights and wrongs, nor did he need one. All that he needed was the opportunity to let his imagination play upon its issues and cross-issues, as they would appear to differing modes and degrees of moral sensibility. And it was in the process of doing this that men and women—not issues—came alive under his hand.

IV

The intense moral realization of his characters gave them, once created, a very tenacious hold upon his imagination: so tenacious that he was often unwilling, almost unable, to let them go. His two most notable creations in *The Warden* were of this kind, and they were carried on into *Barchester Towers* (1857), *Doctor Thorne* (1858), *Framley Parsonage* (1861) and *The Last Chronicle of Barset* (1867). Other characters were added, of course, and some of them obtained almost as close a grip on their author's affections. Other novels were written in the same period, many of them. But Archdeacon Grantly and his father-in-law went on leading their lives in his imagination, growing older as he grew older, yet always themselves as he remained himself. Of the two, the Archdeacon was the more prominent and active, and much more akin to Trollope. His father-in-law, who had been Warden in the first book, stood at the upper limit of Trollope's moral range, and once he had made his great decision in that first episode, there was little for him to do in the world but be gentle to his family and friends, play his 'cello, and take good care of the music in the cathedral. Yet he did all this in such a way that we are made to feel his virtue, his religion even, beyond any description that Trollope felt able to give. The Archdeacon was coarser in grain, quick to anger, but quick to forget his anger, more worldly, but generous and warm-hearted. The two existed side by side, as characters must often do in fiction, making a richer pattern by their contrasting qualities than they could ever have made separately. When the older man came to die, it was through the mouth of the Archdeacon that Trollope expressed his estimate both of the dying man, and of the Archdeacon:

> I feel sure that he never had an impure fancy in his mind, or a faulty wish in his heart. His tenderness has surpassed the tenderness of woman; and yet, when occasion came for showing it, he had all the spirit of a hero. I shall never forget his resignation of the hospital. . . . The fact is,

he never was wrong. He couldn't go wrong. He lacked guile, and he feared God,—and a man who does both will never go far astray. I don't think he ever coveted aught in his life,—except a new case for his violoncello and somebody to listen to him when he played it. Then the archdeacon got up, and walked about the room in his enthusiasm; and, perhaps, as he walked some thoughts as to the sterner ambition of his own life passed through his mind. What things had he coveted? Had he lacked guile? He told himself that he had feared God,—but he was not sure that he was telling himself the truth even in that.

Nothing is more like Trollope himself than this moment of explosive self-perception. The Archdeacon, like his creator, had standards by which to measure his fellow men, and he was tolerably sure of their general rightness. But when he came to ask how far he himself measured up to them, he had his awkward moments. He had coveted many things, greatly: a Bishopric, power, the ruin of his enemies, wealth, and above all in his later days, the glory of his children. He had indeed done his best for them, and they had not done badly for him. His daughter was a marchioness, and though her husband the marquis was unquestionably a moron, she was still unquestionably a marchioness. His eldest son, Henry, had done well in the Indian Army, had won the Victoria Cross, and a wife with a little money. The wife had died, leaving the young widower with a baby daughter, but Henry still had his fine record, some money of his own, and a handsome allowance with his father. He had retired from the Army, and was settling in Barsetshire as a country squire, with land and farms and horses and foxes of his own.

All this had been achieved by stern ambition, and not without guile; and whatever God might think about it, the Archdeacon was usually well pleased with his achievements. In *The Last Chronicle of Barset*, he was sorely tried because Henry fell deeply in love with a young woman, the daughter of a cleric the very opposite of himself, pious, very poor, unworldly, and to make the worst of an already bad job, awaiting his trial on a charge of stealing a cheque. So outrageous was Henry's choice, that his father opposed this new marriage, even threatened to stop the allowance. The struggle between father and son was long and obstinate on both sides, and even the mother's intervention was not able to end it. It was brought to its climax, and at the same instant to its solution, in an interview between the Archdeacon and the girl herself, which illustrates as comprehensively as any passage in Trollope both the emotional force of which he was capable, and the moral standards which he accepted without question. The first part of the interview does her credit—more credit than the Archdeacon had expected. She refers to her father's disgrace, and gives her promise that unless his name is cleared, she will marry nobody:

The archdeacon had now left the rug, and advanced till he was almost close to the chair on which Grace was sitting. 'My dear,' he said, 'what you say does you very much honour—very much honour indeed.' Now that he was close to her, he could look into her eyes, and he could see the exact form of her features, and could understand—could not help understanding—the character of her countenance. It was a noble face, having in it nothing that was poor, nothing that was mean, nothing that was shapeless. It was a face that promised infinite beauty, with a promise that was on the very verge of fulfilment. There was a play about her mouth as she spoke, and a curl in her nostrils as the eager words came from her, which almost made the selfish father give way. Why had they not told him that she was such a one as this? Why had not Henry himself spoken of the speciality of her beauty? No man in England knew better than the archdeacon the difference between beauty of one kind and beauty of another kind in a woman's face—the one beauty, which comes from health and youth and animal spirits, and which belongs to the miller's daughter, and the other beauty, which shows itself in fine lines and a noble spirit—the beauty which comes from breeding. 'What you say does you very much honour indeed,' said the archdeacon.

'I should not mind at all about being poor,' said Grace.

'No; no; no,' said the archdeacon.

'Poor as we are—and no clergyman, I think, ever was so poor—I should have done as your son asked me at once, if it had been only that—because I love him.'

'If you love him you will not wish to injure him.'

'I will not injure him. Sir, there is my promise.' And now as she spoke she rose from her chair, and standing close to the archdeacon, laid her hand very lightly on the sleeve of his coat. 'There is my promise. As long as people say that papa stole the money, I will never marry your son. There.'

The archdeacon was still looking down at her, and feeling the slight touch of her fingers, raised his arm a little as though to welcome the pressure. He looked into her eyes, which were turned eagerly towards his, and when doing so he was sure that the promise would be kept. It would have been sacrilege—he felt that it would have been sacrilege—to doubt such a promise. He almost relented. His soft heart, which was never very well under his own control, gave way so far that he was nearly moved to tell her that, on his son's behalf, he acquitted her of the promise.... As he looked down upon her face two tears formed themselves in his eyes and gradually trickled down his old nose. 'My dear,' he said, 'if this cloud passes away from you, you shall come to us and be my daughter.' And thus he pledged himself. There was a dash of generosity about the man, in spite of his selfishness, which always made him desirous of giving largely to those who gave largely to him. He would fain that his gifts should be bigger, if it were possible.... He had contrived that her hand should fall from his arm into his grasp, and now for a moment he held it. 'You are a good girl,' he said—'a dear, dear, good girl. When this cloud has passed away, you shall come to us and be our daughter.'

It was thus that Trollope created the most solid of his male characters, by a temporary merging of his own personality in theirs: here, he has all but put himself into the Archdeacon's shoes and gaiters. But the merging was never uncritical, because he was critical of himself; he was always capable of qualifying a virtue, of noting an unworthy doubt, and took frequent pleasure in slight backhanded ironies at the expense of their inner weaknesses, as he did at the expense of his own.

As for the girls, he was inclined to be in love with them in the same vicarious fashion. His contemporaries, we are informed by a review written in 1867, liked to make gentle jokes about his intimacy with the minds of his heroines:

how, they asked, had he managed to 'find it all out'? And shortly after his death, Henry James accurately noted the nature of his relation with them:

> Trollope settled down steadily to the English girl; he took possession of her, and turned her inside out. He never made her the subject of heartless satire ... he bestowed upon her the most serious, the most patient, the most tender, the most copious consideration. He is evidently always more or less in love with her.... But if he was a lover, he was a paternal lover.

It was, indeed, the English girl who saved Trollope from the labour of devising plots. She was there to be loved, and love for her was enough to set in motion not only one or two young men, but their families too. For only if the love went hand in hand with an income large enough to support marriage—and marriage in the style to which both parties were accustomed—could it run all smooth. All that was needful then, to produce a story with situations full of doubt and perplexity was to bring the power of love into conflict with the demands of property and social status. The ensuing confusion would involve not only the lovers, but their families and friends, and as wide a circle of acquaintance as might be needed to fill a three volume novel. Trollope made this discovery early in the Barsetshire series, and thenceforward he never bothered his head with plots. 'When I sit down to write a novel', he blandly observed, 'I do not at all know, and I do not very much care, how it is to end.' For this relief, he was almost entirely indebted to the English girl with her ability to inspire love, and to the Victorian sense of property with its inveterate tendency to make love injudicious. As the great tragic conflicts in French classical plays tend to arise from the opposition of love and honour, so Trollope's arose from love and property.

But it would be unjust to present him as becoming thus involved only with young lovers, or with characters on the whole amiable and admirable. Such was his involvement in any creation of his own that he was almost equally capable of becoming devoted to personages neither young nor amiable. In the Barsetshire novels, for example, the Archdeacon's arch-enemy is Mrs Proudie, wife of the Bishop and mistress of the palace which the Archdeacon had coveted so much, and which his father had held before him. Mrs Proudie is probably the best-known virago in English fiction, above all for her achievements in hen-pecking her husband, yet even to her Trollope developed a powerful attachment. The manner of her death was curious. One night at his club, he heard two clergymen criticizing him for carrying the same characters from novel to novel, and they were very hard on Mrs Proudie. 'I got up, and standing between them, I acknowledged myself to be the culprit. "As to Mrs Proudie," I said, "I will go home and kill her before the week is over." And so I did... but I have never dissevered myself from Mrs Proudie, and still live much in company with her ghost.'

V

The Barsetshire novels have come to be regarded as Trollope's chief, if not his only contribution to literature, both by the common reader and by the general run of critics and literary historians. They hold this position partly through their own merits of character and milieu, but partly because they can so easily be made to satisfy the common reader's most common weakness in his choice of fiction, his liking for some more or less adult fairyland where he can take a well earned holiday from the tougher and duller realities of his own life. 'Barset,' J. B. Priestley has observed, 'is a haven of rest.' It is natural enough that novels whose main setting was rural England, and whose main characters were so often country clergy, should have been appreciated in this way. But it is an injustice to this series of novels to perceive in them no more than pleasant placidity, and it can easily lead on to a still greater injustice in estimating Trollope's work. For the more solid qualities in this series are to be found in many of his other novels, where the milieu is less obviously fairy-like, but where his central virtue of moral imagination shows itself both with greater depth and with wider range.

These qualities are nowhere more massively developed than in the linked series of novels which ran through his later life, much as the Barsetshire series had run through his earlier years, the 'political' novels, whose central characters are Plantagenet Palliser and his wife Glencora: *Can You Forgive Her?* (1864), *Phineas Finn* (1869), *The Eustace Diamonds* (1873), *Phineas Redux* (1874), *The Prime Minister* (1876) and *The Duke's Children* (1880).

The main setting has moved from Barsetshire to London, and the main characters are men of wealth and high social status, leaders in their professions and in the House of Commons. The general impression is one of greater 'realism', at any rate in so far as this world is clearly more remote from any conceivable fairyland than Barsetshire had been. But, in following Trollope's achievement in this less idyllic milieu, it is even more necessary to realize how much it issued from his imagination. It had been the dread of his boyhood, as he walked to Harrow along the muddy lanes, that 'mud and solitude and povery' would be his lot through his whole life. 'Those lads about me would go into Parliament, or become rectors and deans, or squires of parishes, or advocates thundering at the Bar,' he supposed; and he told himself that he would never live among them. But with the success of his middle years, he had after all risen to live among them. He knew Members of Parliament, thundering barristers, and the brother of his closest friend was Dean of Ely. And in 1868, he tried to rise still higher, by standing as a candidate for Parliament himself, at Beverley. He was defeated, and both the fact and the manner of his defeat left a very sore place in his spirit. But if he could rise no further himself, his imagination could go where it liked, and its expeditions were the main impulse of the political novels. This was his own view of them—and as usual he saw himself with accuracy:

> By no amount of description or asseveration could I succeed in making any reader understand how much these characters (Palliser and Lady Glencora) with their belongings have been to me in my latter life; or how frequently I have used them for the expression of my political and social convictions. They have been as real to me as free trade was to Mr Cobden, or the dominion of a party to Mr Disraeli; and as I have not been able to speak from the benches of the House of Commons ... they have served me as safety valves by which to deliver my soul.

In this way, his defeat at Beverley gave him a new imaginative impulse, and at the same time ensured that his imagination would not get itself bogged down in too much minute observation. His acquaintance with the political world, like his earlier survey of south-west England, was both wide and vague enough to give him precisely the kind of rich but hazy impression which left his imagination neither starved nor shackled.

In the political novels, as in the earlier series, there is a vast array of characters, and most of them are set and kept in motion by Trollope's usual forces, love and property. But in the central character, Plantagenet Palliser, the chief interest is subtler and deeper. It is a long, full study of a conscience, delicate in itself, and even more perplexed because its owner has wealth, a dukedom, political power, and a very thin skin. The close of *The Prime Minister* is a good example of what Trollope's 'moral consciousness' could make of this material. Palliser has been Prime Minister for three years, as head of a coalition Government. When it falls, his old friend and ally, the Duke of St Bungay, expresses the hope that he will take some office in the next Cabinet. 'I don't think I could do that,' Palliser told him, 'Caesar could hardly lead a legion under Pompey.' But when their talk was over, he found himself regretting 'that apparently pompous speech by Caesar. . . . Who was he that he should class himself among the great ones of the world.' In the days that followed, this moment of unintended arrogance irked him almost more than the end of his power and the formation of a new administration. A few weeks later, he was talking with his late Chancellor of the Exchequer, one of the few political allies he respected, and by him he was given this assurance:

'If the country is to lose your services for the long course of years during which you will probably sit in Parliament, then I shall think that the country has lost more than it has gained by the Coalition.'

The Duke sat for a while silent, looking at the view, and, before answering Mr Monk,—while arranging his answer,—once or twice in a half-absent way called his companion's attention to the scene before him. But, during this time he was going through an act of painful repentance. He was condemning himself for a word or two that had been ill-spoken by himself, and which, since the moment of its utterance, he had never ceased to remember with shame. He told himself now, after his own secret fashion, that he must do penance for these words by the humiliation of a direct contradiction of them. He must declare that Caesar would at some future time be prepared to serve under Pompey. Thus he made his answer.

This is a more interesting process of the moral life than any studied in the Barset novels, and the observation is more penetrating: few moralists have noted so clearly the part which a small phrase, almost a chance phrase, can play in bringing the fluid confusions of the inner life to a point where they crystallize into decision.

But the fine conscience of Plantagenet Palliser is more than an individual study. It is also at the centre of Trollope's political world, and he finds in it the explanation of a process of change in England which was otherwise mystifying. He was himself a Liberal, though with many touches of the Tory in his temperament. He approved in general of the slow process of amelioration which was going on in his day, the gradual spread of democracy and of education to wider sections of the population. He even approved of the extension of the franchise, but at the same time he wondered at the fact that some of the great Whigs, especially those of wealth and title, should be willing to use their political influence for its own destruction, by encouraging it to pass into the hands of millions of men with votes to be cast in secret ballot. Palliser is the type of such a Whig, and in his exact and exacting conscience Trollope finds the explanation of this remarkable change. No other English novelist, and few historians, saw the problem so clearly, and advanced so convincing a solution for it.

It is this extension of his 'moral consciousness' to the whole pattern of English life that informs the political novels, and justifies to the full the remarkable tribute which Henry James paid Trollope a few years after his death:

> Trollope will remain one of the most trustworthy, though not one of the most eloquent, of writers who have helped the heart of man to know itself.... His natural rightness and purity are so real that the good things he projects must be real. A race is fortunate when it has a good deal of the sort of imagination—of imaginative feeling—that had fallen to the share of Anthony Trollope; and in this possession our English race is not poor.

VI

Trollope wrote forty-seven novels, and since few readers will wish to read them all, some answer is needed to the question, which are best worth reading? It is not easy to find one, for quite apart from the large number involved, there are few that fall markedly below his usual level, and perhaps even fewer which rise much above it.

The verdict of the common reader has always been that the Barset series should be regarded as his best and most typical work, and that there is little point in going much further with him. His more serious and persistent readers, however, generally believe that the 'political' series is at least as good, and very probably better. Beyond this, there is confusion. Are the other three dozen novels merely an extension of the Trollopian world over a wider area, a repetition of his favourite themes and his familiar types of character under new names and against slightly shifted scenery? Or do some of them present qualities not to be found anywhere in the two central series?

The second argument has been urged with much force in a study by Mr Cockshut, which sets out to alter radically the accepted view of Trollope's whole work. It contends that Trollope's outlook was, especially in the later part of his life, much less superficial than has usually been supposed, less orthodox, less bluffly optimistic, and more prone to question the assumptions of the age about morality and property. In the light of this contention, the emphasis of attention is changed both within the two main series and in the novels outside them. In the Barset novels, it falls above all on the lonely agony of Mr Crawley, the clergyman wrongly accused of stealing a cheque, but not sure within himself that he is innocent. In the 'political' series, it falls upon the madness of Mr Kennedy in *Phineas Finn* and *Phineas Redux*, and the appalling loneliness of his wife, Lady Laura, who has married him for his money—or at least refused to marry the man she really loved because he had no money. And in *The Eustace Diamonds*, Mr Cockshut finds Trollope's first decisive movement towards satire, and to a view of goods and chattels not wholeheartedly Victorian. With this alteration of emphasis in the better-known novels, there goes the claim that what is most important in them was often more fully developed elsewhere. The gloom and loneliness of the individual, for example, was explored most deeply in *He Knew He Was Right*, which traces the degeneration of a husband from unreasonable jealousy of his wife into actual madness. The fullest development of satire is in *The Way We Live Now*, and of the attack on property and inheritance in *Mr Scarborough's Family*. These, and other of the outlying novels,

Mr Cockshut would place in the forefront of Trollope's work, for these and such-like reasons.

This study has been usefully done; it provokes a more careful reading of some perhaps unduly neglected novels in the later period, and corrects some wrong impressions about those which have been widely read. Mr Cockshut, moreover, has drawn together very skilfully the evidence of Trollope's passionate interest in certain situations and characters: the almost inevitably bad relations between fathers and sons, the 'snarling intimacy of family life', the desperation of girls whose only future is marriage, and whose labour in life is to entrap a suitably endowed husband. And yet the direction of the emphasis is wrong; it runs too directly against the main current of criticism. In his own day, Trollope's reviewers constantly stressed his choice of the middle range of humanity, of the ordinary man or woman, even the commonplace; they only wondered at his power of making it interesting, without distortion and without much apparent imaginative heightening of colour. Henry James's phrase succinctly comprehends the whole contemporary impression: 'His great, his inestimable merit was a complete appreciation of the usual.' The judgement is the more weighty, because a writer's contemporaries very rarely mistake the nature of his merit, though they often misjudge its degree. In concentrating so much attention upon Trollope's handling of the unusual, the heterodox, Mr Cockshut has indulged in an exaggeration, even if a useful one.

My own conviction is that all the essential qualities of Trollope are to be found in the two central series, and that there they are balanced in their right proportions. Outside them, only two novels appear to me to have a really strong claim on the general reader.

The first is *The Way We Live Now*. It was written in 1873, and it savagely satirized the new power of financiers and speculators in English life. Trollope saw them compassing the ruin, or at least the degradation, of the landed gentry, literature, the press, social life, even the Court itself. It is a magnificently sustained piece of anger, imaginatively realized and dramatically presented. The last act of its great villain, Augustus Melmotte, ruined, drunk and defiant, trying to speak in Parliament, and glowering angrily but speechlessly round the House, has a force, both immediate and symbolic, beyond Trollope's usual range. In the previous year, *The Prime Minister* had appeared, and in it the new corruption of finance had been represented by a small-scale swindler, Lopez. Had Trollope but waited for his imagination to devise and select, he might have put the far greater figure of Melmotte in the same place. A novel in which Plantagenet Palliser was opposed to Melmotte, politically, morally and imaginatively, would in all probability have been Trollope's unquestioned masterpiece, his most complete comment on the values of his age. That it did not get written is the heaviest single penalty he paid for his precipitation in covering the daily stint of paper. But even so, *The Way We Live Now* deserves to be read more widely, and to be allowed a distinguished place beside the main political novels.

The second novel which I would specially commend is *The Claverings*, published in 1867. It is a work of a very different kind. It is short, and has a concentration of effect unusual in Trollope. There is no sub-plot to distract the development of the central situation, and all the characters play real parts in it. The main problem it explores, the hesitations and weaknesses of a young man between a beautiful but poor young girl to whom he is engaged, and an equally beautiful but rich widow whom he had loved before her marriage, is exactly of the kind to display at its best Trollope's ability to analyse the unheroic but not quite base man of common mould. But it is above all in its style that it is distinctive. For the most part, Trollope's manner of writing is adequate rather than eloquent, and so impersonal that one often feels it might have been practised by almost anyone else in the same period: though it is remarkable how surely, in fact, a fair specimen of his work can be recognized for what it is. In *The Claverings*, however, more than in any other book, he showed what he could do when he was neither writing against the clock, nor merely 'for length'—the dreadful phrase is his own. It is not merely that as a whole the book is better written than most of the others, but that it also shows some of his subtler qualities of style more clearly than the rest.

There is, for example, a turn of phrase almost peculiar to him, and very characteristic of his ironically intimate report of the inner life: it depends upon the addition of some slight qualification to a previous statement. An example has been given already from the Archdeacon's reflections:

> He told himself that he had feared God,—but he was not sure that he was telling himself the truth even in that.

Here are others:

> He thought that he could give up racecourses; but he was sure that he could at any rate say that he would give them up. (*Sir Harry Hotspur of Humblethwaite*)
>
> Colonel Osborne knew that his visit had been very innocent; but he did not like the feeling that even his innocence had been made the subject of observation. (*He Knew He Was Right*)
>
> It cannot be said of him that he did much thinking for himself;—but he thought that he thought. (*The Prime Minister*)

In *The Claverings*, this characteristic Trollopian turn of phrase is used frequently, and especially in the depiction of the wavering hero. 'He told himself that he was an ass, but still he went on being an ass.' Thus he got himself into his trouble between the old love and the new, and in the midst of it, when he was being true to neither, Trollope concludes an address to the reader on the failings of his hero: 'He should have been chivalric, manly, full of high duty. He should have been all this, and full also of love, and then he would have been a hero. But men as I see them are not often heroic.'

Another of Trollope's characteristic devices was the repetition of a short phrase, at brief intervals but with such shifts of context, such exaggeration, that it acquired the ironic power conferred in the same manner on the phrase 'honourable men' in Antony's speech in *Julius Caesar*. In *The Claverings*, there are two fine example of its use. One is in the twelfth chapter, describing the visit of the beautiful young widow to the splendid estate she had won by her loveless marriage, and the phrase woven through it is 'She had the price in her hands'. It gathers weight continually through the chapter, which ends upon the final bitter variation: 'She had the price in her hands, but she felt herself tempted to do as Judas did, to go out and hang herself.' Five chapters later, the same device is put to more openly comic and hostile uses, when the best mode of wooing this same rich young widow is discussed by Captain Clavering and Captain Boodle, after dinner at their club:

'Well, now, Clavvy, I'll tell you what my ideas are. When a man's trying a young filly, his hands can't be too light. A touch too much will bring her on her haunches, and throw her out of step. She should hardly fell the iron in her mouth. But when I've got to do with a trained mare, I always choose that she shall know that I'm there! Do you understand me?'

'Yes; I understand you, Doodles.'

'I always choose that she should know I'm there.' And Captain Boodle, as he repeated these manly words with a firm voice, put out his hands as though he were handling the horse's rein.

After the phrase has been relished a further half-dozen times, Boodle leaves his friend alone to mediate upon it:

He sat the whole evening in the smoking-room, very silent, drinking slowly iced gin-and-water; and the more he drank the more assured he felt that he now understood the way in which he was to attempt the work before him. 'Let her know I'm there', he said to himself, shaking his head gently, so that no one should observe him; 'yes, let her know I'm there.' Everything was contained in that precept. And he, with his hands before him on his knees, went through the process of steadying a horse with the snaffle-rein, just touching the curb, as he did so, for security. It was but a motion of his fingers and no one could see it, but it made him confident that he had learned his lesson.

And in this way the phrase is made to undermine these two men, to reveal all their coarseness, their monotony of mind, their pompous ineptitude.

An acquaintance with *The Claverings*, then, is worth making not only for its own sake; it is probably the readiest way for a reader to sensitize himself to the subtler aspects of Trollope's style, and above all to his characteristic modes of irony. Without this sensitivity, none of his novels can be read rightly, for even in his dealings with the characters he knew and loved best—indeed especially with them— this irony is never far away. But its quality is so quiet, its onset so unostentatious, that it can easily be missed.

For these reasons, then, these two novels seem to deserve attention. But it must at once be added that many of the others are as good, and very possibly better. *Ralph the Heir*, for example, has some fine political scenes, and at least one character, Sir Thomas Underwood, profounder in conception than any in *The Way We Live Now*. *The Belton Estate* is comparable with *The Claverings* in its compression, and has a parallel theme, the hesitations of a young woman between two lovers, developed with all that power of creating a dramatic scene which has been illustrated above in the encounter between the Archdeacon and Miss Crawley. Others of the lesser-known novels which certainly deserve to be much better known are *Orley Farm*, *Sir Harry Hotspur of Humblethwaite*, *Is He Popenjoy?*, *Dr Wortle's School* and *Ayala's Angel*. The list could easily be made much longer, but the reader who wishes to explore these novels further has no lack of guides. If he is interested in the gloomier and less 'usual' aspects in them, he cannot do better than follow Mr Cockshut; if, on the other hand, he prefers a more orthodox and central view, he should consult the *Commen-*

tary of Mr Michael Sadleir, to whom this generation owes much for defending and explaining a writer who seemed on the very point of slipping into oblivion.

But whatever he may choose to read, he should guard against two misconceptions which can prevent him from giving both himself and Trollope a fair chance. He should not, under the impression of length and weight of circumstance, mistake what is before him for mere photography, and so miss the real, though unostentatious imagination which has moulded it; nor should he let the apparent uniformity and directness of the style lull him into a hypnotic automatism, insensitive to those subtler turns of phrase which are so characteristic an expression of Trollope's 'moral consciousness', of his kindly but ironic perception of the gap between what we are, and what we ought to be, wish to be, or believe ourselves to be.

TROLLOPE

A Select Bibliography

(Place of publication London, unless stated otherwise)

Bibliography:

ANTHONY TROLLOPE: A BIBLIOGRAPHY, by M. L. Irwin; New York (1926)
—contains useful references to early reviews, articles in periodicals, etc.

TROLLOPE: A BIBLIOGRAPHY, by M. Sadleir (1928)
—based on the compiler's renowned collection now in the Parrish Collection in the Princeton University Library: *Supplement*, 1934, and additional material in Sadleir's *XIX Century Fiction*, 1951. The final authority on the works of Trollope themselves, with a fascinating section on the extent of their popularity, as measured by the book market.

A GUIDE TO TROLLOPE, by W. G. and J. T. Gerould; Princeton (1948)
—contains bibliographical tables, and a dictionary of characters, places and events in the novels.

Collected Works:

Note: There is no complete edition of Trollope's works, and it now seems unlikely that there ever will be, for the Oxford University Press has been forced to discontinue the Oxford Illustrated Trollope which was begun in 1948, at a point when it included only nine titles (in fifteen volumes). Many of the novels, however, with the *Autobiography*, are published in the World's Classics series by the same publishers, and for most purposes this can be regarded as the standard, if not complete, edition. Several of the novels are also available in Everyman's Library and in Nelson's Classics.

THE BARSETSHIRE NOVELS, ed. F. Harrison, 8 vols (1906).

THE BARSETSHIRE NOVELS, ed. M. Sadleir, 14 vols; Oxford (1929)
—Shakespeare Head edition.

THE OXFORD TROLLOPE, ed. M. Sadleir and F. Page, 15 vols (1948—)
—includes the following nine titles: *Can You Forgive Her?* 2 vols, 1948; *Phineas Finn.* 2 vols, 1949; *The Eustace Diamonds*, 2 vols, 1950; *An Autobiography etc.* 1950; *Phineas Redux*, 2 vols, 1951; *The Prime Minister*, 2 vols, 1952; *The Warden*, 1952; *Barchester Towers*, 2 vols, 1953; *The Duke's Children*, 1954.

THE LETTERS OF ANTHONY TROLLOPE, ed. B. Allen Booth (1951)
—uniform with volumes of Oxford edition.

Selections:

THE TROLLOPE READER, ed. E. C. Dunne and M. E. Dodd; New York (1947)
—gives few of his dramatic scenes, but exemplifies very well his range of observation.

THE PARSON'S DAUGHTER AND OTHER STORIES, ed. J. Hampden (1949)
—includes *Katchen's Caprices*, not reprinted since its first appearance in *Harper's Weekly*, 1866-7, and four other stories.

THE BEDSIDE BARSETSHIRE, ed. L. O. Tingay (1940)
—has its uses, but proves very clearly that Trollope needs space and time to develop his effects.

MARY GRESLEY AND OTHER STORIES, ed. J. Hampden (1951)
—includes five stories.

Separate Works:

THE MACDERMOTS OF BALLYCLORAN, 3 vols (1847). *Novel*

THE KELLYS AND THE O'KELLYS: A TALE OF IRISH LIFE, 3 vols (1848). *Novel*

LA VENDÉE: AN HISTORICAL ROMANCE, 3 vols (1850). *Historical Novel*

THE WARDEN (1855). *Barsetshire Novel*
—with an introduction by A. D. J. Cockshut, 1955.

BARCHESTER TOWERS, 3 vols (1857). *Barsetshire Novel*
—with introduction by P. Hansford Johnson, 1952.

THE THREE CLERKS, 3 vols (1858). *Novel*

DOCTOR THORNE, 3 vols (1858). *Barsetshire Novel*

THE BERTRAMS, 3 vols (1850). *Novel*

THE WEST INDIES AND THE SPANISH MAIN (1859). *Travel*

CASTLE RICHMOND, 3 vols (1860). *Novel*

TALES OF ALL COUNTRIES, 2 series (1861-3). *Stories*

FRAMLEY PARSONAGE, 3 vols (1861). *Barsetshire Novel*

ORLEY FARM, 2 vols (1862). *Novel*

NORTH AMERICA, 2 vols (1862). *Travel*
—ed. D. Smalley and B. A. Booth, New York, 1951

RACHEL RAY, 2 vols (1863). *Novel*

THE SMALL HOUSE AT ALLINGTON, 2 vols (1864). *Barsetshire Novel*

CAN YOU FORGIVE HER?, 2 vols (1864-5). *Political Novel*

MISS MACKENZIE, 2 vols (1865). *Novel*

HUNTING SKETCHES (1865). *Sketches*
—ed. J. Boyd, 1934 and L. Edwards, 1952.

THE BELTON ESTATE, 3 vols (1866). *Novel*

TRAVELLING SKETCHES (1866). *Sketches*

CLERGYMEN OF THE CHURCH OF ENGLAND (1866). *Essays*

NINA BALATKA: THE STORY OF A MAIDEN OF PRAGUE, 2 vols (1867). *Novel*

THE LAST CHRONICLE OF BARSET, 2 vols (1867). *Barsetshire Novel*

THE CLAVERINGS, 2 vols (1867). *Novel*

LOTTA SCHMIDT: AND OTHER STORIES (1867). *Stories*

LINDA TRESSEL, 2 vols (1868). *Novel*

PHINEAS FINN, THE IRISH MEMBER, 2 vols (1869). *Political Novel*

HE KNEW HE WAS RIGHT, 2 vols (1869). *Novel*

DID HE STEAL IT? (1869). *Drama*
—privately printed. An adaptation by Trollope from the central episode of the *Last Chronicle of Barset*, ed. R. H. Taylor, Princeton, 1952.

THE VICAR OF BULLHAMPTON, 2 vols (1870). *Novel*

AN EDITOR'S TALES (1870). *Stories*

THE STRUGGLES OF BROWN, JONES AND ROBINSON: BY ONE OF THE FIRM (1870). *Novel*
—a pirated edition, reprinted from the *Cornhill Magazine*, had appeared in the U.S.A. in 1862.

THE COMMENTARIES OF CAESAR (1870). *Translation*

SIR HARRY HOTSPUR OF HUMBLETHWAITE (1871). *Novel*

RALPH THE HEIR, 3 vols (1871). *Novel*

THE GOLDEN LION OF GRANPÈRE (1872). *Novel*

THE EUSTACE DIAMONDS, 3 vols (1873). *Political Novel*

AUSTRALIA AND NEW ZEALAND, 2 vols (1873). *Travel*

LADY ANNA, 2 vols (1874). *Novel*

PHINEAS REDUX, 2 vols (1874). *Political Novel*
—Oxford Illustrated Edition, 2 vols, 1951.

HARRY HEATHCOTE OF GANGOIL: A TALE OF AUSTRALIAN BUSH LIFE (1874). *Novel*
THE WAY WE LIVE NOW, 2 vols (1875). *Novel*
THE PRIME MINISTER, 4 vols (1876). *Political Novel*
THE AMERICAN SENATOR, 3 vols (1877). *Novel*
CHRISTMAS AT THOMPSON HALL; New York (1877). *Story*
SOUTH AFRICA, 2 vols (1878). *Travel*
IS HE POPENJOY?, 3 vols (1878). *Novel*
THE LADY OF LAUNAY; New York (1878). *Story*
HOW THE 'MASTIFFS' WENT TO ICELAND (1878). *Travel*
—privately printed.
AN EYE FOR AN EYE, 2 vols (1879). *Novel*
THACKERAY (1879). *Criticism*
JOHN CALDIGATE, 3 vols (1879). *Novel*
COUSIN HENRY, 2 vols (1879). *Novel*
THE DUKE'S CHILDREN, 3 vols (1880). *Political Novel*
THE LIFE OF CICERO, 2 vols (1880). *Biography*
DR WORTLE'S SCHOOL, 2 vols (1881). *Novel*
AYALA'S ANGEL, 3 vols (1881). *Novel*
WHY FRAU FROHMANN RAISED HER PRICES AND OTHER STORIES (1882). *Stories*
LORD PALMERSTON (1882). *Biography*
THE FIXED PERIOD, 2 vols (1882). *Novel*
MARION FAY, 3 vols (1882). *Novel*
KEPT IN THE DARK, 2 vols (1882). *Novel*
MR SCARBOROUGH'S FAMILY, 3 vols (1883). *Novel*
THE LANDLEAGUERS, 3 vols (1883). *Novel*
AN AUTOBIOGRAPHY (1883).
AN OLD MAN'S LOVE, 2 vols (1883). *Novel*
THE NOBLE JILT: A COMEDY, ed. M. Sadleir (1923). *Drama*
—written in 1850, but never acted; used as the main plot of *Can You Forgive Her?* and mentioned in *The Eustace Diamonds*.
LONDON TRADESMEN, ed. M. Sadleir (1928). *Sketches*
—from the *Pall Mall Gazette*, 1880.
FOUR LECTURES, ed. M. L. Parrish (1938).

THE TIRELESS TRAVELLER, ed. B. A. Booth; Cambridge (1941)
—letters contributed to the *Liverpool Mercury*, 1875.

THE TWO HEROINES OF PLUMPLINGTON, ed. J. Hampden (1953). *Story*

Some Critical and Biographical Studies:

REVUE DES DEUX MONDES (1855 and 1858)
—studies by Emile Montegut, a French critic who specialized in the interpretation of English literature. The first of these reviews contains a long study of *The Warden*, the second deals fully with *Barchester Towers* and *Dr Thorne*. They illustrate very clearly the general superiority of the French critical approach to fiction over that of the English reviewers of the same period. It was this superiority in skill and seriousness which enabled Montagut to perceive in Trollope, not simply a naïve realist, but a writer who imposed upon his report of life a pattern of his own, with a style of his own. Both reviews were reprinted in the first volume of his *Ecrivains Modernes de l'Angleterre*, Paris, 1892.

PARTIAL PORTRAITS, by H. James (1888)
—the most perceptive of the early estimates of Trollope's quality.

STUDIES IN EARLY VICTORIAN LITERATURE, by F. Harrison (1895)
—a short essay, but of special interest because it gives a first-hand impression of Trollope himself, and of the surprise felt by the writer that such fine qualities should have happened to lodge in so bluff and noisy a man.

CORRECTED IMPRESSIONS, by G. Saintsbury (1895)
—the short discussion of Trollope in the essay called 'Three Mid-Century Novelists', is a shallow and contemptuous attempt to record his 'comparative oblivion'. It may be of some interest as marking the nadir of his reputation. In his 'Trollope Revisted', *Essays and Studies by Members of the English Association*, Vol. VI, 1920, the same author copiously but indecisively admits that the oblivion had been, after all, only very comparative.

STUDIES OF A BIOGRAPHER, Vol. IV, by L. Stephen (1902)
—the essay on Trollope is short and pleasantly nostalgic; it treats him as a pleasing record of a peaceful but bygone age, and is the first expression of this mode of appreciating him.

A BOOK OF ESSAYS, by G. S. Street (1902)
—a short essay on Trollope claims for him a higher place than was usual at the time, and discusses his 'realism' with some penetration.

ANTHONY TROLLOPE: HIS WORK, ASSOCIATES AND LITERARY ORIGINALS, by T. H. S. Escott (1913)
—the first full-length biography. Many details were filled in by a writer who knew Trollope personally.

THE POLITICAL NOVEL: ITS DEVELOPMENT IN ENGLAND AND AMERICA, by M. E. Speare; New York (1924)
—some interesting points are made about Trollope's treatment of politics, but the author is prevented from doing justice to him by his admiration of Disraeli, whom Trollope disliked both as a politician and as a novelist.

THE SIGNIFICANCE OF ANTHONY TROLLOPE, by S. van B. Nicholas; New York (1925)
—only 490 copies of this booklet were printed. Some of its literary judgements are too enthusiastic, but it contains one of the first attempts to draw a map of Barsetshire, and to classify the novels.

TROLLOPE: A COMMENTARY, by M. Sadleir (1927)
—revised editions 1945, 1961.

ANTHONY TROLLOPE, by H. Walpole (1929)

PORTRAITS, by D. MacCarthy (1931)

FEMALE CHARACTERS IN THE WORKS OF TROLLOPE, by C. C. Koets; Amsterdam (1933).

EARLY VICTORIAN NOVELISTS, by Lord David Cecil (1934)
—a judicious estimate of Trollope is given, containing some valuable comparisons between him and some of his contemporaries, especially Jane Austen, who was his favourite novelist in his youth.

THE TROLLOPIAN, ed. B. A. Booth; Los Angeles (1945-49)
—a quarterly, continued after 1949 as *Nineteenth Century Fiction*.

THE TROLLOPES: THE CHRONICLE OF A WRITING FAMILY, by L. P. and R. P. Stebbins (1945)
—contains much biographical information about Trollope's mother and his eldest brother Thomas Adolphus, and one of the first attempts to emphasize the gloomier and less orthodox strains in Trollope himself.

TROLLOPE: A NEW JUDGEMENT, by E. Bowen; Oxford (1946)

ANTHONY TROLLOPE, by B. C. Brown (1950)
—a sympathetic attempt to define the 'theme' common to the novels, and some illuminating suggestions about the effect of Civil Service experience upon Trollope's approach to life and people.

ANTHONY TROLLOPE: A CRITICAL STUDY, by A. O. J. Cockshut (1955).

A CENTURY OF TROLLOPE CRITICISM, by R. Helling; Helsinki (1956)
—a detailed survey of the ups and downs of Trollope's reputation from his own day to the present, with a good selection of quotations from the original reviews, and a good bibliography of Trollope criticism.

THE HERO IN ECLIPSE IN VICTORIAN FICTION, by M. Praz (1956)
—the long chapter on Trollope is perhaps the most favourable and discriminating judgement so far made by a writer neither English or American.

ANTHONY TROLLOPE: ASPECTS OF HIS LIFE AND WORK, by B. A. Booth (1959)
—this very learned study is specially interesting on the social background, and the vagaries of Trollope's fame.

WRITERS AND THEIR WORK

General Editor: GEOFFREY BULLOUGH

The first 55 issues in the Series appeared under the General Editorship of T. O. BEACHCROFT
Issues 56-169 appeared under the General Editorship of BONAMY DOBRÉE

General Surveys:
- THE DETECTIVE STORY IN BRITAIN: Julian Symons
- THE ENGLISH BIBLE: Donald Coggan
- ENGLISH VERSE EPIGRAM: G. Rostrevor Hamilton
- ENGLISH HYMNS: A. Pollard
- ENGLISH MARITIME WRITING: Hakluyt to Cook: Oliver Warner
- THE ENGLISH SHORT STORY I: & II: T. O. Beachcroft
- THE ENGLISH SONNET: P. Cruttwell
- ENGLISH SERMONS: Arthur Pollard
- ENGLISH TRAVELLERS IN THE NEAR EAST: Robin Fedden
- THREE WOMEN DIARISTS: M. Willy

Sixteenth Century and Earlier:
- FRANCIS BACON: J. Max Patrick
- BEAUMONT & FLETCHER: Ian Fletcher
- CHAUCER: Nevill Coghill
- RICHARD HOOKER: A. Pollard
- THOMAS KYD: Philip Edwards
- LANGLAND: Nevill Coghill
- MALORY: M. C. Bradbrook
- MARLOWE: Philip Henderson
- SIR THOMAS MORE: E. E. Reynolds
- RALEGH: Agnes Latham
- SIDNEY: Kenneth Muir
- SKELTON: Peter Green
- SPENSER: Rosemary Freeman
- THREE 14TH-CENTURY ENGLISH MYSTICS: Phyllis Hodgson
- WYATT: Sergio Baldi

Seventeenth Century:
- SIR THOMAS BROWNE: Peter Green
- BUNYAN: Henri Talon
- CAVALIER POETS: Robin Skelton
- CONGREVE: Bonamy Dobrée
- DONNE: F. Kermode
- DRYDEN: Bonamy Dobrée
- ENGLISH DIARISTS: Evelyn and Pepys: M. Willy
- FARQUHAR: A. J. Farmer
- JOHN FORD: Clifford Leech
- GEORGE HERBERT: T. S. Eliot
- HERRICK: John Press
- HOBBES: T. E. Jessop
- BEN JONSON: J. B. Bamborough
- LOCKE: Maurice Cranston
- ANDREW MARVELL: John Press
- MILTON: E. M. W. Tillyard
- RESTORATION COURT POETS: V. de S. Pinto
- SHAKESPEARE: C. J. Sisson
  - CHRONICLES: Clifford Leech
  - EARLY COMEDIES: Derek Traversi
  - LATER COMEDIES: G. K. Hunter
  - FINAL PLAYS: F. Kermode
  - HISTORIES: L. C. Knights
  - POEMS: F. T. Prince
  - PROBLEM PLAYS: Peter Ure
  - ROMAN PLAYS: T. J. B. Spencer
  - GREAT TRAGEDIES: Kenneth Muir
- THREE METAPHYSICAL POETS: Margaret Willy
- IZAAK WALTON: Margaret Bottrall
- WEBSTER: Ian Scott-Kilvert
- WYCHERLEY: P. F. Vernon

Eighteenth Century:
- BERKELEY: T. E. Jessop
- BLAKE: Kathleen Raine
- BOSWELL: P. A. W. Collins
- BURKE: T. E. Utley
- BURNS: David Daiches
- WM. COLLINS: Oswald Doughty
- COWPER: N. Nicholson
- CRABBE: R. L. Brett
- DEFOE: J. R. Sutherland
- FIELDING: John Butt
- GAY: Oliver Warner
- GIBBON: C. V. Wedgwood
- GOLDSMITH: A. Norman Jeffares
- GRAY: R. W. Ketton-Cremer
- HUME: Montgomery Belgion
- JOHNSON: S. C. Roberts
- POPE: Ian Jack
- RICHARDSON: R. F. Brissenden
- SHERIDAN: W. A. Darlington
- CHRISTOPHER SMART: G. Grigson
- SMOLLETT: Laurence Brander
- STEELE, ADDISON: A. R. Humphreys
- STERNE: D. W. Jefferson
- SWIFT: J. Middleton Murry
- SIR JOHN VANBRUGH: Bernard Harris
- HORACE WALPOLE: Hugh Honour

Nineteenth Century:
- MATTHEW ARNOLD: Kenneth Allott
- JANE AUSTEN: S. Townsend Warner
- BAGEHOT: N. St John-Stevas
- THE BRONTË SISTERS: P. Bentley
- BROWNING: John Bryson
- E. B. BROWNING: Alethea Hayter
- SAMUEL BUTLER: G. D. H. Cole

BYRON: Herbert Read
CARLYLE: David Gascoyne
LEWIS CARROLL: Derek Hudson
CLOUGH: Isobel Armstrong
COLERIDGE: Kathleen Raine
DE QUINCEY: Hugh Sykes Davies
DICKENS: K. J. Fielding
DISRAELI: Paul Bloomfield
GEORGE ELIOT: Lettice Cooper
SUSAN FERRIER & JOHN GALT: W. M. Parker
FITZGERALD: Joanna Richardson
MRS. GASKELL: Miriam Allott
GISSING: A. C. Ward
THOMAS HARDY: R. A. Scott-James and C. Day Lewis
HAZLITT: J. B. Priestley
HOOD: Laurence Brander
G. M. HOPKINS: Geoffrey Grigson
T. H. HUXLEY: William Irvine
KEATS: Edmund Blunden
LAMB: Edmund Blunden
LANDOR: G. Rostrevor Hamilton
EDWARD LEAR: Joanna Richardson
MACAULAY: G. R. Potter
MEREDITH: Phyllis Bartlett
JOHN STUART MILL: M. Cranston
WILLIAM MORRIS: P. Henderson
NEWMAN: J. M. Cameron
PATER: Iain Fletcher
PEACOCK: J. I. M. Stewart
ROSSETTI: Oswald Doughty
CHRISTINA ROSSETTI: G. Battiscombe
RUSKIN: Peter Quennell
SIR WALTER SCOTT: Ian Jack
SHELLEY: Stephen Spender
SOUTHEY: Geoffrey Carnall
R. L. STEVENSON: G. B. Stern
SWINBURNE: H. J. C. Grierson
TENNYSON: F. L. Lucas
THACKERAY: Laurence Brander
FRANCIS THOMPSON: P. Butter
TROLLOPE: Hugh Sykes Davies
OSCAR WILDE: James Laver
WORDSWORTH: Helen Darbishire

Twentieth Century:
W. H. AUDEN: Richard Hoggart
HILAIRE BELLOC: Renée Haynes
ARNOLD BENNETT: F. Swinnerton
EDMUND BLUNDEN: Alec M. Hardie
ELIZABETH BOWEN: Jocelyn Brooke
ROBERT BRIDGES: J. Sparrow
ROY CAMPBELL: David Wright
JOYCE CARY: Walter Allen
G. K. CHESTERTON: C. Hollis
WINSTON CHURCHILL: John Connell
R. G. COLLINGWOOD: E.W.F. Tomlin

I. COMPTON-BURNETT: Pamela Hansford Johnson
JOSEPH CONRAD: Oliver Warner
WALTER DE LA MARE: K. Hopkins
NORMAN DOUGLAS: Ian Greenlees
T. S. ELIOT: M. C. Bradbrook
FIRBANK & BETJEMAN: J. Brooke
FORD MADOX FORD: Kenneth Young
E. M. FORSTER: Rex Warner
CHRISTOPHER FRY: Derek Stanford
JOHN GALSWORTHY: R. H. Mottram
ROBERT GRAVES: M. Seymour-Smith
GRAHAM GREENE: Francis Wyndham
L. P. HARTLEY & ANTHONY POWELL: P. Bloomfield and B. Bergonzi
A. E. HOUSMAN: Ian Scott-Kilvert
ALDOUS HUXLEY: Jocelyn Brooke
HENRY JAMES: Michael Swan
JAMES JOYCE: J. I. M. Stewart
RUDYARD KIPLING: Bonamy Dobrée
D. H. LAWRENCE: Kenneth Young
C. DAY LEWIS: Clifford Dyment
WYNDHAM LEWIS: E. W. F. Tomlin
LOUIS MACNEICE: John Press
KATHERINE MANSFIELD: Ian Gordon
JOHN MASEFIELD: L. A. G. Strong
SOMERSET MAUGHAM: J. Brophy
GEORGE MOORE: A. Norman Jeffares
EDWIN MUIR: J. C. Hall
J. MIDDLETON MURRY: Philip Mairet
SEAN O'CASEY: W. A. Armstrong
GEORGE ORWELL: Tom Hopkinson
POETS OF 1939-45 WAR: R. N. Currey
POWYS BROTHERS: R. C. Churchill
J. B. PRIESTLEY: Ivor Brown
HERBERT READ: Francis Berry
FOUR REALIST NOVELISTS: V. Brome
BERNARD SHAW: A. C. Ward
EDITH SITWELL: John Lehmann
OSBERT SITWELL: Roger Fulford
KENNETH SLESSOR: C. Semmler
C. P. SNOW: William Cooper
STRACHEY: R. A. Scott-James
SYNGE & LADY GREGORY: Elizabeth Coxhead
DYLAN THOMAS: G. S. Fraser
EDWARD THOMAS: Vernon Scannell
G. M. TREVELYAN: J. H. Plumb
WAR POETS: 1914-18: E. Blunden
EVELYN WAUGH: Christopher Hollis
H. G. WELLS: Montgomery Belgion
PATRICK WHITE: R. F. Brissenden
CHARLES WILLIAMS: J. Heath-Stubbs
VIRGINIA WOOLF: B. Blackstone
W. B. YEATS: G. S. Fraser
ANDREW YOUNG & R. S. THOMAS: L. Clark and R. G. Thomas

PROGRESS AND SCIENCE

PUBLISHED ON THE
KINGSLEY TRUST ASSOCIATION
PUBLICATION FUND

PROGRESS AND SCIENCE

ESSAYS IN CRITICISM BY

ROBERT SHAFER

NEW HAVEN · YALE UNIVERSITY PRESS
LONDON · HUMPHREY MILFORD · OXFORD UNIVERSITY PRESS
MDCCCCXXIII

Copyright, 1922,
By Yale University Press

First published, August, 1922
Second printing, April, 1923

TO
CHARLES WILLIAM HENDEL, JR.

PREFACE

This volume does not contain a systematic treatment of its large subject. I have sought to indicate its character in the subtitle.

I am indebted to the editors of *The International Journal of Ethics, The Open Court,* and *The North American Review* for permission to make use of material first published in these periodicals. Parts of the fourth and sixth essays were first published in *The International Journal of Ethics,* parts of the first and fifth in *The Open Court,* and a few sentences from the third in *The North American Review.*

I wish also to acknowledge the kind permission of several publishers to quote from a number of books: *The Direction of Human Evolution,* by E. G. Conklin; *Saint's Progress,* by John Galsworthy; *Character and Opinion in the United States,* by George Santayana (published by Messrs. Charles Scribner's Sons); *Modern Science and Materialism,* by Hugh Elliot; *The New State,* by M. P. Follett (Messrs. Longmans, Green, & Company); *The American College: A Criticism,* by Abraham Flexner (The Century Company); *Self-Government in Industry,* by G. D. H. Cole (Messrs. Harcourt, Brace, & Company); *Chaos and Order in Industry* and *Social Theory,* both by G. D. H. Cole (The Frederick A. Stokes Company); *The Education*

PREFACE

of Henry Adams (The Houghton Mifflin Company); *The Living Past* and *The Century of Hope*, both by F. S. Marvin (Oxford University Press); *The College and New America*, by Jay William Hudson (Messrs. D. Appleton & Company); *The Degradation of the Democratic Dogma*, by Henry Adams; *Higher Education and the War*, by John Burnet; *The Idea of Progress*, by J. B. Bury; *Democracy and Education*, by John Dewey; *Marius the Epicurean, The Renaissance, Miscellaneous Studies,* and *Appreciations*, by Walter Pater; *Syndicalism and Philosophical Realism*, by J. W. Scott; *Theories of Social Progress*, by A. J. Todd; *The Outline of History* and *The Salvaging of Civilisation*, both by H. G. Wells (The Macmillan Company).

The dedication of this volume to Dr. Hendel, of Princeton University, is an acknowledgement of a debt, happily extending through many years, which no words can describe or pay. I owe another and similar debt to my wife, without whose constant help this book could hardly have been written.

R. S.

Aurora-on-Cayuga, New York,
   21 April, 1922.

CONTENTS

		PAGE
I.	Progress through Science	1
II.	Social Progress	45
III.	Education and Progress	102
IV.	Science and History	155
V.	Walter Pater	194
VI.	Conclusion	219
	Index	241

'Αρχὰ μεγάλας ἀρετᾶς
ὤνασσα 'Αλά-
θεια, μὴ πταίσῃς ἐμάν
σύνθεσιν τραχεῖ ποτὶ ψεύ-
δει . . . .
      Pindar.

I

PROGRESS THROUGH SCIENCE

"PROGRESSIVE human activity subduing the world"; "a common human society, working together for the conquest of nature and the improvement of life"; "the evolution of that collective human force which is growing and compassing the conquest of the world";—who has not heard these or similar phrases? They belong to the intellectual groundwork of the age, and in popular thought are the key to its significant activities. As has recently been said, the doctrine of progress is now "the animating and controlling idea of western civilisation. For the earthly progress of humanity is the general test to which social aims and theories are submitted as a matter of course. The phrase *civilisation and progress* has become stereotyped, and illustrates how we have come to judge a civilisation good or bad according as it is or is not progressive."[1]

[1] *The Idea of Progress,* by Professor J. B. Bury, Preface. This is a well-written history of the doctrine, containing material of which I have been glad to make use. The Romanes Lecture for 1920, by Dean Inge, is on the same subject and bears the same title.

This is a fair statement. Yet the doctrine of progress is, as such things go, not old. It had no real existence either in classical antiquity or in the mediæval age. We can now see that the Renaissance prepared its foundations, and it was distinctly foreshadowed by Bacon, but the doctrine did not receive definite expression until well into the seventeenth century. Even then, however, it remained for several generations the possession of a few. Towards the close of the eighteenth century it gained in strength and prominence, but it was not until the nineteenth century that the doctrine of progress became a broadly popular article of faith—faith buttressed, as it was thought, by modern science. And then it rapidly became central to men's thoughts, the test of all proposals, "the animating and controlling idea of western civilisation." In general the doctrine of progress means that humanity is advancing towards perfection, that it always has been doing so and always will. It is not enough to conceive that civilisation has advanced from time to time, or even continuously, in the past; it is necessary also to believe that civilisation must continue always to advance in the future. This is clear enough, but if one asks further questions—if one asks what are the bases of progress, what its path, what does perfection mean—to these and the like one gets no united answer. Answers are loud enough, but they are various. And this alone may indicate that the doctrine of progress needs criticism. There are, indeed, many signs that people are beginning to ask themselves what all along they have meant in using the word glibly, assuming that everybody agreed upon its meaning, assuming too that it expressed at length the final truth.

In undertaking this inquiry I propose to deal in turn with the chief forms which the doctrine of progress appears at present to take. In the oldest form of the doctrine—and the form which to-day is doubtless most widely and prominently in men's minds—progress is said to consist in the increase of exact and verifiable knowledge.[2] This is progress through science. The phrases which I quoted at the beginning of this essay came from a book, by Mr. F. S. Marvin, called *The Living Past*. In this and in a later volume, *The Century of Hope*, Mr. Marvin has sought to expound this form of the doctrine of progress. His method is historical; he calls the former volume "A Sketch of Western Progress," and the latter "A Sketch of Western Progress from 1815 to the Great War." He says of *The Century of Hope* that it "endeavours to exhibit the growth of humanity in the world, taking as a leading—though not exclusive—thought, the development of science and its reactions on other sides of national and international life." He explains somewhat more fully in the Preface to *The Living Past* that his interpretation of history "first came clearly into view with Kant and the philosophers of the eighteenth century. Take Kant's theory of universal history as the growth of a world-community, reconciling the freedom of individuals and of individual states with the accomplishment of a common aim for mankind as a whole. Add to this the rising

[2] "Human progress is largely mental progress, a clearing and an enlargement of ideas."—H. G. Wells, *The Outline of History*, II, 429.

power of science as a collective and binding force which the century since Kant has made supreme. You have then one strong clear clue which, with the necessary qualifications, seems to offer in the field of history something of the guidance and system which Newtonian gravitation gave to celestial mechanics in the seventeenth century. The growth of a common humanity; this is the primary object to keep in view. But it will prove vague and inconclusive, unless we add to it a content in the growth of organised knowledge, applied to social ends."

The recipe for history, then, is implicit belief in 'science organising industry in the service of an united humanity.' Mr. Marvin, it should be said, is a representative figure amongst those who hold to this view. He endeavours to be frank and straightforward; he is at once rather more thoughtful and more temperate than are some of his fellow-spokesmen[3] for the believers in progress through science; and consequently it seems just to centre in the two books I have mentioned a consideration of the doctrine. One of these books, it is true, was written before the War, but the War has not changed Mr. Marvin's mind any more than it has changed the minds of countless others. In 1915 Mr. Marvin undoubtedly spoke for very many besides himself when he asserted that "catastrophes such as we are now witnessing can only delay, but not defeat, the

[3] See Professor W. Libby's *Introduction to the History of Science*, particularly the last chapter and the Preface; also M. George Sarton's article, "The Teaching of the History of Science" (*The Scientific Monthly*, September, 1918).

purpose of the ages and the nature of man." Later he was even able to persuade himself, as can be seen in *The Century of Hope,* that the War was actually furthering his notion of "the purpose of the ages."

Belief in progress through science did not, as I have said, become a broadly popular and dominant article of faith until the nineteenth century; yet it was some hundreds of years ago that the compass and gunpowder first notably showed men the power and consequent profit that might accrue from putting natural forces to work for human purposes. These discoveries, however, were not quickly followed by others, and it was not until late in the period of the Renaissance that anyone appeared who was able completely to express their implications. Only then came Francis Bacon, sharing "to the full the enthusiasm and the sense of power which the age of discovery had inspired in western Europe," and adding "to these the two fundamental traits which distinguish the great founders of modern science in the seventeenth century. One is the critical spirit, determined to sweep away the false Aristotelianism and mere authority which obstructed the progress of effective knowledge: the other, the new impulse to turn to nature as the source and material of truth, and on the truth of nature to build a system for the general amelioration of mankind." Bacon was not one of the actual builders of the new structure. "He was distracted by his erudition and his literary gifts"— qualities surely evil if one can judge from the distrust or hostility which they often evoke—"and still more fatally by the interests of wealth and worldly success," whereas "the actual builders were men of intense and unbroken devotion to the pursuit of truth."

They were, in the first instance, Italians; but the pursuit of truth soon became "an international work, within the area of that smaller progressive world, which Greek intellect, supported by Roman power, had divided from the rest of mankind." The kind of truth specially pursued "in common by many minds in all the leading nations"—"forming a model, as well as a stimulus, to human co-operation"—was what the founders of the Royal Society elegantly called "Physico-Mathematicall Experimental Learning." Whether or not the mathematical and astronomical developments in the sixteenth and seventeenth centuries were regarded by those who took part in them as steps towards "the amelioration of mankind," the advances made at least "show the natural co-operation of several independent minds, working consecutively to attain the one simplest and most consistent explanation of a vast number of hitherto uncorrelated facts." Newton, in whom the development culminated, had "the genius which perceives true resemblances between remote and apparently disconnected facts," and his achievement is "the most fruitful instance in history of the unifying tendency of thought, seen more or less in all its aspects, but above all in mathematics, the 'art of giving the same name to different things.'"

Earlier than Newton, however, there had appeared in Descartes one comparable in some ways of thinking to Bacon. For Descartes shared Bacon's confidence in the meliorative efficacy of exact science. Mr. Marvin quotes his prophecy: "We shall be able to find an art, by which, knowing the force and action of fire, water, air, stars, the heavens and all other objects, as clearly as we know the various trades of our artisans, we may be able to employ them in the same way for their appropriate uses, and make ourselves the masters and possessors of nature. And this will not be solely for the pleasure of enjoying with ease and by ingenious devices all the good things of the world, but principally for the preservation and improvement of human health, which is both the foundation of all other goods and the means of strengthening and quickening the spirit itself." Descartes, we are told, "was the first clearly to suggest" a reconciliation "between the fullest individual culture and the pursuit of a social end"; and "the three centuries since Descartes have brought more and more fully into prominence the social harmony between science and life." In a specifically scientific direction Descartes's greatest achievement was the "mathematical expression of that fundamental conception in modern science which distinguishes it from the science of the Greeks, the idea of movement and continuous growth." This was an achievement which he shared with Newton and Leibnitz, and "with the invention of the calculus in the seventeenth century we reach the last stage yet known to us in the art of measuring which brings the world into subjection to man."

The nature of this achievement indicates for us the general trend of seventeenth-century science. It was, as the founders of the Royal Society had adumbrated, "a physico-mathematical movement, and as such it ran its course before the more complex sciences of life took definite form. It has grown continuously ever since, and by its connexion with industry and the practical arts has become the most powerful and typical branch of science as the agent in subduing the forces of nature to the use of man." Yet there were in the seventeenth century isolated advances in other sciences, such as Harvey's anticipation of the founding of biology and John Mayow's discovery, through experiments with candles and small animals, of the existence and fundamental property of oxygen; and—though we are not told why—these "instances bespeak the intimate similarity of all scientific truth."

The eighteenth century witnessed two great results of the scientific development of the seventeenth. In England it saw the industrial, and in France the social and political, revolution. The former led to the socialisation of science, for science "did not affect the whole of society, until the sweeping changes in the life of the people, which resulted from the union of science and industry, brought men together in masses and made all men think." This union of science and industry "is really another example of that integration of human powers of which science by itself offered so many striking instances." What happened essentially was that, first through the steam-engine and ever since through a miraculously increasing number of other devices, science actually began to be applied to the satisfaction of human needs and desires. Practical fulfilment came to the prophecy of Bacon and Descartes. Thus in one sense the English mine-owners and cotton-mill operators of the eighteenth century were really the great humanitarians of the period, although the merely superficial results of their enterprise were such that Mr. Marvin admits that "the condition of the mass of the people of England was probably worse than it had been at any previous period, while landlords, manufacturers, and capitalists generally, were making larger profits than ever." This was the temporary result of sweeping changes. The permanent result was the utilisation, made possible by capitalists and manufacturers, of the almost unimaginably great stores of power for the control of nature opened up by iron and steam. One aspect of this industrial revolution calls for special notice. Wherever modern industry has developed it has gathered men closely together into towns. This has been essential "for the work in hand in the world." "The assimilation of the vast resources which the new science and mechanical inventions had put in man's command, and the organisation of a society strong, keen, and united enough to grasp and utilise them," has demanded a "quick exchange of ideas, vigorous combination of many minds and many wills. This is the gift of the town."

"The gift," Mr. Marvin sagely observes, "must be studied with discernment and the eye of faith." Proper discernment and faith show, in the first place, that the highly specialised work necessitated by modern industry is an important step towards human unity; it is, "from one point of view, narrowing, mechanical, monotonous; from another, an impressive lesson in the dependence of every particle in the social organism on every other and on the whole. To the countryman, to the workman in a simple state, the fact, equally true, is more remote; the factory worker is surrounded by his fellows and depends at every step on what others send him. . . . This co-operation, which we take for granted in any running concern or running engine, is really the expression in concrete fact of a vast force of organising mind, which has itself grown up with the system, making and being made by it together. Nor does it reside exclusively in any one set of minds, though there must be special organisers, such as foremen and directors. Every person taking part in such a system has in some degree his spirit of co-operation heightened." And in the second place Mr. Marvin, with continued discernment and faith, says that "the town even more than the trade encourages this tendency. . . . For the business-relations, which gave rise to the town, become but a small part of all the forms of association by which its members are developed in co-operative activity; and it grows by its own growth. It is Aristotle's city-state, writ large, in letters of steel. The necessities of machine production made the modern town: its organisation offers to the citizens a larger and fuller life. Iron for marble, smith's work for sculptor's and mason's—much of the difference between the modern state and its archetype is expressed in that change—both as a fact and as a symbol. Less beauty, less individual work, less freshness of thought mark the modern structure: but its material is more durable, the lines of the building are larger, and the ties and stresses

PROGRESS THROUGH SCIENCE

are arranged in the light of a higher mechanical science."

Such, then, were some of the earlier results of the application of science to the amelioration of mankind. They gave, as Mr. Marvin says, definite primacy to the leading nations of western Europe. He adds, however, in seeming forgetfulness of the whole purpose of his writings, that England in particular now "indisputably took the lead of the world" because of her early use of her providentially given "sinews of the new war."

Concurrently with this English development there came into prominence in France a group of thinkers, commonly known as the Encyclopædists, who united to preach the perfectibility of man. The doctrine was in the air. All of the enlightened were beginning to believe in it, yet each one had his own theory for attaining the easy felicity of the race, and it is sometimes difficult to discover their common element. Diderot and some of his immediate associates derived the idea as well as the inspiration for the Encyclopædia largely from Bacon. As Mr. Marvin correctly says, "They refer constantly to Bacon as their apostle and use his language to express their purpose. Like him they set out to found an 'empire of virtue' and to increase human happiness by the growth and spread of science." They went further, however, than Bacon expressly did —though not further than most have thought he should have gone on his principles—in denying the validity of all revealed religions, most of them showing a special and venomous hostility to Christianity. Our sole source of knowledge, they said, is the observation of nature, and all knowledge is thus summed up in the descriptive and generalising exact sciences. They saw that Bacon already had been proved correct in his prophecy that we should learn to command nature by observing or discovering her laws and obeying them; and they looked forward to a progressively increasing command over nature for the satisfaction of human desires as the exact sciences should further develop. Thus these sceptical materialists, flushed with optimism, dreamed that at last humanity was on the true path leading to a perfect state where misery should no longer exist, and where all should dwell in happy concord.

But the precept to obey nature's laws led also to a somewhat different argument. Were not men's miseries due simply to the human institutions of civilisation which had resulted from the pursuit of mischievous and perverse ideals and wrong-headed aims? Did not men become vicious just through their failure to obey nature's laws in their highly artificial organisation of society? Would they not, therefore, speedily attain perfection if they resolutely struck off their fetters of custom and law, and so achieved freedom to be their naturally good selves, to satisfy their naturally good desires? Such a view puts the responsibility for men's present miseries and imperfections entirely upon society, and accordingly it was asserted that the immediate condition of indefinitely great progress for humanity was revolutionary change in the direction of securing for all men freedom, equality, and unity or concord.

A still different yet allied view of progress came a

PROGRESS THROUGH SCIENCE

little later in the biological speculations of Lamarck. He had been, it is true, anticipated in some respects by Diderot, and in others by other thinkers of the period. But he it was primarily who brought the theories of the time to bear upon the subject-matter of biology. "We find in him," Mr. Marvin says, "frequent mention of an inherent tendency to progressive improvement in living things. Nature was compelled, by a law the Supreme Being had imposed, to proceed by the constant fresh creation of the simplest forms, the monads of life which are the only beings directly created. These then develop by gradual steps towards the highest level of intelligence and organisation, partly through their own innate tendency to perfection, partly through the force of external circumstances, the variations in physical conditions on the earth and their relations to other beings." "What is this," Mr. Marvin asks, "but a short and general statement of beliefs held by a large part of all subsequent thinkers on the subject?"

Mr. Marvin goes on to say that Lamarck in his investigations foreshadowed later geology as well as biology, and so supplied "the first hint of the correlation between earth and life, . . . Lyell and Darwin, which was ultimately to win universal assent for the doctrine of evolution." And in the middle of the nineteenth century Darwin, "and his fellow workers on the doctrine of evolution, transformed the old simple faith in human perfectibility by two additions. They gave a body of facts, a set of operative causes to fill out the vague and somewhat empty formulæ which satisfied the first enthusiasts. And they supplied the other complementary term which any sound notion of progressive life requires, the idea of the environment upon which the developing organism acts and which reacts upon it. To Condorcet, to the enthusiasts of the Revolution, the future was a vision of 'mankind marching with a firm tread on the road of truth, virtue, and happiness,' a road on which 'we could see no limits to our hopes.' To Darwin, to anyone who had studied the facts of life from the new perspective, progress was no less real, it was a palpable and concrete thing, but its reality could and should be measured by the adaptation of the living being to its environment, including in its environment those fellow creatures with whom it lives." Mr. Marvin is aware that biological science has not the exactness of physical science, and he instructively compares the former to a journey by aëroplane: "There is no permanent way. We travel quickly; we feel our way and dart hither and thither to escape a contrary wind. But the speed, the exhilaration, the prospect are superb, and the solid world recedes beneath our flight." Yet, he says, "however Darwin's theory is finally modified, it remains the dominating influence in all the sciences of life. It transferred the centre of interest from the life of the individual to the growth of the species. . . . Darwin's law, moreover, becomes itself another and potent link in the unification of mankind, for like all science it brings together the co-operating and consenting minds, and also gives us an objective unity among things outside us which were before regarded as separate beings. In the light of a general law of evolving life, all animal and vegetable species appear as branches and twigs and flowers of one great tree springing from a common root."

This I think is true. Darwin, Lyell, and their coworkers and followers seemed to prove what many had already in substance said and what many were anxious to believe. Not all were thus anxious, it is true, for the great nineteenth-century controversy over evolution should be neither ignored nor forgotten; but most have come to feel that the battles against Darwinism, as they were actually conducted, were lost before they were begun. Those on both sides of the conflict felt that the Darwinians 'had the goods.' The Darwinians seemed to prove that worldliness was right, and at the same time this was becoming, through industrialism, the dominant characteristic of society. To the social forces actually at work they gave high sanction; industrialism was a forward step along the path of progress. And the Darwinians seemed to guarantee progress towards perfection as a fact—as an inherent natural tendency of all living things. It is plain enough now how social fact and biological theory happened at the moment to play into each other's hands; so that, spite of great controversies at the time, it seems as if most men were merely waiting for the theory of progressive evolution. When it came it was seized upon with a feeling of relief; it meant "a fuller life on all sides, the fullest life of which the individual is capable," as something all might count on in the future. And whose future was scarcely asked, in an age of action rather than of meditation. It was sufficient for an increasing number of men that the new facts gave substance "to a view in which all good things, the beauty of nature and the joy of living, as well as knowledge itself, are all included in that manifestation of the Highest to which our being tends. The barriers of asceticism, partly mediæval, partly puritan, have been broken down, and our ideal of the Best does not now seem to grow only as one side of our nature by some stern law imposed from without, but embraces all congruent things, and will, as the self develops, embrace still more." Doubtless it is a pleasant view; and men have felt that science is the sufficient instrument of progress—science which has done so much and which inevitably must end by doing everything.

Important for progress is the increasing unity of mankind, without which, indeed, its chief benefits can never be achieved. Mr. Marvin, however, is certain that much has been accomplished towards this end. The first steps were taken in the building-up of the ancient empires in the rude religious infancy of the race. "For the task of building up a great society round one centre of government, the scientific intellect is of itself unsuited: it is a probe before it is a link." But the beginnings once safely made, science became in modern times 'link' as well as 'probe.' This in fact is Mr. Marvin's fundamental claim, which he never wearies of repeating. "The earlier developments of applied science . . . tended on the whole in a very marked degree to the unification of the world. Steam-ships, steel-rails, and telegraph-wires were the chief agents, and later improvements, the turbine engine, the internal-combustion engine worked by oil, wireless telegraphy, are all developments . . . tending in the same direction. The inhabited world thus moves on clearly to a common goal just as the members of the solar system are all one in their concerted movements round the one source of light and heat and motion." Mr. Marvin goes on to remind his readers that this alone is a stupendous fact, full of lessons. It may both inspire and guide us. In these achievements "man has found himself as the continuous creator. His thought, growing from age to age, has linked itself in the work with his active and inventive powers, and gone on adding strength to strength. It is the application of his knowledge which proves to him both its foundation in reality and his own capacity for using these realities for his own ends. From this comes confidence and a vista of fresh conquests awaiting him in the future. The guidance comes from reflecting on the conditions which have made this progress possible. The thought lying at its basis is a collective thing, not limited by any national boundaries, but spreading freely wherever it finds congenial elements, just as a Frenchman, an Englishman, and a German co-operated to establish the law of the conservation of energy. The fact that such co-operation is often unconscious is the strongest evidence of the inherent likeness in the workings of all human minds and of the common process which unfolds itself continually throughout the world. Unconscious and obscure as the first workings of this thought may be, when once announced and applied to the world of facts it proceeds to create an organisation of life as complete and unbreakable as the links which bind the thoughts themselves together. This is the patent and most significant result of the triumph of applied science in the last century, as true and striking as the social nature of the science itself. Society has become, in all those countries where industry has been organised and developed by science, a far more united and stable thing than it was before, or than it is in other regions less advanced in this respect."

This and preceding quotations exhibit Mr. Marvin's reasons for asserting that science is the greatest agent, and a demonstrably efficacious agent, for unifying mankind. Yet he should be quoted further upon so fundamental an assertion: "This growth of science," he says, "is by no means the whole of civilisation, but it holds a commanding position in it, and several features in the scientific evolution seem identical with the conquering social spirit itself. Like language, the method of exact science has a double aspect, the external facts which it brings together and arranges, and the human minds of which it correlates and expresses the thought. Now on each side of this double process the unifying action of scientific thought is its most striking feature. On the objective side it carries the generalising process of language much further and applies it exactly. Where language gives the same name to like things, science, seeing deeper, can give it to the superficially unlike, and express by the same equation the fall of the stone and the revolution of the planet. . . . It is the logical essence of the process, though we are here rather concerned with the social aspect of the fact. Just as the method consists objectively in collecting resemblances

PROGRESS THROUGH SCIENCE

from the complex of phenomena and expressing them in the simplest exact general statements or laws, so, on the side of the human minds perceiving the resemblances and formulating the statement, there is a corresponding process of comparison and unification. The differential equation, though Leibnitz suggested its precise form, sums up the consensus of innumerable minds, the earliest savages who noticed the likenesses of things around them, the first measurers who agreed to lay out their fields and decorate their buildings on a common scale, the Greeks who formulated the similarities of figures in the first equations, the Arabs who improved the notation, the thinkers of the seventeenth century whose genius, co-operating, through many minds, carried the idea of a common law into the recesses of space, and expressed it so concisely that it has become the universal and permanent intellectual currency of mankind." Thus "scientific method" is "firmly established as the natural and fundamental link of progressive human society." And, further, both the history and the use of science "proclaim the necessary unity of human effort. For science arose from the simplest facts of common experience, and grew by the co-operation of the mass of men with human intellect at its highest. And when developed it returns again to widen and strengthen the common intelligence and increase the common good. Above all, more perfectly than any other form of thought, it embodies the union of past and present in a conscious and active force."

Thus science is said to exert its unifying influence in several directions. It unites diverse appearances in the world of phenomena, knitting up lightning and magnetism, falling stones and the revolving earth, plant and animal and man, past and present, into one coherent whole. Likewise through the steam-ship, the railroad, the aëroplane, the telegraph, the telephone, it makes our world more compact, throwing all men closely together and making them rub elbows, as we say. Hence it is no longer possible for us to escape our fellows if we would, but, as never before, necessary for us to accommodate ourselves to each other, suppressing our peculiarities or 'unsocial' qualities in the process. Further, science unites men's minds; it "is man's true universal language"; and in its theoretic aspect it is both international and co-operative in character in the greatest degree, while in its applications in industry it again brings home to every worker the fundamental importance of co-operation in human effort for the common good and exhibits to him the complete dependence of each human being upon all others. Regarding this Mr. Marvin says that "just as the humblest worker in a great observatory may feel some glow in the revelations of the telescope above him, or the fitter on the railway bridge reflect that his work is vital to the lives of thousands and the welfare of a continent, so we may believe that all organised industry is capable of inspiring this feeling and giving the worker this foothold in a universal scheme."

I do not know how real all this may seem to informed and sober persons. Using as far as possible Mr. Marvin's own words I have tried to sketch the development of the gospel which he preaches. A critical history of its

PROGRESS THROUGH SCIENCE

development would be, I may say, a different thing; but I have been concerned simply to present this doctrine as it is conceived by those who believe in it. Its adequate criticism in this form is not easy, but I wish at any rate to suggest some considerations which an adequate criticism would have to take into account.

In the first place Mr. Marvin pretends to write history, and to prove this doctrine by the sanction of historic fact. He candidly tells his readers, it is true, that while "the growth of a general or European frame of mind" is evident to all, still, "it is one thing to believe in and realise this, and quite another to trace its workings in the manifold difficulties and turnings of practical life." Yet he has an easy way of surmounting this and similar difficulties. His method is just to disregard everything that does not support his "strong clear clue." "We are surely justified," he says, "in giving the first place in our treatment to those sides of human nature in which the historic development is most marked." And again: "From tool to tool, from flint axe to steam-engine, is a striking, palpable measure of man's achievement from his earliest beginnings to our own days. This must not be understood to confine the idea of progress within the limits of the mechanical arts or to suggest that mechanical tools are the highest product of human intelligence. . . . But man's tool-making is so characteristic and progressive, it brings together and exhibits in working order so many of his powers, that if we were isolating one aspect only of his activity, the series of his tools would best display the growth of mind." Mr. Marvin shows skill in achieving plausibility, but his procedure which these words seek to justify is the simple one that I have mentioned, of disregarding whatever does not suit his plan. By this method, of course, one can make history 'prove' anything one wishes; it has often been done. And accordingly one who wants to be convinced rather than hypnotised must throughout Mr. Marvin's work rewrite it for himself as he reads. Evidently his books are scarcely 'history' at all, though their disguise may be effective for capturing those persons who swallow propaganda whole.

A case in point is Mr. Marvin's treatment of religion. He is struck by the religious basis of ancient civilisations, such as that of Egypt, and he sees that the formation of strong and stable governments, extending over great areas, apparently had then to depend upon the development of the religious spirit. Accordingly he says that the religious spirit was valuable for the beginning it alone could make towards the organisation of humanity for the conquest of nature; it alone was able to bring and hold together great societies around one centre of government, to inspire individuals with such passion for the social structure as to forget themselves for its sake. We owe, he continues, the same debt to mediæval Christianity. At the break-up of the Roman Empire Christianity providentially stepped in, not merely to rebuild an old civilisation, but to widen and strengthen its germ of permanent truth; that is, to implant in men's hearts the hope of a world-polity in which all humanity should be harmoniously united in the pursuit of a common social end. The consequence

PROGRESS THROUGH SCIENCE

is that the Middle Ages, which apparently contributed nothing to progress through science, in reality gave us the very possibility of such further progress. It is true "that at the close of the Middle Ages man was not on the whole better equipped by his knowledge of the laws of nature than he was in the hey-day of Greek science. . . . But on the other side of the picture we see the social force and unity of the vanguard of mankind immensely strengthened by the process of these unscientific centuries; and this development was no less essential to the coming conquests of mankind than scientific knowledge itself." "The social unity of all mankind, the common action and purpose of the universe," we are told, "became articles of faith, guaranteed by the most powerful organisation in the world." And mediæval Christianity culminated in the 'demonstration' "that there is one principle which rules the heavenly bodies in their certain courses and by the same law the souls of men. As surely as we see the former revolve in their orbits, so surely is mankind created to work together for the salvation of all." Thus the "ideal purpose" of the Papacy was "to bring together the two realms of man and nature under one Law of Love."

Mr. Marvin unobtrusively makes the transition from talk about the social benefits resulting from religious faith to talk about religion as being itself essentially socialistic propaganda. This is a sufficiently remarkable transition, but the passages just quoted show its accomplishment. Accordingly it is easy for Mr. Marvin when he reaches the nineteenth century to say that in this period, particularly during the last thirty years of it, there was real and great 'religious' progress, and that it centred in "the growing devotion of religious people to good works, especially of an organised kind." "The progress of religion," he says, "consists essentially in bringing its conceptions more and more nearly into harmony with the highest moral ideas of mankind." Now "in our own and recent times both the public and the preachers are turning to the good will, the good life, the desire to help one's neighbours, as evidence of religion, apart from creed or formal practices. . . . The modern parish and diocese is a network of societies and agencies for improving the moral and social condition of its members."

Plainly here is falsification of two kinds. In the first place, Mr. Marvin misrepresents the well-known character and essential nature of mediæval Christianity. Christians did indeed preserve much of the old Greek and Roman civilisation through the long period of barbarism and slow rebuilding; they did hasten the development of a new European civilisation. Yet it can be said in a sentence that civilisation was not the Church's aim. Whatever its failures and lapses, the Church did not aim at the creation of an Earthly Paradise. Often unwillingly and always with difficulty, the Church still did contrive to preach the depravity of the natural man and the sinfulness of all earthly and fleshly desires. Not social amelioration but the greater glory of God through the redemption of men's souls from temporal corruption was the Church's aim. Certainly a vague sense of human solidarity did arise in isolated instances from the reflexion that God's grace might come equally to all men, irrespective of race or social condition, but this is a very different thing from saying that the Church taught as an article of faith "the social unity of all mankind." To recognise this it is enough to remember that the Church never discouraged the private accumulation of wealth, that it never sought to relieve temporal injustice or oppression, that it never attempted to level social inequalities—that, in a word, it frankly left worldly affairs to the children of this world, being itself concerned with the totally different, eternal realm of the spirit. So far, moreover, as it failed of this general aim, as too frequently it did, failure did not come from any bias in favour of social amelioration.

In the second place, Mr. Marvin misrepresents the nature of religion itself. Did any man or woman—it may be asked, with no intention of flippancy—ever worship God in spirit and in truth for the sake of providing the children of the poor with pasteurised milk, or in order to found homes for orphans?—did any man or woman indeed ever worship God in spirit and in truth for the sake of making his neighbours across the street or next door more honest? A plain answer to this question puts the matter in a clear light. To anyone who has known religion even at a distance the question will seem perhaps worse than absurd, yet it makes a fair summary of Mr. Marvin's assertions. The truth is that a religious person may partially express or give outward result to his religion through good works, even of 'an organised kind.' He may thus, for instance, help to support 'fresh-air homes' for city children or, more questionably, he may see to it that his neighbours do not disobey the prohibition law or falsify their income-tax returns. But others may do the same things from quite other motives, from simple good will or benevolence, from devotion to efficiency, from the itch which allows no rest to the meddlesome busybody. Good works thus are not even certain evidence of religion, and are by so much the less religion itself. Religion is a condition of the inward man—an inner, personal experience in which the individual finds new life in the consciousness of the grace and the fatherhood of his God, and in the assurance thereby given him of the eternal peace which passeth understanding. This means that essentially religion is not a social activity at all, and that, moreover, the very entrance-way to religion is a deep conviction of the relative emptiness of the mutable things of the outward world. This truth is as old and as generally known as it is fundamental; yet to many, perhaps to most, it seems now unreal. As Mr. Marvin says, 'both the public and the preachers' turn elsewhere their faces in this generation. But so far as this is so, if we are frank with ourselves we can only confess the obvious reason—that we are strangers to the religious experience. Such confession, however disagreeable it may be to some well-meaning people whose morals are unimpeachable, is at least serviceable to the cause of truth. Nothing worth the having can be got through palpable misuse of words; and religion is a word whose right meaning has long since been definitely fixed. Self-deception is in fact the most innocent name

PROGRESS THROUGH SCIENCE

one can give to attempts at the transference of a creditable name to secular activities howsoever meritorious.

There is an old-fashioned aphorism by Benjamin Whichcote which runs to the effect that "among politicians the esteem of religion is profitable, the principles of it are troublesome." Mr. Marvin's perversion of truth in his effort to write history according to his own preconception appears to give a new meaning to the old saying. Yet Mr. Marvin could justly claim, of course, that here as well as in his general exposition of progress through science he has only mirrored a popular contemporary point of view. There is, in fact, a connexion here which will presently become plain. First, however, it is necessary to glance at several aspects of the doctrine of progress through science.

Knowledge, said Bacon, is power; we may command nature in so far as we learn her laws and obey them. Bacon's full meaning became plain only from the moment when men discovered how to transform latent natural power into contemporary terms; that is, into money. Then it became plain that science opens the way to material wealth otherwise unobtainable. And from this profitable character of science has come its popular justification and its immense prestige. Men have, of course, always sought power for themselves; though the fact is sometimes obscured because the extent to which power is measured in terms of money has not been the same in all ages. In considering the human craving for power the following words of Thomas Hobbes are worth remembering. "In the first place," Hobbes wrote, "I put for a general inclination of all mankind a perpetual and restless desire of power after power, that ceaseth only in death. And the cause of this is not always that a man hopes for a more intensive delight than he has already attained to, or that he cannot be content with a moderate power; but because he cannot assure the power and means to live well, which he hath present, without the acquisition of more." Whatever may now be thought of Hobbes's philosophy in general, no candid person is likely to dispute these words, but they bring to light a problem. For the desire of power means primarily power for one's self, or at the least power that one can feel a definite share in. It is a commonplace that we feel pride in our country's power so far as we benefit from it in material prosperity;—that, on the other hand, our feeling tends to be one of resentment, making more or less violent 'reformers' of us, in proportion as we are conscious of not receiving a fair share of the general wealth. This certainly is the common rule. And we want wealth ourselves for our own private purposes, which are diverse. This it is which makes power a neutral thing, perhaps good for the individuals who fortunately possess it, but at least as likely to be evil in the long run for them, and altogether likely to be evil for the generality of mankind. For power always involves control over other human beings, the use of other men as instruments for one's own ends. This is an unescapable fact, though many habitually and conveniently forget it, no matter what the form of one's wealth and, it may be added, no matter what the form of our political institutions.

The demagogue proposes an easy remedy for the

evils of power. He would simply make it 'public' instead of private; and it is always possible that his appeal to the gullible may so succeed as to effect a redistribution of power. From this he and his friends may benefit. But the very nature of material power is such that it can be made 'public' in only a fictitious or verbal sense. An individual or group of individuals must always control it, and in so doing must use other human beings as means to their own ends. Demagogues may be more conscientious and humane than other men or they may not—but we can have nothing save their own assertions for surety. And even granting their sincerity, it is notorious that politicians become—from conviction it cannot be doubted—more conservative as they attain actual power and experience the difficulties of administration. One still cannot tell whether the new distribution of power in Russia is 'succeeding' or not, but one significant fact about the Russian experiment has definitely emerged. It was early discovered by the present rulers that they could not hope to succeed without governmental compulsion to industrial work. Granting that the government was composed of perfect and incorruptible beings, it thus became conceivable that stable prosperity might in time result for the *community*. But prosperity conditioned by the tyrannical oppression of the individuals who make up the community can in the end prove only an empty mockery, no matter how widely it is distributed.

Mr. Marvin is rather hypnotised by the contemplation of power. There is an emotional ring in all that he says about its increase through science. This is, he says, 'stupendous,' which no one would deny. Yet Mr. Marvin is no sophistical advocate of the 'public' control of power, nor does he quite commit himself to the position that power is necessarily and in itself a good thing. Concerning the latter, "it would be well for the world," he says, "if the unification of scientific theory had had its counterpart in the unification of sentiments and aims in life. But progress in inventions . . . has been as fruitful in producing more and more effective ways of destroying the life and work of man as it has been in protecting and promoting them. One hopeful fact, however, may be recorded. Nearly all the achievements of science in fabricating weapons of destruction can be converted with little change into constructive channels. The process of manufacturing the most deadly explosives is near akin to that of producing the most effective fertilisers of the soil. Dynamite prepares the way for railroads as surely as it levels forts." This of course is true, but Mr. Marvin succeeds in quite begging the question which he himself has raised, and we shall presently see that there is little enough basis for hope that men's aims will soon cease to conflict with each other. The more perfect, in fact, the unification of such sentiments and aims in life as Mr. Marvin has in mind, the more certain are future conflicts amongst men.

It must be remembered that the goal of progressive humanity is "the fullest life of which the individual is capable"; in other words, the attainment of a state of affairs in which the individual may freely satisfy all his desires, which are assumed to be naturally good. About their natural goodness no question need now be raised, but men's desires are also numerous. "Man is a great deep," wrote S. Augustine, "whose very hairs, O Lord, thou hast numbered and they are not lost in thee; yet more easily numbered are his hairs than his affections and the motions of his heart"—*et tamen capilli eius magis numerabiles quam affectus eius et motus cordis eius*. And modern experience, whatever some modern theory or propaganda may say, proves this still true. Men's desires, free rein being given them, are inordinate; they endlessly grow in intensity, in number, and in conflicting diversity. Old desires increase through satisfaction and new ones are added to them. Periods of satiety and disgust do not perceptibly retard their march. Everyone knows that commerce finds its readiest and largest, if not always its surest, profits in novelties; and the rapidity with which fashions, not alone in clothes, alter themselves is proverbial. This 'expansion of the spirit,' as Mr. Marvin loosely and admiringly calls it, is a restless longing for change and new excitements which from its very nature can never be satisfied. Growing upon itself, satisfactions only increase it.

One may wonder if 'progress' of this sort is worth serious effort, and if its contemporary apologists are really understood by their energetic and unreflective disciples. Yet the problem of satisfying an infinity of desires is not the only one to be taken into account in understanding its nature. One of the remarkable and, it would seem, still insufficiently pondered results of the union of science with industry has been an increase—it is said of well over four hundred *per cent.* in a hundred years—in the population of the western hemisphere. As power of satisfying desires has increased so has the number of those who insistently desire. The development of organised industry, too, has been largely dependent upon this increase in the army of workers. We may in time develop both the means and the requisite sentiment for the control of our numbers; indeed it is certain that in no very distant period we shall have to do so, but if population in the western hemisphere becomes stationary or dwindles, so inevitably will further progress through science cease or retrogression begin. From this there is no escape; the fact is only evaded, not met, by loose conjecture, which can derive no sanction from history, concerning man's inventive capacity. That capacity is admittedly marvellous, but it operates within strict limits, of which requisite man-power is one. Moreover, the term 'labour-saving device' is little else than a fool's coinage. Thus far productivity alone has increased, and if increased productivity is not eaten up in the future by the growing numbers of our own or another race, it will be eaten up by new necessities bred by new desires.

It is well to ask what has actually been accomplished through applied science. Thus far science has contrived for a brief space, as such things go, to improve the material well-being of a large minority of the population of about half the globe. That this material betterment has been extraordinarily great everyone knows, but for it a price has been paid which is only beginning to be realised. Even Mr. Marvin admits, as has been seen, that in the early nineteenth century progress

PROGRESS THROUGH SCIENCE

through science brought it about that "the condition of the mass of the people of England was probably worse than it had been at any previous period." Then and later industry has succeeded only through oppression, through the degraded or ruined lives of the multitude. In the last eighty or ninety years the material condition of working people has slowly but greatly improved, yet no one can pretend that even at present the lives of the great majority are other than a sorry makeshift, and the concessions of capitalism apparently do little or nothing to allay black discontent and class-hatred. The fact is that industrialism and the rewards of wealth not only depend for their existence upon poverty, but that industrialism constantly accentuates its evils. In some societies a man may be poor and yet not discontented, but this is no longer possible wherever industrialism has developed. The attention then paid to material benefits has its natural consequence in materialising, narrowing, and indeed debasing the lives of rich and poor alike. Yet what has been paid in these ways is perhaps nothing to what must still be paid in the future. In 1914 a new period of payment was inaugurated which will be with us for many a weary year. "Competition of riches," wrote Hobbes, "honour, command, or other power, inclineth to contention, enmity, and war; because the way of one competitor to the attaining of his desire is to kill, subdue, supplant, or repel the other." And as such competition brought on the War, so did exact science make it the most destructive and cruel struggle within recorded history. And being over now it is yet not over, for no man can see any end to its all-pervasive, dangerous economic and political consequences. Furthermore the kind of 'progress' possible through applied science by its nature promotes such wars. That 'progress' is nothing other than a competition for riches or other power—a competition which must continue so long as its reward is limited in extent.

If, however, the aim of making mankind more comfortable were somehow attainable, and if the price paid for material benefits were not far greater than the benefits themselves, there would still be the question whether this would contribute, as Descartes and countless others have thought, to the real betterment of humanity. Perhaps this question has already been answered, but it deserves explicit recognition. Wise men of all ages have laid it down that human betterment can come only through the development of our spiritual capacities, and that all other things should serve as means to this end. Without being for the present more precise, we may accept this as a truism which no one can seriously deny. It is easy to see that a starving man's greatest need is food, and a freezing man's, warmth, and that without these and similar elements of material well-being a man cannot, if he would, cultivate his higher faculties. It is also easy to say in consequence that if men are once made sufficiently comfortable and given sufficient leisure they will all straightway turn to the cultivation of their higher faculties. That is the argument, and Mr. Marvin like the rest looks forward to the attainment in this way through science of the spiritual betterment of the race. But argument is too dignified a word for such reasoning.

Patently nothing of the sort actually happens, nor is there any good ground for hope that it may. What does happen is that concentration of attention upon material well-being blinds men to benefits of any other kind. The power to secure material advantages breeds, as has been said, simply the desire for more. The 'sufficiency' of which Mr. Marvin and others dream is never achieved because this desire is infinitely expansive, growing upon its food. Yet so far as it is satisfied it inclines men to believe there is no reality or meaning in spiritual values. Their materialised lives are good enough for them. Anyone who has never learned and relearned this from his neighbours is singularly fortunate, but even such an one can scarcely be blind to the more general lessons furnished by this age. One of the most significant, if not the most striking, of these is the decline during the last thirty or forty years of liberal education. Another and more striking one is the spectacle of the American people inveterately, desperately amusing themselves.

It seems to me that in the light of these considerations Mr. Marvin's loose talk about the unifying efficacy of science loses its plausibility. Men are not necessarily united by being brought, physically, more closely together. This has been known, indeed, rather to kindle antipathies which, if repressed, sooner or later break forth with preternatural vigour. This at the most produces a dull uniformity of manner and appearance which bears no relation to the unity of which Mr. Marvin speaks. Nor are these results attained by teaching men the interrelations of phenomena and so, amongst other things, emphasising their kinship with beasts. Again, the modern worker's realisation of the dependence of others upon his execution of his task is not so likely to fill him with love of humanity as with the sense of power. In proportion as he realises the necessity of co-operation amongst men he tends to turn that need to his own private advantage, holding up his industry or society at large for a higher material reward. No one blames him for doing this who does not also blame his employers, who are playing exactly the same game; but surely to the fact no one can be blind. Nor can there be any reasonable expectation of a different state of affairs. Moreover, granting Mr. Marvin's claim that science has united us all in the common pursuit of 'conquering' nature, this is a singularly different thing from that human unity which he visualises. From this unity of effort competition can never be eliminated because of the object of strife—and the greater the unity the greater must be the competition. Material rewards are always either yours or mine, and we will only unite to share them in order to obtain an advantage over some third competitor. Chaucer's Pardoner long ago knew all about this, and the men of his brief tale are still alive. The only sort of common effort which promotes human unity in any significant sense of the phrase is strife after a spiritual reward, which alone is not vitiated by vulgar competition—which alone may be shared by all men alike without dimming its lustre or lessening its value for each one. Here alone the strife is not against one's fellows, but against one's self.

Indeed Mr. Marvin is himself strangely conscious that science has not accomplished what he is so anxious to claim for it. As he ambiguously puts it in a passage already quoted, 'the unification of scientific theory has not had its counterpart in the unification of sentiments and aims in life.' On one occasion he throws out a hint that this will be remedied when the 'humane sciences,' slower in development than the mechanical ones, shall have attained their full growth. Whether through accident or wisdom, however, he does not develop this hint. Instead he finally swings in another direction. It might be supposed that in his recognition of a need for 'unification of sentiments and aims in life' Mr. Marvin perceives man's real trouble to lie after all within himself. It might be supposed that he is preparing the way for an inconsistent recognition of the necessity of a regimentation of men's desires—of a self-discipline resting upon discrimination between good and evil in human nature. Such a supposition would, however, be distant from the truth.

The truth is that Mr. Marvin does in the end implicitly abandon his whole case for science considered by itself; that he admits the power or wealth made available by science to be a neutral thing, constantly turned to 'unsocial' uses; and that he admits that science can provide no check upon the 'unsocial' use of wealth. Mr. Marvin does this; yet he still maintains that the goal of progressive society is a condition wherein each individual may freely satisfy to the utmost his natural desires. Of course, for the attainment of such an aim the exact sciences are supremely needful, and they remain in Mr. Marvin's scheme the necessary instruments of progress. But for securing that the wealth created by science is put to purely social uses he turns to social sympathy and relies upon it as an equally necessary copartner in the work of progress. This has, I must say, the appearance of being an unhappy afterthought or concession to stubborn facts in Mr. Marvin's scheme of things; and at any rate it introduces a new and alien factor into the argument for progress through science.

Mr. Marvin is accordingly constrained to speak of science and sympathy as if they were inseparable partners, though he is not guilty of actually confounding them with each other. "Side by side with the growth of science," he says, "which is also the basis of the material prosperity and unification of the world, has come a steady deepening of human sympathy, and the extension of it to all weak and suffering things. . . . Science, founding a firm basis for the co-operation of mankind, goes widening down the centuries, and sympathy and pity bind the courses together." The general intention of such words is plain enough; yet it takes no great amount of reflexion to see, even from Mr. Marvin's admissions, that science and sympathy bear no organic relation to each other except that of enemies. Vivisection is a fair example of what happens when they meet on common ground. But if the spirit of theoretical science is one from which all feeling is rigidly banished, it might still be claimed that the purpose of applied science is humanitarian in nature. It exists only to serve human desires; but on the other hand it has grown only because it is profitable. Mechanical inventions were no more than interesting toys before their commercial possibilities were realised. And everyone knows the extent to which commerce now depends upon the creation of new desires. The truth is that the transparent disguise of humanitarian activity has been insisted upon just to render personal profit respectable. And that humanity has not yet sunk below the uneasy feeling that personal profit is after all ignoble is proved by the boast of scientists themselves that they never derive such profit from their discoveries, but leave that for other men. This too is the meaning of the respect generally accorded anyone who acts, as we say, disinterestedly.

But aside from the partnership between science and sympathy which Mr. Marvin seeks to imply, he finds definite proof of the increase and spread of social sympathy in state regulation of the conditions of labour and, even more, in such organisations as the Boy Scouts, the Girls' Friendly Society, and the Student Christian Movement—analogous apparently to the American Y. W. C. A. and Y. M. C. A. He says that "such bodies are very characteristic of recent times; they are largely religious in spirit, and their religion has certain common features. . . . They are without exception humanitarian in a definite and formative sense. They all train their members to believe, and to act in the belief, that the good of others is our own good also, that we develop our powers by such action, and that this in fact is the nature and genesis of all true progress in the world. . . . It should be . . . clear to the student of history that this expansion of the essential and immemorial principle of all morality is on a wider scale and affects more sides of life than anything we have seen before. . . . This fact of triumphant association is indeed so indubitable and so impressive that we might be inclined to rest in it alone as sufficient evidence of the progress of humanity."

I quote these words for whatever they may be worth. They at least throw light upon Mr. Marvin's attempt, already noticed, to identify religion with humanitarian propaganda. Like other observers, he is impressed with the altogether remarkable force often exerted by religion in reshaping the life of the individual. This compelling sanction he covets for the new gospel of social sympathy, and he seems seriously to believe that by using the name he can secure the thing. As to that, however, there are no hopeful facts to bear him out. The only successful instances of co-operation hitherto have been those which directly minister to self-interest. Mr. Marvin's own arguments make the same appeal. So also, if the account just quoted is correct, do the arguments of those well-meaning people who are attempting through various organisations to infuse our children and youths with an up-to-date social consciousness. Plainly there is nothing in any of this which shows the working of sympathy;—there is nothing here but calculated self-interest. Nor is it easy to see how sympathy, often weak when it does exist and always a capricious emotion quickly spent in proportion as it is violently felt, can ever be so fundamentally remade as to form a positive and efficacious guiding principle

PROGRESS THROUGH SCIENCE

for society.[4] Indeed the term 'social sympathy' is itself a contradiction, expressive of nothing real. For sympathy, like all emotions, demands a concrete object, and in proportion as its object is distant or abstract it becomes vague and unreal. A man is aroused to violent action at the sight of a dog or a horse being cruelly

[4] One of Dr. Johnson's candid talks on the subject is worth hearing again: "Talking of our feeling for the distress of others;—JOHNSON. 'Why, Sir, there is much noise made about it, but it is greatly exaggerated. No, Sir, we have a certain degree of feeling to prompt us to do good: more than that, Providence does not intend. It would be misery to no purpose.' BOSWELL. 'But suppose now, Sir, that one of your intimate friends were apprehended for an offence for which he might be hanged.' JOHNSON. 'I should do what I could to bail him, and give him any other assistance; but if he were once fairly hanged, I should not suffer.' BOSWELL. 'Would you eat your dinner that day, Sir?' JOHNSON. 'Yes, Sir; and eat it as if he were eating it with me. Why, there's Baretti, who is to be tried for his life to-morrow, friends have risen up for him on every side; yet if he should be hanged, none of them will eat a slice of plumb-pudding the less. Sir, that sympathetic feeling goes a very little way in depressing the mind.'

"I told him that I had dined lately at Foote's, who shewed me a letter which he had received from Tom Davies, telling him that he had not been able to sleep from the concern which he felt on account of *'This sad affair of Baretti,'* begging of him to try if he could suggest anything that might be of service; and, at the same time, recommending to him an industrious young man who kept a pickle-shop. JOHNSON. 'Ay, Sir, here you have a specimen of human sympathy; a friend hanged, and a cucumber pickled. We know not whether Baretti or the pickle-man has kept Davies from sleep; nor does he know himself. And as to his not sleeping, Sir; Tom Davies is a very great man; Tom has been upon the stage, and knows how to do those things. I have not been upon the stage, and cannot do those things.' BOSWELL. 'I have often blamed myself, Sir, for not feeling for others as sensibly as many say they do.' JOHNSON. 'Sir, don't be duped by them any more. You will find these very feeling people are not very ready to do you good. They *pay* you by *feeling*.'" (Boswell's *Life*, ed. Hill, II, 108-109.)

treated;—the same man reads of the massacre of fifty thousand Armenians or of a distant famine killing its hundreds of thousands without, as we say, turning a hair. He may feel, a little uncomfortably, that he ought to be disturbed, but he is not. The Armenians, or the stricken Chinese or Russians, are concrete objects, but they are distant. By so much the less is there any reason for expecting men to feel active sympathy for humanity at large. There is, on the contrary, every reason for suspecting those who pretend to such sympathy. For the truth is that inculcation of social sympathy opens the way for much fine talk unaccompanied by action—for sheer sentimentalism—and thus it is certain of popularity. Yet of course this leaves the individual and society quite unchanged, and so effects no positive result except its encouragement to self-deception.

However, it is to be wished that we would sometimes ask ourselves if, supposing a condition of universal brotherly love were attainable, this would be a desirable state. No one can answer this question completely, howsoever gifted with imagination, because none can definitely picture such a condition. I shall not here make the attempt, yet some things are plain. Such a society from its very nature would be soft, spineless, and poor. It would be poor both spiritually and materially; with easy-going nonchalance it would neither penalise the slothful nor reward the industrious. It would be completely indiscriminate in all its judgements, the ooze of fraternal sentiment blurring every outline and swiftly unmaking painfully built-up standards of character. Indeed it is difficult to resist the

PROGRESS THROUGH SCIENCE

conclusion that relapse to savagery would be swift and complete. These are sweeping statements, but I can see no ground for assuming that such a society would retain the institutions on which civilisation has hitherto rested. Neither could it nor would it wish to do so. Those institutions rest at every point upon the recognition of actual differences amongst men which it would be a chief purpose of completely humanitarian society to ignore. Thus the institutions upon which organised community life depends would inevitably vanish. Further, I can see no ground for assuming that such a society would preserve any characteristics not demonstrably necessitated by a condition of brotherly love, and savage tribes now exist in which the social bond is extraordinarily strong.[5] It is, however, important that we should not lose ourselves in necessarily vain dispute concerning the precise character of such a society, but that we should awaken to realisation of our almost total ignorance of the condition into which many 'social reformers' of the day would plunge us if they could.

These considerations suggest that social sympathy

[5] Not without interest here are some remarks in Kant's *Idea for an Universal History,* a treatise with which Mr. Marvin plays fast and loose in an effort to make it out that it fully supports his own views. Kant writes: "Without those, in themselves by no means lovely, qualities which set man in social opposition to man, so that each finds his selfish claims resisted by the selfishness of all the others, men would have lived on in an Arcadian shepherd life, in perfect harmony, contentment, and mutual love; but all their talents would forever have remained hidden and undeveloped. Thus, kindly as the sheep they tended, they would scarcely have given to their existence a greater value than that of their cattle." (The translation is Edward Caird's, *The Critical Philosophy of Kant,* II, 550.)

cannot be relied upon as an agent of progress. Yet, as we have seen and as Mr. Marvin himself admits, neither is progress through science alone a possibility. Moreover the popular notion, fostered by Mr. Marvin, that science has proved progress to be in the nature of things is, as we shall presently see, a delusion. It is an echo of the over-confident science of forty or fifty years ago, and no scientist of any repute now dares to make such claims. The truth appears to be that science is an effective means to a kind of progress which has necessary limits, stopping far short of what we should like. And even such progress is attended by a grave danger. For if we expect too much we shall be grievously disappointed, yet the development of science has encouraged precisely such expectations. Thus have men been wrapped up in the material and outward circumstances of their lives, and in visions of an Earthly Paradise in which they could have no share even were it other than an empty dream. Thus science has made some of us more comfortable, but has blinded very many of us to all the deeper values of life, so that we have paid dearly for our comforts. It would be a truer view to regard the applied science of the last hundred years as an agent of the acceleration simply of change rather than of any process which deserves the name of progress. And if this be so it follows that men such as Mr. Marvin are hardly doing us any good, are promoting rather beliefs and hopes which may in the end work an intolerable mischief in the world.

II

SOCIAL PROGRESS

WHEN, towards the end of the seventeenth century, the doctrine of progress, as I have said, first definitely appeared in European thought, it was confined to progress in knowledge. It was asserted that there was and would always be a necessary progressive improvement in men's knowledge of the world, but that was all. Human nature and human capacity would remain unchanged, howsoever the veneer of civilisation should change under increasing knowledge. It was only in the eighteenth century that the doctrine of progress received additions which enable us now to recognise it as a friend. These additions it seems first to have received at the hands of the Abbé de Saint-Pierre, an extraordinary and now little-known figure who devoted his life to unsuccessful projects of moral and social reform. The Abbé was a 'natural utilitarian,' a believer in the Cartesian principles of the supremacy of reason over authority and of the invariability of natural law, a believer also in the necessary progress of knowledge.

PROGRESS AND SCIENCE

From these beginnings it was an easy step to the notion that exact moral and political sciences would contribute to human happiness in the same way as physical science. The Abbé took this step and became a believer in social progress. He believed that rational consideration of the means to social betterment, together with governors wise enough to carry out the conclusions arrived at, would insure continuous progress towards general happiness. For he believed also in 'the omnipotence of governments and laws to mould the morals of peoples' and thus to bestow happiness upon them.[1]

Naïve in many ways as the Abbé de Saint-Pierre certainly was, he was yet the natural precursor of the Encyclopædists of the latter half of the eighteenth century, who in the main only extended and consolidated his views. The Encyclopædists in general had a clearer view of the difficulties of social amelioration, but to offset this they were confident in the power of legislation and systematic propaganda completely to remould human nature. The sensationalist psychology of Locke, conveyed to France and extended in scope by Voltaire and Condillac, was the foundation of their faith. Helvétius argued thence that intellectual and moral inequalities between men arise wholly from differences in education and social environment; he argued also that moral science is equivalent to the science of legislation, so that in a wisely governed community all men are equally capable of reaching the highest mental development. All men's faculties are naturally equal!—hence it was supposed that if reason should rule and knowl-

[1] J. B. Bury, *The Idea of Progress*, Chap. VI.

edge spread the perfection of humanity would slowly, perhaps, but surely appear.

Rousseau, it is true, is still thought by some not to have shared his friends' belief in social progress. This is not the place to argue the question, but it may be observed briefly that this opinion appears to have arisen largely because his scale of values was different from that of many of his contemporaries. That he condemned the contemporary development of the arts and sciences means, not that in his opinion social 'progress' was synonymous with degeneration, but simply that social development had gone off at a tangent from its true line. In the possibility of what he considered true social progress he firmly believed, and thought, moreover, that he knew how to bring it about. All men, he held, were naturally good; the evil nature of actual men was due to their perversion by evil institutions. The means of preserving their naturally good selves lay in political liberty and equality. The foundation of social progress, then, lay in a political state in which all the members united to guarantee the natural rights of each member —a state in which each one, united with all in this common purpose, obeyed only himself and so remained completely free. What such freedom would in fact amount to we need not ask; but it can be seen that Rousseau was more nearly in agreement, concerning social progress, with contemporary apostles of enlightenment than has at times been supposed. In fact Rousseau deepened profoundly the popular appeal of this doctrine by placing the seeds of social progress not in the informed reason alone but also in the emotions and will, and by postulating as its condition political equality and substantial economic equality. The assertion of the natural goodness of men was immensely flattering and, so to say, convenient, and the means of bringing it into play were such as promised tangible assets to the poor and the unfortunate.

Rousseau said, somewhat oddly perhaps, in the opening paragraph of *The Social Contract* that he meant to take men as they were and laws as they might be. This also was the aim of a group of economists in the latter half of the eighteenth century who formulated a theory of social progress from their characteristic viewpoint. Taking men as they were, they sought the principles of a natural order in society which would insure to all men temporal happiness. "Humanly speaking," one of them said, "the greatest happiness possible for us consists in the greatest possible abundance of objects suitable to our enjoyment and in the greatest liberty to profit by them."[2] Liberty was necessary not only for enjoyment but also for production, because of its stimulation of effort. And for enjoyment security of individual property was equally indispensable. Hence the proper function of government was limited to the protection of individual property, and complete freedom should be secured for private economic enterprise. Through such comparatively simple means, it was thought, would universal happiness result. These economists, however, did not advocate political liberty nor were they equalitarians.

Such, very briefly, was the general character of these

[2] Mercier de la Rivière. Quoted by Bury, *op. cit.*, p. 173.

SOCIAL PROGRESS

early theories of social progress. It is easy nowadays to pick flaws in them, yet on the other hand we still recognise them as friends. The doctrine of social progress is a living force; and its foundations, under the surface of contemporary discussion, have not greatly changed since the eighteenth century. In the interval, however, the doctrine has gained an increasing hold upon the popular mind. To-day we divide all people awkwardly, inaccurately, but unhesitatingly into progressives and reactionaries. Under the banner of progress all manner of men flock. In its name the Russian Bolshevists have been doing their suicidal work—but equally are conservative Americans 'the most progressive people on earth.' Social progress has in short, as was in effect said in the preceding essay, become a species of popular religion of which the chief articles of belief are: that earthly life is in and for itself a good thing, that terrestrial happiness is possible for all men, that applied science and industry have given us the means for abundant enjoyment, and that it is now the task of social science and government so to order our common life that toil shall not rest heavily upon any of us and that the means of enjoyment shall be equally open to all. It is, moreover, generally believed not only that terrestrial happiness is possible for all men, but that it is infallibly coming to pass—that is, that social science and government are bound to succeed in their task.

If, however, one asks what the grounds of this belief are, one discovers that it rests at no point upon anything which can be called proof. This is the surprising, outstanding fact about the doctrine of social progress

PROGRESS AND SCIENCE

which ought to be known by those who put their faith in it. It is in the strict sense of the word a dogma; there are no known facts which force its acceptance. Triumphant opponents of religion have termed it a monument of human egoism, and have delighted in the discomfiture which they have caused in pointing out how religious creeds have embodied, not what men knew, but what they merely wanted to believe. However it may be with religious creeds of the past, this is the truth about the modern gospel of social progress.

In the nineteenth century the great support of the believers in social progress was the doctrine of evolution. Herbert Spencer, the industrious philosopher of evolution, guaranteed it. "Always towards perfection," he said, "is the mighty movement—towards a complete development and a more unmixed good; subordinating in its universality all petty irregularities and fallings back, as the curvature of the earth subordinates mountains and valleys. Even in evils the student learns to recognise only a struggling beneficence. But above all he is struck with the inherent sufficingness of things." And further, "The ultimate development of the ideal man is logically certain—as certain as any conclusion in which we place the most implicit faith; for instance, that all men will die."[3] But it is now definitely recognised, I think, that this and all similar statements are really little better, to speak plainly, than balderdash. Evolution proves nothing about progress. Evolutionary science formulates the 'laws' of change which organisms obey. In so doing it is forced to use terms, such as

[3] *Social Statics*, First Ed'n, quoted by J. B. Bury, *op. cit.*

'development,' which are also used in connexion with human scales of value. This, however, while in some cases it may indicate a certain disingenuousness, in general indicates only the poverty of language; for 'development' and similar words as the evolutionist uses them have no connexion with human values. Progress means an unified, purposive process, but some natural 'laws' are apparently irreconcilable with others and nature knows nothing of human purposes. Evolution does not reveal successive stages of life, nor life on a continuously ascending scale. Neither the amœba, the microbe, the ganoid fish, nor the monkey disappeared when man arrived. As for life on an ascending scale—what then are we to make of the facts of reversion and retrogression, as real and as familiar as the opposite kind? The fact is that evolution is as often a downward process as an upward one; and on the other hand when it is 'upward'—that is, moving towards increased complexity and specialisation of function—in all organisms it reaches insuperable limits. This is what happened thousands of years ago to the amœba and to the ganoid fish, to monkeys, ants, and bees, and to the whole series of parasites which attained 'fitness' by retrogression or simplification. 'Fitness,' of course, is another of those scientific terms which confuse the unwary; for it too bears no relation to fitness in any scale of human values.

To assert that increasing complexity of structure and specialisation of function is a 'law of nature' is, it is now known, simply untrue. "Evolution has proceeded," writes a well-known biologist of to-day, Professor E. G.

PROGRESS AND SCIENCE

Conklin, "along many lines and not along a single one; it is best represented, not by a ladder or scale but by a branching tree in which growth has ceased in certain branches but is still going on in others, and while many branches grow upward, some turn down. In one case it is progressive, and in another retrogressive, in one case it leads to increased and in another to decreased size and complexity of structure; in one case to physical strength and combativeness, in another to weakness, cunning, and concealment."[4] Moreover, where increasing complexity is occurring there is progress from the biological but not necessarily from the human point of view. The climax of heterogeneity or complexity is chaos. And if co-ordination or order be added to the concept we have to remember that precisely the trouble with many savage communities seems to be that they live in a too elaborate network of ceremonies which have hardened into system. Simplification, which is always retrogression from the biologist's point of view, may equally well be progress from the viewpoint of human values.

These in summary form are some of the considerations which have, in recent years, forced a profound modification of that fancy picture of evolution as invariable and infinite upward progress with which scientists in the past have filled the popular mind. It now appears that earlier views of evolution were in part the result of ignorance and in part the result of what

[4] *The Direction of Human Evolution.* (Direction in this title seems to mean path, not control.) Other quotations from Professor Conklin are taken from the same book.

has somewhat awkwardly been termed man's egocentric predicament. This is, simply, that we look for what we like. Men have begun investigations with the idea of progress in their minds; then, from the confused welter of contradictory natural processes of change, they have arbitrarily selected those which tend to 'prove' their case. These they have strung together on an ascending line, remaining silent about the facts which they have consciously or unconsciously neglected. It has become increasingly plain, however, that the results of such a method, whatever other value they may have, are not science. Yet unfortunately they still find a large reading public, as has been proved by the sales of Mr. H. G. Wells's *Outline of History,* in the field of history one of the latest of those fancy pictures of evolution which a more developed and critical science has discredited.

But, it may be said, while we cannot now regard progress as a certainty or even as the general rule, man in point of fact has progressed, is progressing, and we can set no limit to his future possibilities; so that, while we now have to modify Spencer's language, we may still believe in the coming of the ideal man. This, however, is not true. In the first place Spencer's prediction depended, as many people apparently do not realise, upon the heritability of acquired characters. But such heritability has been notoriously a disputed point, and at present it seems no longer to find any serious defenders. Professor Conklin writes: "In spite of much controversy, due largely to lack of clear thinking, it is now practically certain that characters acquired by the mortal body are not inherited; that is, are not transmitted to the germ-plasm. . . . The hope of permanently improving the human race, or any other species, in this manner can only lead to disappointment and failure." Yet this is not the only reason for modifying our hopes. Where biological progress does occur it always reaches insuperable limits. The resources of organisms are finite. If they develop in one direction they are correspondingly cut off from development in others. The path of history is strewn with the wrecks which have resulted from this fact, and a whole science, palæontology, is mainly devoted to the classification of their remains. This rule is absolute, and man is no exception to it. When an organism's inherent limits of progress are reached development ceases, and the organism then remains in all essential respects stationary. If an organism transgresses these limits it gets killed for its mistake. Otherwise, so far as is known, nothing short of cataclysmic change in environment will cause further change in the organism. The amœba thus has remained stationary for millions of years, and it is no longer alone. Lice, guinea-pigs, dogs, and men are all in the same boat.

"The conception of unlimited evolutionary progress in any particular line, whether among plants, animals, or men, is a mere chimera," says Professor Conklin, and at present in all organisms from the lowest to the highest the inherent limits of progress appear to have been reached. In the case of man Professor Conklin seems to be as confident of this as in the cases of other animals, nor is it easy to see how his conclusions can be controverted. He says, "there can be no doubt that human evolution has halted, either temporarily or permanently, and when we consider the fact that in every line of evolution progress is most rapid at first and then slows down until it stops, we cannot avoid the suspicion that in those lines in which human evolution has gone farthest and fastest it has practically come to an end." Professor Conklin considers this to be as true of man's intellect as of his bodily structure. He admits, of course, that anyone can see plenty of room for further improvement, and that indeed in the majority of men intellect seems to be just doubtfully emerging. "Surely," he says, "there is great room for improvement here, but so, also, is there room for intellectual improvement in monkeys and dogs and all other animals below man. The fact that there is room for improvement by no means signifies that improvement will take place. Just as in the case of physical evolution, so here, also, there are limits beyond which intellectual evolution cannot go, and these limits are far short of ideal perfection." There has been in the past a great accumulation of knowledge by which we to-day benefit but, as everyone must know, the accumulation of knowledge is a very different thing from increasing intellectual capacity. In the latter there has been no increase in several thousand years; nor is this all, for, in the opinion of those who best know, the Greeks in the two centuries between 500 and 300 B. C. showed greater intellectual capacity than has any people since that time.

Hence it is that we have to say good-bye to the ideal man. He has gone to the land of romance, from which he came. We do not even build upon sand, rather upon nothing at all, if we look forward to a great society composed ultimately of ideal people. The perfect intellect in the perfect body is a beautiful dream, but it is something not of this earth. However, as anyone can see, we do in fact build upon each other. Knowledge may be and often has been, but is not necessarily, lost with him that knows; and the poet's words, or the prophet's, echo, though sometimes faintly, down the ages. Each generation builds upon the last and, though some add not much, others add immensely. Thus through our always accumulating social inheritance progress becomes a reality, and we have only to survey our contemporary level in order to be convinced that it has no limits short of ultimate earthly perfection.

In some such words the modern self-confident belief in social progress might be justified of its children. Professor Conklin, from whose recent book I have been quoting, himself disposes of one view of progress only to replace it by another, and believes that through our accumulating social inheritance progress not only may but will certainly continue until we have achieved a perfectly organised society. Professor Conklin's view will be examined presently. First, however, it should be observed that if such progress can be predicated it should take place in accordance with some general law. In the nineteenth century notable efforts were made to formulate such a law. Superficially it seems an easier thing to do than what biologists and geologists have managed to accomplish, because our knowledge of man's past is comparatively so extensive; there is more evidence, more crude fact, in this field of knowledge than in that of any other of the historical sciences. Yet the many workers in this field have accomplished nothing. Those who have begun with some preconception have, of course, found evidence to support it, just as it has been wittily said that no generalisation about women can be wrong; and as a result many contradictory 'laws' of progress have been announced. But these 'laws' have in general satisfied no one except their authors, for reasons beyond their frequent contradiction of each other. And they have been unsatisfactory because they plainly have not fitted even generally known facts of human history. I do not propose here to review any of these 'laws' because it is so widely admitted that none hitherto propounded has any claim to finality. This indeed is shown in the efforts still being made to discover such a law.

It is nearer the present purpose to inquire why prolonged search has met with no result. The reason lies in the complexity of the phenomena to be accounted for. So far this complexity has proved an insuperable barrier, and there are reasons for believing that it must always do so. John Stuart Mill pointed out long ago the extreme difficulties attendant upon any effort to treat this subject scientifically.[5] He showed that even were it possible to discern a law of uniformity in any succession of events this would be only an 'empirical law,' not a causal one, and that, while it might thus shed light on the past or some portion thereof, it would afford no basis for prediction. Further, Mill showed that a law of progress which might serve as a basis for

[5] *Logic,* Bk. VI, Chaps. vi-xi.

prediction would have to be one which, first ascertained empirically, could then be deduced from an already established body of laws for mind and character—from psychology and ethology. The method, in other words, would have to be the concrete deductive method of astronomy. But the phenomena to be accounted for by social science are of almost infinitely greater complexity than those which astronomy embraces. Consequently Mill felt that the task of formulating a law of human progress was one beyond human capacity.

Mill's opinion is the more impressive because he felt that there was a law of progress awaiting discovery, were that possible. He was himself deeply impressed by the method of Comte in attempting to formulate a satisfactory law, and he was convinced of the usefulness of such attempts. Nevertheless, critical and dispassionate consideration forced him to recognise the insuperable difficulties in the way of actual discovery. One of these difficulties, only alluded to by Mill, would seem in itself to make not only the discovery but the existence of a definite law of progress impossible. This is the part which sheer accident plays in history. Many nowadays, owing to the triumphs of science, seem to have no true conception of the part played by accident in the world. It is the work of science to discern order regulating the apparent diversity of phenomena—the so-called laws of nature. This is the aspect of nature with which scientists deal, and thus inevitably they come to emphasise, in one sense truly, the all-pervasiveness of unvarying sequences. Yet this should not blind us to the equally pervasive reality of accident; and it should be realised that the existence of accident is entirely consistent with the assumptions and discoveries of science. From the scientist's viewpoint the universe is presumably a cosmos, under the reign of universal law; given a cause, and everywhere and at all times it must have the same effect. This of course is truism, but it is necessary also to realise that the universe is full of causal chains which are independent of each other and which yet may at any time collide. When they do, accidents happen. One who wishes to see what this means in the sphere of natural knowledge may profitably contrast the facts at present known in astronomy with the crude popular notion of the fixed and orderly relations of the heavenly bodies. As regards human history the point is simple, and means that any sequence of events might equally well have been radically different from what it has been. But if this is so, it follows that there cannot be in the nature of things a definite law of progress, as the French philosopher Renouvier contended a generation ago. Professor J. B. Bury has recently given an illustration of this difficulty which I cannot do better than quote. "It may plausibly be argued," he says, "that a military dictatorship was an inevitable sequence of the French Revolution. This may not be true, but let us assume it. Let us further assume that, given Napoleon, it was inevitable that he should be the dictator. But Napoleon's existence was due to an independent causal chain which had nothing whatever to do with the course of political events. He might have died in his boyhood by disease or by an accident, and the fact that he survived was due to causes which were similarly independent of the causal chain which, as we are assuming, led necessarily to an epoch of monarchical government. The existence of a man of his genius and character at the given moment was a contingency which profoundly affected the course of history. If he had not been there another dictator would have grasped the helm, but obviously would not have done what Napoleon did."[6]

Illustrations of this sort could of course be multiplied without number, and it must be admitted that they make the notion of a definite law of human progress seem chimerical. If the factor of accident does not entirely destroy the possibility of a law, at any rate any law which allowed for it would be so far removed into the region of vacuous generality as to have no positive value. Moreover, there is another profoundly disturbing factor which a satisfactory law would have to take into account; this is human consciousness. Self-consciousness, of course, is to the scientist little less than a scandal. His field of work is elsewhere, and when he cannot disregard consciousness he perforce attempts to explain it away. Very recently Mr. J. W. Scott has pointed out how Karl Marx's prediction of the class war illustrates this difficulty inherent in a 'natural science of man.' Marx, fundamentally defective though his analysis was as an universal law of progress, nevertheless had sufficient insight and intellectual power to formulate a law astonishingly near accuracy for a brief segment of European and American development. Mr. Scott points out, however, that Marx's prediction is

[6] *Op. cit.*, p. 303.

SOCIAL PROGRESS

already seen to have been inaccurate, and that it is seen to have been inaccurate because Marx left out of account one fact—the fact that by his very discovery of the class war he himself brought about an alteration in its character. He altered it simply in awakening the classes concerned, in making them conscious of the fact of its existence. No sooner were they conscious of it than movements set in on both sides which have had the net result of greatly ameliorating the very conditions which, according to the prediction, were bound to get progressively worse until the class war should reach its bloody climax. As Mr. Scott puts the general fact, "The difficulty of reducing the facts of man's social behaviour to natural law, as we might the behaviour of animals, is simply that the natural law which governs men has a trick of ceasing to be a law whenever it is proclaimed. In the present instance, whenever the two classes learn what the 'law' of their action is supposed to be, they see it to be discreditable, begin to remember their humanity, and refuse to have it."[7]

The fundamental nature of this difficulty in the way of formulating a law of human progress is so apparent that it needs no emphasis. These, then, are some of the reasons why the contemporary notion of social progress is fitly to be termed a dogma; there is neither any known law of human progress nor any likelihood that one will ever be discovered. There is good reason for suspecting that this may be not only because of the limits of human capacity but because none exists. Further, no help can be derived from biological science.

[7] *Syndicalism and Philosophical Realism*, p. 34.

Evolution has to do only with the fact of change, which is equally consistent with progress or retrogression. Biological progress, moreover, is not synonymous with human progress, and when it does occur it always has inherent limits which force its cessation far short of ideal perfection. So far as biology does contribute anything to the question it tells us that there is no ground for hoping that man will ever be essentially different from what he is now.

However, were such considerations as these more generally known it is doubtful if contemporary faith in social progress would suffer any immediate diminution. A faith which has not only persisted but has been immeasurably strengthened in the face of much heartbreaking experience during the nineteenth century and the early years of the twentieth is not likely to diminish without a considerable struggle. Prophets who have caught sight of the millennium will not easily forgo publication of their cheering messages. They may grow more wary in language, but they know their audience, and know that there is always a career for him who tells the people what the people wish to believe. Hence our air is long likely to be distracted by breezes blown from the land of romance. Mr. G. D. H. Cole in his recent book on *Social Theory* announced that he intended therein to elaborate principles of 'right,' that he intended to treat of what ought to be, not of what is. If such claims have any meaning at all they mean one thing—that Mr. Cole aimed at proclaiming principles of universal validity; as he says himself, "it is . . . essential to understand that these principles . . . are, however imperfectly, at work everywhere around us in society." But in the same breath he goes on to warn his readers that he would not think of testing his conclusions anywhere save in western Europe, that he fears they would not apply even to Russia, much less to civilisations of the East. And Mr. Cole frankly adds that his principles are in reality based on observation of contemporary society alone in two or three small countries of northern Europe. It is impossible to say whether or not Mr. Cole felt a suspicion of foolishness in thus contradicting himself, but he obviously felt secure. And, consciously or not, he felt secure because he was engaged in telling people what they want to hear; he was holding forth alluring prospects of a good time about to be had by all.

Here is the dangerous aspect of the gospel of social progress. It matters not whether its propagandists are sincere or unscrupulous—and as far as the present argument goes we may assume them all to be sincerely well-meaning and altruistic in disposition—equally in either case these propagandists are engaged in depicting prospects which as far as anyone actually knows have no possibility of fulfilment. All of us like to hear good news; all of us interpret as being good any news that we hear, as long as we can; but if the facts of experience indefinitely persist in disagreeing with what we have been told and have been promised—sooner or later inevitably follows a day of bitter disillusionment. Such a day the propagandists of social progress seem to be preparing; and it may well turn out that those who are to-day most bitten by reforming zeal will presently be those most directly responsible for disintegration and decay.

It is best to take a concrete case. Mr. G. D. H. Cole is prominent amongst contemporary reformers. He is a man of keen and active mind who by dint of much hurried, energetic writing has carved out for himself a position of leadership in the movement of the guild socialists. In his thinking there is much that is true, much that is salutary which we need to be told. Of this there can be no dispute, and many of us are considerably in Mr. Cole's debt for the vigour and alertness which he has infused into his political writings. If I am not here concerned with this aspect of his work it is not because I am unaware of it, but because there is another side to his remarkable activity. Mr. Cole sees nothing good in the present organisation of society. On all sides wherever he looks, except in the ranks of the trade-unionists, he sees only perversion and decay. Society is far sunk in a stupor of immorality; social practice is synonymous with organised and brazen theft, while social theory is sterile. All this and more is the result of the pervasive tyranny of capitalism. For in these days "economic power is the key to political power, and . . . those who control the means of production are able, by means of that control, to dominate the State. Nor is their power dependent on an actual organisation of the machinery of State in their interest. However the State may be organised, and whatever parliamentary system may exist, economic dominance will find its expression in political dominance. . . . The fact that . . . institutions are largely democratic in

SOCIAL PROGRESS

form does not make them democratic in practice, because the power of capitalism stands behind the State. Capitalism controls the funds of the great parties, and thereby controls their policies: capitalism controls the press, and thereby twists and deforms public opinion to its own ends: and, even if these expedients fail, no Government dares to run seriously counter to the wishes and interests of the great economic magnates."[8] The capitalist is immoral because his motive is greed, instead of service to the whole community; and he further attempts with persistent immorality to force others, through fear of starvation, to work for him, instead of allowing them freely to work in service of the whole community. "To do good work for a capitalist employer is merely, if we view the situation rationally, to help a thief to steal more successfully."[9] Consequently "with the capitalists there is often an armistice, but there is never peace."[10] And all the while "orthodox social theory is bankrupt."[11] But amidst this gloom Mr. Cole sees one ray of light. Industrial workers are imbued with the spirit of rebellion against the whole system; let them once dominate society, and righteousness then, and then alone, will rule. There must first be a confiscatory revolution in which capitalism must be abolished root and branch. If society can be intimidated, through constant strikes, into allowing the change peacefully, well and good; but the great change

[8] *Self-Government in Industry,* 5th ed'n, p. 123.
[9] *Ibid.,* p. 189.
[10] *Chaos and Order in Industry,* p. 157.
[11] *Social Theory,* p. 209.

must come speedily[12] if open violence is to be avoided. This vast revolution once accomplished, industry is to be turned over to the actual workers therein, who will henceforth run it to suit themselves in the interest of the whole community. The workers then will be free men, not exploited slaves as they are and must be under capitalism, and they will themselves choose all their foremen, managers, and the like by election. These and all other elected officials will be subject to the constant criticism and advice of those who elect them, and will also be subject to recall. Each craft-union, or guild, is to have coercive power—power of imposing fines, imprisonment, or other penalties—such as the state alone now wields, though only the state is to be allowed to maintain an army and navy. Further, along with capitalism wages are to be abolished, and men are to receive the fair profits of the industry in which they engage, subject, however, to the maintenance of universal economic equality—an important restriction indeed.

Of course it is impossible briefly to summarise the whole structure of guild socialism, which Mr. Cole is fond of sketching in bold outline. It is likewise impossible to ask Mr. Cole and his friends about perplexing questions of detail. Mr. Cole wisely deprecates such questions, pointing to the difficulty of prophecy—which he apparently feels more at some times than at others—and relying upon the inspiration of the moment later to settle satisfactorily all troublesome minutiæ when the time of revolution arrives. I have accordingly attempted only to indicate some of the salient characteristics of

[12] *Chaos and Order in Industry*, p. 271.

this New Order which is to insure universal righteousness and happiness. About such results Mr. Cole has no doubts or qualms, for reasons which his readers would do well to examine. He says himself that his only assumptions are "that the object of social organisation is not merely material efficiency, but also essentially the fullest self-expression of all the members," and "that self-expression involves self-government."[13] These, particularly the first, are worth pondering, but they are neither Mr. Cole's only nor his largest assumptions. For he also takes over two important assumptions which first proved popular in France in the eighteenth century. These are the natural goodness of man and its corollary that man is not responsible for his sins or defects, which are caused wholly by perversion and wickedness in his environment, and which will disappear with proper change in the structure of society. "Man is not naturally a rebel against order, unless the order," says Mr. Cole, "is itself unjust"; but at present the individual is "subject to an autocracy which at every turn stifles, instead of developing, his natural capacity for self-government and self-assertion."[14] However, under the New Order "good work done for the Guild will be done in the interests of a society of equals, and will appeal to the highest and strongest of human motives—the sense of fellowship. Even a purely rational man would work well for his Guild: how much more willing will be the service of the average man, a creature of sentiment, ever more inclined to give than

[13] *Social Theory*, p. 208.
[14] *Self-Government in Industry*, p. 188.

PROGRESS AND SCIENCE

to take, if only he can feel that in giving he is serving a fellow and an equal!"[15] Such quotations could easily be multiplied were it necessary, and they are conclusive. The key, in fact, to Mr. Cole's whole enthusiastic projection of a new and righteous society lies in his acceptance of this exploded dogma of man's natural goodness. All the data of experience, the positive knowledge of science, and the inner knowledge of the individual unite to expose the falsity of the notion, yet Mr. Cole builds his structure upon it and finds that readers still swallow it eagerly—so comfortable a doctrine is it to believe.

One perforce recalls again the famous scene in the Champ-de-Mars on the 14th of July, 1790, when the sovereign people of France gathered together to swear loyalty to the new constitution which was to insure a reign of justice and happiness for all. The trappings of the festival were cheap enough, but those who took part in it really believed that by the magic of legislation their minds and hearts had suddenly been transformed; they really believed that their natural goodness had been reinstated in its true place as the regnant motive of life and that earthly felicity was at hand. We all know the sweeping and terrible refutation which closely followed, we all know that there was no magic change beneath the surface; and so clear was the lesson that the naïveté of the French revolutionary spirits has become a byword. That it is a sheer absurdity to suppose that one can transform the springs of feeling and of action by legislation is now a truism; yet so dear to the

[15] *Self-Government in Industry*, p. 189.

obstinate heart of man has been this glittering supposition that it has not yet been allowed to die. One might suppose that, even if the shocks of experience could not do so, the example of the very believers in this supposition would before now have killed it. But not even William Godwin nor the futile experiments and writings of Robert Owen in England, nor yet Fourier in France, with his notable discovery of a law for so harmonising the passions that none of them should need to be curbed or restrained—neither these nor lesser figures have sufficed to make ridiculous this baseless supposition, which is cherished by others of the present day besides Mr. Cole. Yet that he bases his projects on such a foundation ought in itself to be sufficient evidence that Mr. Cole is engaged in arousing hopes which have no possibility of fulfilment.

There is, moreover, another way of looking at Mr. Cole's picture of the New Order which forces the same conclusion. For the purpose of practical agitation, to increase their self-confidence and feeling of solidarity, Mr. Cole and his friends urge workingmen continually to strike for whatever most appeals to them—chiefly more pay and less work. They so strike, Mr. Cole of course says, for the sake of the whole community, though it is not always easy to distinguish this high motive. What is always easy to see is that workingmen are interested because they perceive the immediate rewards for themselves and are out to get them. In other words, with well-meant intention, with an underlying altruistic purpose, groups of workingmen are recklessly being encouraged to believe that they can obtain whatever they want by a sufficient show of force. And what workingmen want is—at least in the present decayed and perverted state of society—not perceptibly different from what other men want. Not all men by any means are cursed by the desire of great wealth—probably very few are, and fewer still by the desire of wealth for its own sake. But on the other hand nobody wants to be poor, unclothed, and without bread. And practically all men, in consequence of this fact, want greater security of income than they now have and want a larger income than they now have. For poverty, as everyone knows, is relative, within limits, to the individual's habits and standards. Probably, in addition, there are as few men who love a really idle existence as there are who love wealth for its own sake. Yet practically all men want more leisure than they now have, and want freedom to enjoy it in their own ways.

Greater security of income, more income, more leisure—these things are elementary human desires, whatever varied motives beyond them may inspire the efforts of this man or that. And when groups of workingmen discover, as sooner or later they must, that Mr. Cole and similar leaders are endeavouring to manipulate them for quite other purposes will they—even though they are carefully assured that it is for the ultimate good of society—prove docile and obedient? Or will they throw aside leaders no longer useful to them and proceed to use their self-confident power, their developed solidarity, for their own immediate ends? And are they likely to endeavour to make themselves the servants or the masters of society? If they should follow the latter course, moreover, they would only be putting into practice the sort of 'freedom' which Mr. Cole now preaches to them, telling them, as he does, that a set of thieves—the capitalists—are unscrupulously denying them a kind and degree of autonomy which it is safe to say no large group of men has ever yet enjoyed upon this earth.

There can be no reasonable doubt about the answer to the questions just asked. It is notorious that mass movements have a way of getting beyond the control of their leaders. Scarcely a season passes without the lesson being brought home to us in one connexion or another, often with tragic impressiveness. In America, during the War and immediately after, there were two unusually plain cases of this phenomenon on a large scale. In both cases mass movements, once they had gathered momentum, went their own way, leaving their first leaders dismayed and helpless. When America entered the War patriotism was zealously organised to help along the cause. Unquestionably many good things were thus accomplished which might otherwise have gone undone, but those things were accomplished at a price. Everybody entered in and waved his flag, but immediately very many began to use the one great cause for the achievement of smaller causes nearer home. Bumptious authoritativeness blossomed forth everywhere. Organised patriotism became in hundreds of communities synonymous with organised persecution and bullying. A great wave of self-righteous intolerance swept over the country, and generous idealism was transmuted into blind and unmeaning hatred of the 'Huns' and, incidentally, of all other 'damned ignorant foreigners.' Nor was this all, for intolerance was frequently too heated for nice discrimination, and persecution extended to all manner of dissenting opinions having no relation to the War and its issues. Likewise immediately after the War, as, it is to be hoped, some yet remember, an epidemic of casual, local, and apparently purposeless strikes broke out in all parts of the country. It seemed like a new disease. Crazy demands were made and, if they were granted, new strikes with new crazy demands were straightway inaugurated. Labour leaders struggled with obvious honesty but no success to master the situation, and the trouble only disappeared when industrial depression began to settle over the country. There was no mystery in this; it happened, as some people seemed to understand, because during the War these men had learned that they could get anything they asked for.

The lesson of these episodes, and of mass movements generally, is plain; and it is certain that Mr. Cole's workingmen will go on their own road at just the time when he thinks them ready to begin realising his purposes. If they do, obviously they will make impossible the fulfilment of the New Order which Mr. Cole depicts. Nor, on the other hand, will they realise their own hopes. The reason is simple: there are too many of them, even though it is true that the organised groups form an aristocratic minority amongst wage-earners. Dazzled by the increased productivity of this age too many have forgotten, as was said in the preceding essay, that population has increased neck and neck with productivity. The result is that, for all the increased wealth of modern industrialised countries, the standard of living cannot be largely raised for any great number of people. If organised workingmen dominate society they may arrange things howsoever they please and yet will find that they cannot appreciably better their material condition, though their leaders may be more comfortably circumstanced. The expropriation of capitalists would make so little difference in the workingman's income that it has more than once been pointed out that the only substantial arguments in favour of the step are not at all economic in their nature, but 'social'; that is, such an act would remove an eyesore from the workingman's gaze or, in different words, appease his envy. Some theorists, of course, have argued that the abolition of capitalism would save for workingmen not only the incomes of capitalists but also the far larger sums which, it is claimed, are expended wastefully in capitalistic production. No one doubts the existence of waste, but equally there is no reason for doubting its perpetuity under any other system of management. It is easier to talk about waste than to remove it. And, moreover, not only is there no evidence that communal ownership of industry would be economical, but all existing evidence indicates that it would be more wasteful than is private ownership. Nor is the reason far to seek; universal experience proves that the more attenuated responsibility is, the more careless is management. What a large group of people may be responsible for, in effect nobody is responsible for, which means that under collective ownership industry would ride hastily for a fall. Workingmen will only deceive and in the end ruin themselves if they fancy that, through some magic, their favourite theorists will be able to produce money out of nothing. Finally, any candid inquiry must take it into account that, in proportion as workingmen do now succeed in raising their standard of living at the expense of the rest of society, they are making themselves the more unfit to meet the ruinous competition of Asiatic labour which is infallibly in store for them. Asia is just beginning to be industrialised, but the present tactics of European and American workingmen are hastening the process. Whatever changes—and undoubtedly they will be many—the development of industry brings about there, it is certain that for a very long period the standard of living will be, as it now is, almost incredibly lower than in Europe and America.

This last consideration would of course apply to Mr. Cole's New Order equally well if we should assume that he could realise it just as he pictures it in his vivid day-dreams. Plainly, then, Mr. Cole and his like are engaged in arousing hopes which can never be fulfilled, and which consequently, so far as they are seriously grasped at, can end only in the reactions of bitter disillusion. The trouble is not, it should be observed, that such reformers as Mr. Cole are aiming at bad ends. Mr. Cole and the other guild socialists, Mr. Bertrand Russell[16] who has closely connected himself with them, and Mr. R. H. Tawney who, in his *Acquisitive Society*,

---

[16] There is a penetrating criticism of Mr. Russell's political programme in Mr. J. W. Scott's *Syndicalism and Philosophical Realism*.

has outlined a programme of modified guild socialism, all have in view a general end which is certainly good. They all aim ultimately at the maximum of liberty for the individual consistent with equality of opportunity. Some may not agree with the interpretation of this end given by one or another of these gentlemen, some may not agree that their proposals even if they could be carried out would conduce to this end, but all surely must agree that such an end is certainly good. The trouble is precisely that although the end proposed be never so good, it is a far different thing to pronounce it feasible. Reformers too generally seem never to consider the distinction, yet in practice it is fundamental. We might like to have wings as well as hands. Animals, however, may have only one or the other; no matter what good results might be achieved through the combination it remains a sheer impossibility. Man alone, thanks to his rational intellect, is able finally to achieve something 'just as good.' And this is the point. If we recollect the thousands of years which have had to pass before the invention, its enormous cost in money and in human life, and its extreme limitations now that we do have it, no one could possibly term it 'just as good.' The wonder is, of course, that we have aëroplanes and dirigible balloons at all, poor and hazardous as they are and must remain, whatever further improvements they may undergo. And wings themselves we can never have upon this earth.

The aëroplane, moreover, such as it is, we have paid for heavily, not alone in the respects just mentioned, but also, as Dean Inge has candidly remarked, in that thus far in its actual uses the invention has proved an almost unmitigated curse to humanity. So likewise if we could have wings we should have to sacrifice our hands to pay for them. Equally in either case we have to pay, as we always have and always shall. And thus even an enthusiast such as Mr. Cole cannot escape this difficulty when he bends to explanation of the structure of the New Order. In his effort to give the citizen more 'freedom' he inevitably has to extend the mere quantity of governmental machinery until he involves society in so complex and all-pervasive a network of political device that the hardiest imagination can scarcely visualise it. The consequence is that a very large portion of every man's time must be expended in working this machinery. Present experience more than proves this to be an impossible condition, but this is not all. In addition, the vast number of elected officials have to be subjected to such restrictions and dangers—constant advice and criticism from their constituents, and the recall, for example—that it would certainly be much more difficult to induce self-respecting men to incur the punishment of election than now it is, and, consequently, offices would the more readily fall to rogues, charlatans, or popular flatterers. His readers may have noticed that Mr. Bertrand Russell avoids exposing such difficulties as this by a simple device. He just does not attempt to explain the actual procedure by which his day-dreams are to be realised. In consequence Mr. Russell achieves unexampled freedom in picturing the desirable changes in the organisation of life which we might effect, as he assures us, simply by wanting them badly enough.

SOCIAL PROGRESS

Indeed, Mr. Russell's political writings form the real modern Book of Wonder Tales, and one finally concludes it is not for nothing that Mr. Russell has observed that "there is often in men of science, even when they are quite old, something of the simplicity of a child."[17]

There are, however, reformers who are not so simple as to suppose that by changing institutions one can suddenly and radically change human nature. Amongst them Miss M. P. Follett has recently become an outstanding figure. Her programme of meliorism, *The New State*, has been very generally felt to be one of the notable additions in recent years to political literature. And for Miss Follett's scheme of social progress there is this to be said: it is not based—as are the schemes of all revolutionary propagandists—upon a consideration of human nature apart from its present environment. Miss Follett realises that if a new period of social progress is to be inaugurated it must begin with real changes in individuals and that these changes will only then begin to express themselves in institutions; she realises that such progress must have small beginnings and must be a slow growth; and she bases her whole plan upon a process which she believes to be a practical possibility because she has already seen it working. This certainly is, as we say, all to the good. Yet on the other hand Miss Follett is enthusiastically sure that she has discovered the royal road to perfection, that if we but follow her advice all will be for ever well with us, that, in short, to her has been communicated "a secret

[17] *Proposed Roads to Freedom*, p. 207.

... which is going to revolutionise the world."[18] This, of course, is not necessarily an absurd conviction. Miss Follett may be quite right, but when one encounters such confidence that the secret of earthly felicity has at last been revealed it is a plain duty to ask on what precisely this confidence is based. Everything depends, not at all upon Miss Follett's fervour, which is unexcelled, but upon the reason for her conviction. *The New State* is one continuous exhortation; it engenders in the suggestible and uncritical reader the same emotional assurance which the author so obviously feels, and leaves that reader certain that infinite progress is in the nature of things, certain that if we do but acquire the proper 'technique'—which this book sets forth—nothing can prevent progress towards ultimate perfection and the reign of justice and earthly happiness.

If, then, Miss Follett cannot produce a sound basis for her assertions she has been engaged in a practice as dangerous as that of other and more obviously unwise reformers; for she has, to speak plainly, cruelly deceived her readers. Consequently it is hardly reassuring to be told, "This is what we need to learn—that we can walk in any direction we choose." The reason for learning this extraordinary thing is that each human being is, according to Miss Follett, infinite in capacity for expansion. "No 'whole' can imprison us infinite beings. The centre of to-day is the circumference of to-morrow." And "to speak of the 'limitations of the individual' is blasphemy and suicide." The individual is

[18] *The New State*, p. 97. All later quotations from Miss Follett are taken from the same book.

infinite because no one person can live, as the saying is, unto himself, in separation from his fellows. We are all united one to another in intricate bonds of interdependence. This, it is true, is hardly news; but from this follows, we are told, the great point—that, since none of us is self-sufficing, we live our fullest lives when we are in fullest association with others; and not merely association but something more, which Miss Follett calls interpenetration. Hence, "the aim of each of us should be to live in the lives of all. Those fringes which connect my life with the life of every other human being in the world are the inlets by which the central forces flow into me. . . . Then do we find reality, only in union, never in isolation. . . . To go out to meet our fellows is to go out and let the winds of Heaven blow upon us—we throw ourselves open to every breath and current which spring from this meeting of life's vital forces." Once we have begun there is no limit assignable to the degree and extent of possible interpenetration, and with each step we grow towards perfection, for each step is a release of vital forces hitherto imprisoned. Further, "as soon as we are given opportunities for the release of the energy there is in us, heroes and leaders will arise among us. These will draw their stimulus, their passion, their life from all, and then in their turn increase in all passion and power and creating force."

Thus the infinity of the individual is a paradox, for it arises from his insignificance, his complete dependence upon society. We might go on indefinitely with Miss Follett to behold the gorgeous future which this surprising infinity insures to man, but the primary question for us is, How did Miss Follett learn that we live our real lives only through our interpenetration with others? For it is one thing to say, with obvious truth, that our lives both physical and intellectual depend upon others, and a very different thing to go on to say that our lives are consequently at their fullest and best when we most fully and closely associate with others. The difference, it is true enough, is merely one of emphasis, but the changed emphasis which Miss Follett puts upon the external life of the individual has profound meaning. If from the point of view which she takes it means for each of us the capacity for infinite expansion, so also—as she does not tell us—does it mean the disintegration of the individual. Miss Follett, spite of the self-contradictions in which her book abounds, cannot have it both ways. The spontaneous life of unleashed impulse which is her ideal, in which free expansion is given to all the energies which spring from the 'vital urge,' can be attained only at the sacrifice of the individual's inner integrity, only at the expense of the integrating guidance and criticism of the rational intellect.

What, then, makes Miss Follett willing to pay this price for the primacy of the individual's external life? It is apparently this, that she sees no other way of further social progress. She is, moreover, convinced that unlimited further social progress is open to us with the development of 'interpenetration.' She obtained this idea, so far as one can learn, from experience and observation of a process which most of us have at one time or another shared in. She has observed that committees or other small groups occasionally end their deliberations with a programme which in the beginning had been suggested by no one individual, which is not the result simply of compromise, which yet satisfies everyone, and which is in fact something *better* than any one person working alone would have been able to devise. In other words, the varying and sometimes apparently opposed ideas of the several individuals seem in the course of discussion to interpenetrate so that finally a composite yet organic result comes into view which all recognise to be something better than what any single individual had had in mind in the beginning. Each one feels that this is what he was really, though obscurely, aiming at; yet the result has been made possible only by group organisation and seems to be the creation of the group itself. This occasionally—though I must say, as far as my own observation may go, most rarely—does happen; and it is the element of reality which forms the starting-point of Miss Follett's programme of meliorism. For she draws thence these large conclusions: that in such group action the individual reaches his highest peak; that if this happens now occasionally it can be made to happen more and more, so that eventually the lives of all will be wholly united in the achievement of transcendent group purposes; that all aspects of local and national life may be thus organised; and that consequently the organised group should be the political unit of the future, through which will come a new epoch in human affairs and the accomplishment of all good things. In order to bolster up these large hopes Miss Follett insists upon the subtlety and mystery of the group process and asserts that the group itself possesses an independent personality which transcends that of every individual composing it. In this specious manner she establishes the validity and even apparently the infallibility of what used to be called the general will.

It all depends upon the initial paradox of the infinity of the individual. "The non-existence of self-sufficing individuals gives us the whole of our new theory of democracy. . . . When we can give up the notion of individual rights, we shall have taken the longest step forward in our political development." "The group-spirit is the pillar of cloud by day and of fire by night—it is our infallible guide—it is the spirit of democracy." "Democracy is the actual commingling of men in order that each shall have continuous access to the needs and the wants of others." "We can satisfy our wants only by a genuine union and communion of all, only in the friendly outpouring of heart to heart." This comes in group organisation. "Much of the evil of our political and social life comes from the fact that we crave personal recognition and personal satisfaction; as soon as our greatest satisfaction is group satisfaction, many of our present problems will disappear." Perfect freedom, amongst other things, will have been gained. "Freedom is the harmonious, unimpeded working of the law of one's own nature. The true nature of every man is found only in the whole. A man is ideally free only so far as he is interpermeated by every other human being; he gains his freedom through a perfect and complete relationship because thereby he achieves his whole nature." Hence one can "have no liberty except as an essential member of a group.... We see that to obey the group which we have helped to make and of which we are an integral part is to be free because we are then obeying ourself. Ideally the state is such a group, actually it is not, but it depends upon us to make it more and more so. The state must be no external authority which restrains and regulates me, but it must be myself acting as the state in every smallest detail of life. Expression, not restraint, is always the motive of the ideal state." Hence "we are beginning to know now that our freedom depends not on the weakness but on the strength of our government, our government being the expression of a united people." "And with this unity will appear a sovereignty spontaneously and joyfully acknowledged." "Our political forms will have no vitality unless our political life is so organised that it shall be based primarily and fundamentally on spontaneous association."

Spontaneity is the real word. "What we must get away from is 'the hell of rigid things.' There is a living life of the people. And it must flow directly through our government and our institutions, expressing itself anew at every moment. We are not fossils petrified in our social strata. *We are alive.* This is the first lesson for us to learn. That very word means change and change, growth and growth. To live gloriously is to change undauntedly—our ideals must evolve from day to day, and it is upon those who can fearlessly embrace the doctrine of 'becoming' that the life of the future waits.

All is growing; we must recognise this and free the way for the growth. We must unclose our spiritual sources, we must allow no mechanism to come between our spiritual sources and our life. The *élan vital* must have free play." "It is the creative spontaneity of each which makes life march on irresistibly to the purposes of the whole." "This is the universal striving. This is the trend of all nature—the harmonious unifying of all."

I cannot here, of course, howsoever freely I should quote, do justice either to the comprehensiveness of Miss Follett's exposition or to her passionate reiterations of personal conviction. I have, nevertheless, quoted so much in the hope that Miss Follett's own words might sufficiently show two things. First, the immense structure which she raises upon a slender if not shadowy foundation. The mystical, rapturous group process, as she describes it, is admittedly a rare phenomenon. There is at present nothing to show that it is feasible to make it common. Miss Follett talks of its transcendent benefits like a prophet, but this, if I may so put it, gets us nowhere. It raises our hopes to the skies but leaves us where we are. And Miss Follett has nothing at all to say about the practical means of extending and deepening group organisation; she contents herself with mere talk of what might be accomplished if such organisation were once perfected. This being so, it may be permitted us to doubt the practical significance of her book, for this is the crux upon which her whole programme depends. *The New State* is indeed a demonstration on a large scale of the folly of building dream-castles upon a series of hypothetical guesses, and then easily assuming it to be legitimate to speak fervently of these splendid structures as if their real existence had already been proved.

In the second place I hope it is plain that, even if we assume Miss Follett's plan to be feasible, it would necessitate an extraordinary sacrifice from each of us. So great would be the price that it is a serious question if we should not lose more than we could possibly gain —in which case progress would hardly be the word for what we had done. We should inevitably lose in two ways. For one thing, Miss Follett's New State would open hitherto undreamed-of opportunities for busybodies; it would be a paradise for the unofficial tyrant who longs for just the chances which she provides for meddling with the needs and wants of his neighbours. Many of us have quite enough trouble with unofficial guardians of our welfare as it is. Miss Follett herself, though for another reason, quotes a poor schoolboy; "I hate this school, I wish it would burn up," he wrote, "there's too much old self-government about it, you can't have any fun." Every right-thinking person who knows what this boy really meant will sympathise with him. As anyone who has been a 'self-governing' schoolboy will know, this youngster was crying out against the unofficial, all-pervasive tyranny of his schoolfellows who had eagerly seized the opportunity of robbing life, with the very best intentions, of every shred of independence.

This surely is something to give us pause before we enter into the New State, where everybody will have to be not only interested, but 'passionately and joyously' interested, in other people's business. And, in the second place, if we reflect upon the general atmosphere of continuous passion and joy necessary in the New State, we shall realise that all who enter here must abandon for ever the rational, critical intellect. The New State can flourish only in a welter of spontaneous impulse; for it the critical reason is as the hand of death. The responsibility for integration is shifted to the group—that is, it is left to everybody in general and nobody in particular. And for the group to work its work the individual has to disintegrate into the riot of his divine, vital instincts. Miss Follett's only evidence that this would be a gain is the occasional success of her group process. And for this vague possibility she is eager recklessly to abandon, in effect, our present selves. In fact, this effort to centre the individual's life outside of himself; the paradoxical claim that the individual lives his fullest and deepest life in his external acts, when in reality this means the submergence of the individual in the mythical personality of a group; the uncritical, passionate refusal to recognise the inherent limits of political action, and the consequent straining somehow to infuse into the structure of the state, and subtract from the individual, qualities of personality which in fact only the human individual has; —all this is in sober fact not progress, but the very negation of progress.

I do not mean to imply—any more than in the cases of such men as Mr. G. D. H. Cole and Mr. R. H. Tawney—that Miss Follett has not in *The New State* written much that was worth writing and that is worth reading. Beyond doubt she has done so; and indeed one feels that local group organisation, wherever it can and does develop—shorn, however, of its transcendental flavour and mystical unction—may in the course of time do much to enrich and consolidate local community life. But on the other hand there is no discernible ground for elevating group organisation into a panacea for all our ills. To do so, on the showing of Miss Follett's book, would be only to invite ultimate disillusion and tragedy.

In general, one cannot but conclude, after much reading in the literature of social progress, there is a certain reckless abandon which is peculiarly characteristic of the writers of this literature. One is only too likely to discover imagination rather than insight, fervour rather than knowledge, passionate self-confidence rather than the inquiring mind; and one cannot avoid thinking that some publicists and propagandists of the day will sometime have much to answer for. Perhaps nothing else at the present time so brings it home to one that it is not enough to have good intentions. One feels consequently the greater relief when occasionally one does light upon the sober opinions of some writer who has not entirely let his hopes run away with his good sense. This at any rate was my own experience in reading Professor E. G. Conklin's *Direction of Human Evolution*. Professor Conklin, as I have said, believes that, while progressive human evolution has long since ceased, social progress is still in its infancy. He has his own dream of an eventually perfect earthly life, which he voices with something of the social reformer's aban-

PROGRESS AND SCIENCE

don; and he has not perhaps caught all the implications of what he says, so that his book is not free from confusion. Yet, on the other hand, he is aware of the limitations of his subject, and he discusses real possibilities with balance and restraint.

Professor Conklin believes that "the past and present tendencies of evolution justify the highest hopes for the future and inspire faith in the final culmination of this great law in

> " '. . . one far-off divine event,
> To which the whole creation moves.' "

He thinks that "there is good evidence that we have barely begun to realise the possibilities" of the progressive evolution of society, and he says: "The religion of evolution deals with this world rather than with the next. It prays 'Thy kingdom come, thy will be done on *earth.*' It seeks to build here and now 'The City of God.' It looks forward to a time when 'Righteousness shall cover the earth as the waters cover the sea.' It looks forward to unnumbered ages of human progress upon the earth, to ages of better social organisation, of increasing specialisation and co-operation among individuals and races and nations, to ages of greater justice and peace and altruism." This of course is the sort of thing with which the modern prophet's pages are strewn, and Professor Conklin here echoes their tone. But at the same time he has scrupulously provided antidotes which are calculated to cool the glowing anticipations of any careful reader of his book.

SOCIAL PROGRESS

In the first place Professor Conklin has that spaciousness of outlook which is one of the gifts of modern scientific training. The evolution of society, he says, is really in its infancy—yet it is by now some 20,000, or possibly 30,000, years old. At this rate his conjecture of an ultimately perfect society might be correct, yet that society could hardly appear inside of a couple of hundred thousand years, or perhaps inside of a million. Professor Conklin also points out that "just as in the case of the evolution of organisms, so, also, in human history we recognise series of changes genetically connected but leading nowhere except to mere diversity, others which lead to increasing adaptation to peculiar conditions, and still others leading to increasing perfection and complexity of social organisation—that is, *divergent, adaptive, and progressive types of evolution characterise human history as well as the history of animals and plants*. As in the evolution of organisms, so, also, in human history there have been innumerable changes or diversities that have led nowhere; there have been many changes which have led merely to better adaptation to peculiar conditions; there have been very few lines of progress." And he goes on to say later that "even the end of our civilisation need not mean, and probably would not mean, the end of all social evolution. Other civilisations would probably arise on the ruins of ours as ours has succeeded many others. The teachings of biology and of human history indicate that further social progress must lie in the direction of the rational co-operation of all mankind. Whether our civilisation survives or not, the probabilities are, that sometime these ideals of rational co-operation and of democratic fraternity will prevail."[19]

These considerations appear to suggest that after all we might get along as well if we did not think so much about approaching earthly perfection. Progress which for so long a period must be marked by just such struggle and difficulties, such material injustice, such prevalence of sheer accident, of good luck and bad, such tragic imperfections and dangers as most of us now experience—such progress hardly seems to have that immense, immediate significance in our daily lives which its prominence in contemporary thought and popular faith claims for it. Nor is it a question only of time, for the cooling words which I have quoted about

---

[19] Such words as these help one properly to place Mr. H. G. Wells's propagandist book, *The Outline of History*. This is an attempt to picture the period from the origin of the earth to the present time as one continuous progressively evolutionary process. The attempt, naturally, seems to succeed best in the periods about which we know least—those preceding the last several thousand years of human history. For this last period Mr. Wells does not succeed in making his picture look plausible in spite of the omissions and of the distortions of historic fact in which he indulges—as, for instance, in his treatment of the Greeks and Romans, in his defence of nomadic barbarians, in his transference to the papacy of an idea which had its origin in pagan Rome, in his defence of the outrages of the French Revolution. The truth is, Mr. Wells's book is a belated product of the scientific point of view of about thirty or forty years ago. Mr. Wells has replied to some of his critics in an article in the *Yale Review* (July, 1921), in which, amongst other things to be said in his defence, he has called attention to the fact that already some 200,000 people had purchased the *Outline*. But this perhaps only proves that there are many people who enjoy the reading of romances. The book, at any rate—interestingly and vividly written piece of literature though it is—has little claim to be regarded as serious history.

the possibility that social progress may not culminate in our own civilisation, but in one succeeding it or in the last of a series succeeding it, have the same effect. It would thus appear to be the part of wisdom to relegate ideas of unlimited social and material progress to the backgrounds of our minds along with our other purely speculative interests. For, however it may be with 'society,' there is evidently here no ground of hope for us who are now alive, or for our children, or for theirs. Our lives and the lives of our children must be lived in terms of the world as we find it here and now.

Nor is this all; for such further progress as is actually within the limits of possibility may turn out on examination to be, from the human viewpoint, not 'progress' at all. Professor Conklin has already indicated in passages which I have quoted the general nature of possible further progress, but his direct exposition of it should be read in his own words. He points out that progressive evolution, when it takes place, has several practically invariable characteristics. It "invariably and inevitably means increasing differentiation and integration." "In every instance" progressive evolution "has been in the direction of greater specialisation and co-operation. One-celled organisms, in which the greatest amount of individual liberty is preserved to the separate cells, have undergone but little progressive evolution and have remained in practically the same stage of organisation for millions of years. Many-celled organisms, on the other hand, have undergone the most varied and extensive evolution; and this has been due to the fact that the specialisation of single cells and their co-operation in the work of the organism as a whole has made possible the highest types of organisms.

"In a similar way one may trace the evolution of animal societies from a condition in which extreme individualism prevails up to societies of ants, bees, and termites in which the specialisation of individuals is higher, the mutual dependence more complete, and the work which the colony is able to perform is immensely greater and more perfect than could be accomplished by any number of individuals working separately. What the individual cannot do because of lack of strength or specialisation or time, the social group can accomplish with the strength and specialisation of all and through long periods of time.

"What is true of insects in this respect is also true of men. It matters not that in the one case activities are governed by instinct alone and in the other by intelligence as well as instinct; the final result . . . is the same, whether the advantages of higher organisation have been discovered by natural selection or by intelligence. If human society is to be something more than an aggregation of individuals, if it is to accomplish more than can be performed by separate persons, it must be through higher and higher organisation, that is through greater specialisation and more complete co-operation. There is no doubt that the evolution of human society has been in this direction, and the entire past history of living things indicates that further progress of society must be along this line."

SOCIAL PROGRESS

Professor Conklin is of the opinion that "the incompleteness of integration, co-operation, and harmony in human society is due to the fact that imperfect intelligence and freedom have come in to interfere with instinct. Disharmony in ourselves and in society is the price we pay for personal intelligence and freedom." But "the personal freedom which endangers human co-operation opens at the same time a new path of progress along rational lines. In our individual behaviour and in our social activities we now seek the ideal harmony of the hive, but on the higher plane of intelligence, freedom, and ethics." Professor Conklin recalls it to his readers' attention that some ancient states apparently achieved a more perfect specialisation and co-operation than has any modern one. But, as he says, those states were powerful autocracies, and they are dead. If, consequently, we are to achieve lasting social progress it must be voluntary, not forced. This means that there must be a voluntary progressive subordination of the individual to the welfare of society as an end in itself. We must, in effect, acquire a profound longing to become human cogs. This may come about through the gradual elimination of those in whom selfishness predominates, and through the consequent gradual preponderance of the altruistic. When the altruistic do preponderate, things will begin to move more quickly. There will then prevail the only kind of equality which, as Professor Conklin wisely and candidly reminds us, is now or in the future possible between human beings —that is, equality of opportunity. In the altruistic future equality of opportunity will be maintained through the development of intelligence and aptitude tests which will determine with finality what luck one had at one's birth. Through these tests, in other words, the individual's place in society will be determined beyond appeal. The tested individual will thereafter be free to do his appointed duty nobly—and that is all. Thus if, in the future, 'society' wants several pyramids built it will not be done by forced labour in the barbarous Egyptian manner—it will be done through freely bestowed, self-abnegating sweat.

The ultimate goal—the "far-off divine event"—is what Professor Conklin calls a rationally organised society. This is a society all of whose functions are performed with perfect harmony and fraternity. In it everyone will be entirely satisfied with his infallibly determined place and will stick to it devotedly, deriving his life's satisfaction, apparently, from the perfect way in which the whole vast organism of society works together—like a clock. In the meantime we are to derive our life's satisfaction from the knowledge that we are doing our bit—if, of course, we are—towards this far-off possible consummation. This is 'the religion of evolution' as Professor Conklin has summed it up in sentences already quoted; and he says, to encourage us: "Even struggle and suffering and death have their value if in the long course of evolution they lead to progress. Men do not die and leave only their bones and implements, but 'they rest from their labours and their *works* do follow them.'"

This is a view of further progress which is, generally speaking, possible; and it is more than this, for, as far

SOCIAL PROGRESS

as I can see, it is the only view warranted by the present state of our knowledge. It is, at that, conjectural; but it does not transgress what is now known, nor is it built upon mere guesses or generous hopes. Professor Conklin is not clear whether we are to regard such further progress as inevitable or whether it lies with us to accept or reject it; in a passage which I have quoted he inclines plainly to the former view, but elsewhere in his book he appears to contradict himself.[20] However, in either case, so far as 'this civilisation' is concerned we are free to do as we please. We need not attempt to travel in the direction Professor Conklin indicates if we do not want to. And I doubt if many, actually knowing what that direction is, will wish to go much further; for Professor Conklin's interpretation of life is not likely to seem, to any careful reader of his book, a tolerable one. Moreover, any careful reader, before he finishes this book, is practically certain to ask himself several puzzling questions to which he will find no answer in its pages. And he will find none, I venture to think, because there are insuperable difficulties in the way of defining our ordinarily vague ideas of progress. So far as social progress is concerned, at any rate, even so restrained and circumspect a writer as Professor Conklin has only evaded, not met, these difficulties.

In the first place, if the goal of social progress is a rationally organised society, we have to ask, For what end is it organised? It is surely unintelligible to attempt to say that society is an end in itself, though some in high places—driven, one suspects, by relentless theory

[20] In Section "A" of his last chapter, particularly p. 239.

—have done so. One has only, however, to ask what such a statement can mean in order to discover that it is essentially blind and unmeaning. No coherent answer can be found. The only intelligible one is that society exists for the sake of the individuals who compose it, and that accordingly its only ends are their ends. Yet this makes social progress a curiously circular process: individuals sacrifice themselves for the sake of society which in turn exists solely for the sake of the same individuals. It is hardly surprising that Professor Conklin should have failed to notice this question, since had he done so he would have been forced to write a quite different book. For its only answer is that a rationally organised society could not ask self-sacrifice from any of its members.

Again, Professor Conklin sanely urges the necessity of taking long views in considering social progress, but we may justly complain that he has himself failed to do this. He has arbitrarily limited his view to suit his convenience. He ends with a vision of finally attained earthly felicity, and thus manages to sanction an austerely hopeful outlook, which gives some meaning and value—even though they be tenuous—to our own lives. Modern science, however, is able to pronounce that 'the end of the world' is a certainty. The time finally will arrive when it will become progressively more and more difficult to maintain life on the earth, and then ultimately—no longer possible. After that the earth will be, as we say of the moon, dead. Professor Conklin mentions nothing of this, yet it has, certainly, an intimate connexion with what he does say. For it can mean

SOCIAL PROGRESS

only one thing: that whatever stage of complex organisation society may attain to can be merely temporary—the prelude to a long decline and withering of material civilisation, and to the final earthly extinction of humanity.

> The cloudcapp'd towers, the gorgeous palaces,
> The solemn temples, the great globe itself,
> Yea all which it inherit, shall dissolve;
> And, like this insubstantial pageant faded,
> Leave not a rack behind.

Many have wished that Prospero might have talked a little longer; but, make of the great riddle what we will, we cannot suppose that the goal of all our striving is a rationally organised society. To make that supposition is to empty human life of all meaning whatever. Professor Conklin tells his readers that an interpretation of life based on the intrinsic value of the individual is not of the highest type. One does not know where he got this information, but plainly it was good news for him, because in terms of social progress he can interpret life only as a ruthless sacrifice to a problematic external end. Other meaning there is none; we are cruelly brought into the world to serve as mere stepping-stones to an ultimate possible good which, even if somehow realised, is nobody's good, and which therefore cannot be even the good of the whole. It is difficult to imagine a more effectual way of saying that human life is an empty mockery. And if popular vague notions of social progress as 'a good time coming for all' are vain and futile, so equally, it would appear, is any view of social progress which keeps within the limits of possibility, as these are indicated by the present state of our knowledge.

The truth is that the dogma of social progress is a mischief-making force which increases none of the values of life; instead, it distracts us from life's realities to send us chasing an *ignis fatuus*. From the eighteenth century to the present day it has been productive less of any positive good than of mere restless discontent and disappointment. Miss M. P. Follett says the fact that we have something makes it cease to be worth mentioning, because progress depends not on what we find but on what we achieve. That unfortunately is the inevitable attitude of one caught by the dogma of social progress. And always the same thing is happening or is ominously threatened: the fruits of social progress are never for us, they are only for our children's children; yet the doctrine does not begin really to fire us until, while we perhaps continue to think of it thus, we begin subtly to *feel* it as something for ourselves. It has been said that the doctrine of evolution in the nineteenth century transferred the centre of our interest from the life of the individual to the growth of the species. But so far as this is true it is likely to be long a source of confusion; for we do now talk, indeed, in terms of the species and indulge in hazy visions of its growth, yet inevitably we continue to think and live as individuals. Thus a contradiction is introduced into our lives which turns them all awry and which lends a factitious interest to matters with which we can have no concern. For we begin to feel the benefits of progress as something for ourselves and thus are encouraged to entertain hopes which under no circumstances can be fulfilled. These hopes, moreover, concerning as they largely do material satisfactions, encourage us to blame others rather than ourselves and our notions of the world for our inevitable disappointments. The consequence too frequently is that we turn stubbornly and bitterly to whatever good things we can achieve by immediate action. We set up a guillotine, we strike and strike again and resort to sabotage, we join the I. W. W., we become Bolsheviki—and we eat dust and ashes for our mistakes and crimes. In the name of progress we end with the attempt, so far as in us lies, to destroy society itself.

I do not wish to suggest that we are all really happier than we realise and that we ought to be counting our blessings—nor yet that, bad as it may be, this is the best possible world. It takes neither penetrating intellect to see nor great courage to say that there are all around us a thousand things crying out to be bettered. Nowadays indeed it appears to take more courage to refrain from such obvious and financially profitable remarks than to make them. In many cases, moreover, evils need only to be discovered in order, to a certain limited extent, to be mitigated; showing that our social world can be made better from year to year. But only to a certain limited extent;—for no sooner do old evils disappear than new ones spring up. And there need be no fear that young 'radicals' will ever find themselves out of work for lack of obvious material evils with which to find fault. Industrial and social conditions are to-day in some respects almost unbelievably better than they were seventy-five years ago, yet to-day there is greater and more ominous dissatisfaction with them than there was then. And this dissatisfaction is warranted; the conditions which cause it are bad. Workingmen and their friends, moreover, sometimes complain that they achieve betterment of their condition in one direction only to find that they have to pay for it themselves in another direction which they had not thought of—through their noses, in fact. And so they do. And they may do infinite harm; they may inconvenience us, or starve us, or more expeditiously murder some of us, yet they will not thereby escape their burden.

Some contemporary apostles of social progress, such as Miss Follett, attempt to deal boldly with this embarrassing difficulty by pointing out that the emptiness of achievement follows necessarily from the concept of progress;—what we have is worthless because we have it, progress consisting in what we achieve, which then also becomes worthless. On this basis the reward lies only in the struggle itself, in the experimental attitude involved, which we are invited to regard as the essential meaning of life. This is what Professor John Dewey seems to tell his disciples, who apparently believe they are not cheated. But where on this account is progress? One cannot tell; it has quietly disappeared through a side door. Such a philosophy may indeed serve as an anodyne for the treadmill of earthly experience, and, taken for what it really is, it may have some value. For it may constitute the first step towards a *reductio ad*

SOCIAL PROGRESS

absurdum—the crumbling of the idol of social progress through its own weight.

It is at any rate plain that the concept of social progress—far from doing what to the popular mind it at present seems to do—really empties the individual's life of all meaning and value. Yet this it does in the name of the individual, ostensibly for his sake. And this alone accounts for the active interest which it evokes. But it spells only self-deception if we allow ourselves to suppose that progress under any circumstances can mean anything directly to us. There is an intrinsic value in the life of the individual; of that we may be sure—but we shall have to look elsewhere if ever we are to find it.

III

EDUCATION AND PROGRESS

"IF humanity is to hold the threads of its own destiny and rise from ages of blind drift to a plane of mastery, it will be through discovering and utilising new types of education." So writes Professor Arthur James Todd in the Preface to his *Theories of Social Progress*. It is a soberly written book. Professor Todd does not share the common illusion that social progress is in the nature of things; he quotes approvingly Sir Arthur James Balfour's statement that progressive civilisation "is a plant of tender habit, difficult to propagate, not difficult to destroy, that refuses to flourish except in a soil which is not to be found everywhere, nor at all times, nor even, so far as we can see, necessarily to be found at all." In a word, Professor Todd is cautious if not whole-heartedly sceptical, and from his careful survey there issues no vision of an easily grasped or certainly approaching Utopia. Yet Professor Todd does conclude that further social progress may be assured to us in one way—through the right kind of education. It will not be easy, and Professor Todd frankly mentions a great difficulty; "only when the majority of a social group," he says, "are provided with the means of finding out truth for themselves and actually develop the capacity for constructive thought can we hope to realise the noble vision of the idealists." But he feels convinced that so great a transformation can be brought about by what he calls social education—the deliberate inculcation of a proper attitude towards society along with careful training of the intellect when the child is young and impressible.

This conclusion is significant. Professor Todd is, of course, not alone in his opinion. Principal Alexander Morgan, for example, in his book on *Education and Social Progress* writes that education "can do more than any other agency to remedy our social ills. Social progress cannot be secured by legislation alone, but by the slower and surer plan of educating the people, and of introducing into the schools the reforms we wish to introduce into the life of the nation." Agreement with such opinion as this is probably on the increase at present. And as, through criticism and unfortunate experience, swifter and more direct methods of social progress are found wanting, reformers are likely more and more to discover in education the means of final achievement. Mr. H. G. Wells is perhaps at present the best known case in point, but he will probably be joined by others.

Such a development of opinion is natural enough. Education has from immemorial days been the means whereby the social inheritance of peoples has been passed on to later generations. Education, in the widest sense, has always been the conserver of progress already achieved. What our ancestors learned by accident or from experiment often enough died with them, but not always; at times they succeeded in passing it on to their sons, who thus entered adult life with certain initial advantages. Of course, as civilisation became more complex so did the process of learning, certain aspects of which thus came to be delegated to professional teachers. The business of education has never been a complete success, but it has generally worked fairly well as a conserver of useful knowledge of all kinds; and for a few education has through many ages done more.

Reformers are naturally not satisfied with education of this kind, which is only in a negative sense an agent of social advancement. Positively education has necessarily been conservative in tendency, a necessity which some writers on the subject seem not even to understand. But in any case, for the new purpose, changes are needed, and in some quarters are being urged with confidence. By change, of course, I mean sweeping or fundamental change, since education is in minor ways, like everything else, always changing with altered circumstances. And by way of inquiry into the possibilities of progress through education it is best to examine several concrete proposals of change. I have just mentioned Mr. H. G. Wells, who has recently outlined a scheme of progress through education, and we may begin with some consideration of the measures which he urges.

EDUCATION AND PROGRESS

Mr. Wells has become convinced, chiefly as a result of the War, that the salvation of humanity depends upon the formation of a world-state. Not at all discouraged by the apparent impossibility of such a revolution in the affairs of men, he has with characteristic energy set about the task, if not of bringing the world-state into existence through his own effort, at least of convincing others of the need for it. He has written the already famous *Outline of History* to show that the ideal of ultimate world unification has ever been the true line of human progress, and that when it is achieved all good things will flow therefrom. He has also attempted to show that partial realisations of this ideal in the past have always depended for their measure of success upon what he calls popular education;—though there is grave doubt whether many could agree with him as to the legitimacy of his use of the word. This book he has followed with *The Salvaging of Civilisation*, in which he lays it down that the final complete realisation of world unity is now feasible through a new campaign of education. In this book as well as in *The Outline of History* Mr. Wells is far from clear in his use of the word education; and in particular he not only fails to distinguish it from propaganda, but seems to regard the two as being the same thing. This initial confusion allows him to visualise education vaguely and to talk about it, on occasion, loosely. There is no doubt about the nature of his general conviction, but it is a different matter to form a really clear picture of what he wants or how it is to be accomplished. "The creative responsibility for the world to-day," he says, "passes steadily into the hands of writers and school-teachers, students of social and economic science, professors and poets, editors and journalists, publishers and newspaper proprietors, preachers, every sort of propagandist and every disinterested person who can give time and energy to the reconstruction of the social idea. Human life will continue to be more and more dangerously chaotic until a world social idea crystallises out. That—and no existing institution and no current issue—is the primary concern of the present age." Consequently "the task immediately before mankind is to find release from the contentious loyalties and hostilities of the past which make collective world-wide action impossible at the present time, in a world-wide common vision of the history and destinies of the race." "This means an unprecedented educational effort, an appeal to men's intelligence and men's imagination such as the world has never seen before."

These quotations, I think, sufficiently show the difficulty in understanding clearly what Mr. Wells means by education. However, a considerable portion of *The Salvaging of Civilisation* is devoted to an outline of a new kind of education in the usual and more precise signification of the word. Hitherto, we are told, difficulties of a merely physical sort have made an efficacious educational campaign for world-unity impossible. For such an end universal education the world over on a higher plane than has hitherto been attempted is a primary necessity. And "it is possible now to make . . . a new sort of school, a standardised school, a school richly equipped with modern apparatus and economis-

EDUCATION AND PROGRESS

ing the labour of teaching to an extent undreamed of, in which, all over the world, the same stereotyped lessons, leading the youth of the whole world through a parallel course of schooling, can be delivered." Mr. Wells treats of the matter of apparatus in some detail and with considerable feeling. He has in mind the extended use of motion-pictures, of phonographs for linguistic teaching, of maps and diagrams and the like. He also advocates the making of comprehensive standardised teaching formulæ, lesson notes, digests, and similar material which in his opinion would enable anyone to teach efficiently and with 'undreamed-of' economy of effort. There is a well-known story about a French minister of education who said that on pulling out his watch he could tell exactly what verb was being conjugated at that moment in all the elementary schools of France; Mr. Wells wishes to extend such uniformity in the content and methods of teaching throughout the world.

What is to be taught in these standardised schools? Mr. Wells tells us in a general way. Instruction is to be centred in the idea of world-unity, and for this purpose a new Bible—the 'Bible of Civilisation'—is fundamentally necessary. This is to consist of parts of the present Bible, expurgated, much revised, and, too, supplemented by some of the best things in modern literatures. The historical books of the Bible are to be replaced by a comprehensive picture of world-history—just such a work as Mr. Wells's own *Outline of History*, revised and somewhat compressed. Then will follow the Books of Conduct and Wisdom, which are to include authoritative information about personal hygiene and the facts of sex; and following these will come the Anthologies of Poetry and Literature, containing, in part, passages bearing upon the social and individual responsibilities of men; and the work will be concluded with a "Book of Forecasts, taking the place of the Prophets and Revelations." This book is to be written by statesmen, and is to contain what we in America should call their party-platforms for the coming generation;—naturally this book is to undergo continual revision. The 'Bible of Civilisation' will be "perhaps two or three times as bulky as the old Bible," and will be, in brief, an authoritative, succinct, and yet very comprehensive statement of the background and the meaning of life as we now at length understand these matters. Mr. Wells says: "Our education is, I think, pointless without it, a shell without a core. Our social life is aimless without it, we are a crowd without a common understanding. Only by means of some such unifying instrument, I believe, can we hope to lift human life out of its present dangerous drift towards confusion and disaster."

This book, then, is to be central to the new education. In addition, every child is to achieve a practical mastery of two or three languages besides his mother tongue, and is to study the elements of at least four or five languages more. The sciences of course are not neglected. Besides his mastery of the social idea, of information about sex, of universal history and of geography, and of languages, every youth by the time he is about sixteen or seventeen is to have a much more

EDUCATION AND PROGRESS

advanced knowledge of mathematics than is now attainable in most of our schools, a knowledge of general physical and general biological science, and shall have acquired skill in drawing and manual work of various kinds. All this, Mr. Wells insists, is not a large order; and it is not a large order because of one thing—the capacity of the present age for mass production and standardisation.

It may, however, reasonably be asked why the organisation of such a training system will prove "the key to all our human disorder." We are answered that it will do so because all our present troubles arise from our "ignorance, prejudice, and passion," and these will naturally disappear at "a higher level of intelligence." "The watchword of conduct that will clear up all our difficulties is the *plain truth*. Rely upon that watchword, use that key with courage and we can go out of the prison in which we live; we can go right out of the conditions of war, shortage, angry scrambling, mutual thwarting and malaise and disease in which we live; we and our kind can go out into sunlight, into a sweet air of understanding, into confident freedoms and a full creative life—for ever." Our troubles are as simple as that; knowledge will cure them, and will issue in a world administration and organisation which will insure the permanency of the cure. Upon this Mr. Wells dilates at length, naturally, and leads his readers to believe that nothing too good can be said of the approaching world-state. I must confess, however, that, spite of what I have read, the world-state seems to me forbidding; it looks more like the stifling than the saving of humanity; and indeed I find it difficult to see, as have many reviewers of the book, how any reader can take *The Salvaging of Civilisation* with entire seriousness. Mr. Wells is a man of sudden and variable enthusiasms, and I could not help feeling as I read its pages that this was the product of one of them, and that presently it would be replaced by another. The book was obviously written in a great hurry, which may account for some of its difficulties of construction, but others are probably to be accounted for by the sheer enthusiasm with which Mr. Wells envisages his subject. He is here, as always, immensely in earnest, he has the best of intentions, he gives occasional evidence in this book of an unwonted humility, and yet on the whole he abates none of his usual and remarkable self-confidence. He himself demands that he be taken very seriously indeed; in effect we are given to understand that if we do not all immediately fall in with his whole design, there is revealed in the world "a great and lamentable diversity of opinion and, as a consequence, an enfeeblement and wasteful dispersal of will."

Aside, however, from any conclusions about a possible world-state, one may ask how much hope of social progress there is in Mr. Wells's purely educational proposals. In suggesting an answer to this question I shall not ask if his programme would have the results he claims for it in case it could be carried out; no one, indeed, can say, and no one can doubt that the results, whatever their nature, would be remarkable. I do not wish, either, to dwell disproportionately upon the immediate practical difficulties inherent in his proposals.

EDUCATION AND PROGRESS

These must be obvious to everybody. In *The Outline of History,* which closes with a prophetic vision of the world-state, Mr. Wells says that this future government will be 'sustained' by a highly organised system of universal education. That too would have its own practical difficulties, but it is a very different matter and is, however remotely, conceivable. But the same system of education, understood as propaganda for the coming world-state, simply is not conceivable, and Mr. Wells does nothing to help one's imagination. He just fervently appeals, and that is all. It is true, he seems to mention lightly the possibility of imposing his system upon the peoples of the earth, but this, if it means anything at all, implies a world-government already existing and exerting, in addition, a more active and closer control over human affairs than at present does any national government. It seems plain, in fact, that Mr. Wells's fervour involves serious intellectual confusion. In the closing chapter of the *Outline*[1] he says, "Each one who believes . . . brings the good time nearer; each heart that fails delays it." This sounds like neither science—unless it be Christian Science—nor statesmanship. It is simply Mr. Wells, relying upon the fervour of the revivalist considered apart from what the revivalist says. "Hitherto," he observes in the *Outline,* "men of reason and knowledge have never had the assurance and courage of the religious fanatic." But to-day, he thinks, scholars and teachers may have become at length fanatical, and herein lies his hope of a

[1] My quotations from this book are taken from the first American edition in two volumes.

'vital' movement. He instructively defines a 'vital' movement as one that arises in a "wave of emotion, of unifying feeling," and he discovers the earliest example of such a movement in the first crusade. Here, "the fact of predominant interest to the historian of mankind is this *will to crusade* suddenly revealed as a new mass possibility in human affairs." That effort had the crudity of a first attempt; now, however, we may expect to do better. What Mr. Wells apparently quite fails to realise is that there is no analogy here with his programme of education. Were his proposal translated into really analogous terms it could only mean, as far as one can see, the English and American conquest of the earth and beneficent but 'firm' administration thereof for the sake of the new educational system. This is scarcely likely; nor is it, indeed, in the least what Mr. Wells wants.

It is a necessary conclusion, then, that there are insuperable practical difficulties in the way of putting Mr. Wells's proposals into effect. But if we could suppose these difficulties magically to be done away, there would still remain others not less insuperable. For Mr. Wells's project would depend for its success upon an assumption which, immensely flattering as it is to humanity, is yet radically opposed to all experience.

The assumption is that all human beings are equally capable of high intellectual development. There is also the complementary assumption that all human beings are naturally good. Our present "ignorance, prejudice, and passion" form a sort of outer layer, which needs only to be removed in order to reveal underneath our real and naturally good selves. We are restrained from living "righteously and well" merely by our lack of such information as the exact sciences can now furnish us. In other words, our troubles arise not from any inherent defect in ourselves, but from removable evils in our educational environment. This is pure eighteenth-century French thought, scarcely disguised by its contemporary phraseology or by Mr. Wells's occasional inconsistencies in viewpoint. Mr. Wells represents to-day—though of course he is not alone in doing so—its English tradition, which was inaugurated by William Godwin and continued by Robert Owen. He tells us of Owen, in the *Outline,* that he held men and women to be "largely the product of their educational environment, a thesis that needs no advocacy to-day." It needs none because it is so flattering a supposition that men feel naturally a profound longing to believe it. It is hardly necessary to add, however, that there is no demonstrable ground for such a belief, and that all experience seems radically to contradict it.

There is, moreover, no way of testing such proposals as Mr. Wells makes except by present experience and knowledge. Naturally he would deprecate such a test, since it is the unsatisfactoriness of experience which itself calls forth his proposals. Yet it is certain either that such revolutionary proposals will not work if tried, or that, failing of this certainty, they will never be tried if there is relevant experience and knowledge to which they go too wildly counter. In the present case the assumptions on which Mr. Wells's programme rests point to the conclusion that it is impracticable—

that it would not work if tried. If consequently his proposals are not to be condemned forthwith they can only be tested further by present relevant experience if there is any; and it so happens that several modern countries have attempted universal education within the limits of their own territories. Accordingly we can form some notion of the extent to which Mr. Wells's programme is practicable by contrasting it with such universal education as now exists. For this purpose it would be admitted, I should suppose, that the United States furnish at least as good a field of observation as we can obtain. In the United States we have had popular education continuously since the days immediately following the landing of the puritan colonists in New England. Our educational history is the history of the constant expansion and extension of the public schools. We have aimed to make education universal and, more recently, compulsory in the earlier years. Our efforts have not always been wise, but we have never neglected this problem, and it is safe to say that we have done all that has been humanly possible in our circumstances. From the earliest days of our independence we have been conscious, and have acted on the consciousness, that universal education was implied in the very existence of our democratic form of government. Hence it is that our experience should furnish as trustworthy evidence as can now be got concerning the possibilities of universal education. Some might, it is true, instance pre-War Germany as a country where a higher general level of thoroughness was attained, but it should be remembered that this achievement, so far as it was real, was

EDUCATION AND PROGRESS

bought at the expense of a more centralised administration which easily lent itself to improper manipulation, as, for one example out of several that might be instanced, in the systematic teaching of falsified history. There would now, indeed, probably be few to deny that the German system had inherent defects which more than compensated for its apparently unusual results. Mr. Wells himself says that "by European standards, by the standard of any state that has existed hitherto, the level of the common education of America is high."

But Mr. Wells adds that "by the standard of what it might be, America is an uneducated country." To this everyone must agree. No one is satisfied with American education, from the primary schools through the universities. The system is being subjected to a constant fire of criticism and is constantly being tinkered by the well-meaning. The greatest efforts are and have been expended upon it. Yet spite of all effort we have still some 6,000,000 completely illiterate people in America. And as regards the others, reached by the system, the general conclusion is that in proportion as education has been spread over a wide field it has become thin. As we have multiplied schools we have relaxed our standards. It is particularly to be noted that we have eagerly used the newest paraphernalia which Mr. Wells recommends, sometimes with entertaining effect. Had Mr. Wells taken the trouble to investigate the use in some American schools of all manner of modern apparatus he could never have made his extravagant claims for it; actually tried, mere apparatus is found to leave us very much where we were. So also no country has endured more from the so-called educational expert, with his improved teaching formulæ and his improved standardised and stereotyped lessons and his improved general organisation with its accompanying centralisation of administration—all measurably within sight of what Mr. Wells desires. Yet these things have not availed; no miracle has been worked; "by the standard of what it might be, America is an uneducated country." The trouble lies partly in Mr. Wells's childlike faith—there is no other way of putting it—in mere machinery and organisation. He has apparently reiterated untruths about the achievements of applied science for so long a time that he himself firmly believes them. In *The Outline of History* he has painted a romantically unreal picture of machinery in our age doing all of our mechanical work, so that civilisation has at length dispensed with the human drudge. To such a picture Mr. G. D. H. Cole gives the proper corrective when he says roundly that in the present era "machines do the skilled work and men the dirty work."[2] Something similar may be said about education. As far as actual experience can tell us, nothing in the way of mechanical equipment or standardisation has made the individual human teacher a less basic factor in the work of education. Mr. Wells in *The Salvaging of Civilisation* assures his readers that he speaks as "a trained teacher" and as "an old and seasoned educationist," yet I venture to believe that in general those who know most about teaching know best that the personal factor in education—the personality and

[2] *Self-Government in Industry,* 5th ed'n, p. 232.

inborn ability of the individual teacher—not only is but always must be fundamental.

And the individual teacher, with whatever external helps, can stand and deliver no more than he or she has. That is one of the two major difficulties encountered in extending education. As the army of teachers grows, the teacher necessarily becomes less and less an exceptional person. The vast majority of teachers, from the nature of things, have to be of what we call average human nature, with no special aptitude for their task. Many of them conscientiously, devotedly, do all they can, but none the less do it all badly. We have to get along with hundreds of stupid teachers, incompetent teachers, careless and ignorant teachers—teachers who often know no more than their best pupils, sometimes even less. And as teachers have grown in number the problem of training them has grown an impossible one. In the majority of cases, too, where training has done all it can, one has to recall the ancient, famous dispute as to the relative places of inborn genius and of training in the making of a poet. That dispute was finally concluded by the general decision that, with inborn genius, one had still to have all the training that could be got if one was to be a great poet; and that, without inborn genius, no amount of training could ever make one a true poet. The same conclusion, it is now known, holds for teachers as well. The true teacher, the good teacher, is a very rare find. All of this, I may add, Mr. Wells himself admits to be true; he believes he can safely make the admission because of his faith that the deficiency can be compensated for by machinery and

PROGRESS AND SCIENCE

standardisation; but as to that I have spoken my own belief not only, but that of every practicing teacher whom I have known.

And as it is with teachers, moreover, so is it with pupils. Good ones do not grow in herds. Education is too often found to be, in inverse proportion, like vaccination; even with the utmost care it does not 'take,' as we say. Prolonged effort expended upon the majority of pupils is always likely in the end to prove wasted effort. Beyond the merest rudiments of knowledge, which everyone can be made to learn, the best teacher becomes really effective only as a sign-post. A sign-post is of no earthly use unless one wants to know the way; but if one does want to know the way the sign-post is an invaluable economiser of effort. So precisely with teachers. If their pupils want to learn they can show the way, they can lead onward and upward, in moments of hardship and discouragement they can serve as living example and inspiration;—all this and more they can do, proving themselves invaluable helpers. But their pupils must want such help. Teachers can lead their charges to the water—they cannot make them drink. And for the waters of learning very few are thirsty.

This is the actual situation. It affords small ground for utopian hopes; it gives no encouragement whatever to such proposals as those of Mr. Wells. It is perhaps true, as many maintain, that every human being has some special aptitude which training will improve; it may be novel-writing, or bridge-building, or prophesying, but it may be, too, cotton-picking, or furnace-stoking, or sand-digging, or the handling of pig-iron.[3] But such a fact, if it be a fact, does not help those who prophesy social progress through education. For experience conclusively shows that those who are capable of high intellectual development are a mere handful amongst our millions. And the intelligence tests which, during the War, were administered to the drafted men of the American army show the same thing. I should not wish to defend the strict accuracy of those tests, or of any similar ones, and indeed I am inclined to think that there is at present more harm than good in the hasty, indiscriminate use to which they are apparently being put in some occupations and in some schools. But, allowing for even a wide margin of possible error in individual cases, no one can refuse to credit the information which the American army tests have provided concerning the general level of intelligence. This information has accurately been described as startling. Yet, it is needful to remember, it is startling, not in comparison with what other experience had already told us, but only in comparison with what reckless publicists and dabblers on the borderland of science had led us popularly to expect 'might be' the case. The army tests were of two kinds, one for those who could read and write, another for those who could not, and they "were devised to measure intellectual capacity or inherited ability rather than acquired information or education."[4] This it is important to remember in assess-

---

[3] An instructive paper bearing on this is "The Principles of Scientific Management" by F. W. Taylor (*The World's Work*, May, 1911).
[4] Conklin, *The Direction of Human Evolution*, p. 102. I have

PROGRESS AND SCIENCE

ing the results. These results can best be seen if they are put in tabular form:

Approximate Number Who Were Tested, 1,700,000

Grade	Mental Age	Per cent. of whole
A (very superior intelligence),	18-19	4½
B (superior intelligence),	16-17	9
C+ (high average intelligence),	15	16½
C (average intelligence),	13-14	25
C— (low average intelligence),	12	20
D (inferior intelligence),	11	15
D— (very inferior intelligence),	10	10

Owing to the number who took these tests it is fair to conclude that they represent the levels of intelligence in the American population taken as a whole. If anything the results may be too favourable, inasmuch as no evidently feeble-minded person was drafted into the army. We are brought to see, consequently, that 45 *per cent.* of our whole population can never develop intellectual capacity beyond that of a normal twelve-year-old child, and that another 25 *per cent.* are condemned to hover between the mental ages of thirteen and fourteen. And these two classes alone make up 70 *per cent.* of our population. We know, moreover, that intellectual capacity is inherited, like other personal characteristics, and that people of low intelligence have on the average more children than people of high intelligence. Education unfortunately can do little if anything to change inherited intellectual capacity; it can only develop capacities which are already potentially

adapted the table presented in the text from one used by Professor Conklin.

present. And effort expended upon a child of small capacity is, beyond that child's inherited level, wasted effort, as any teacher knows from hard experience. These, then, are the inherent, necessary limits of universal education.[5] We have perhaps nowhere yet reached those limits; we need, certainly, to keep doing all that we can do; but it is the height of folly to suppose that any programme of education such as Mr. Wells's could be carried out in any country in the world. Education can do much for us; it has probably nowhere yet done all that it can do; but there is no reason for supposing or hoping that it can now or ever accomplish the miracles necessary for the designs of such prophets of social progress as Mr. Wells.

There are others, however, who base, or seem to base, their hopes of social progress through education on a firmer foundation. Professor A. J. Todd, in the book from which I have quoted, particularly mentions Professor John Dewey as being one of the foremost of those who are to-day showing the way to this kind of achievement. And it indeed seems to be true that Professor Dewey has become a powerful leader of those who regard themselves as progressive educators. There is frequent reference to him in their discussions of their aims; and it is generally known that both at the University of Chicago and at Columbia University he has sent out into the country a large number of enthusiastic disciples who have busied themselves in spreading further his influence. Hence it is necessary that we ask what Professor Dewey's hopes are and what his method

[5] For these statements see Conklin, *op. cit.,* pp. 103-105.

for achieving them. There is in this a certain difficulty which might well give us pause were it needful here to attempt anything like a thorough canvass of his pragmatical philosophy. For Professor Dewey is on occasion disarmingly obscure; to the ordinary mind his writings seem to contain many contradictions. He appears at times to give his reader something with one hand while he quietly takes it away with the other. He often seems, at any rate, to offer a solution of all our problems by blandly leading us a long way around to the conclusion that there are no solutions. One sometimes wonders, indeed, if the secret of Professor Dewey's temporary power may not lie partly in his very circuitousness, although probably this notion is too simple to be worth consideration.

Fortunately, however, it should not be necessary for the present purpose to go very far into Professor Dewey's vaguer complexities. It is, in fact, comparatively easy to see both the ground and the appeal of Professor Dewey's major point regarding education. This is that education is not 'preparation for living,' nor any one aspect of living, such as the acquisition of knowledge or of skill, but is life itself. This seems slightly blind, on account of the narrow meaning which we ordinarily attach to the word education. But of course everyone knows that a young child begins to learn practically from the moment of its birth, and that by the time the child begins its formal schooling it has already learned a vast number of things. It has learned these for the most part informally, as member of a family, and through what it is the fashion to call social activity. Before the advent of complex civilisation probably children got all their education in this manner. But as civilisations have developed and knowledge has accumulated it has apparently always been found necessary in the course of time to erect formal schools. In our own age developed industrialism has in unprecedented fashion robbed family life of its educational values—robbed it, that is, of opportunities for the child to learn its way about as a social being, through sharing in the activities of housekeeping. In consequence a greater burden has been thrust upon the school. But the modern school has devoted itself chiefly, if not exclusively, to the intellectual development of the child;—the means of acquiring knowledge, reading, writing, and the like, and the rudiments of knowledge have been its specialties. For reasons of expediency, too, the rudiments of knowledge have been taught abstractly, and a passive receptivity on the pupil's part has been regarded as a virtue.

This state of affairs Professor Dewey disapproves; and all must agree with him that our complex civilisation has developed certain disadvantages, in education and in other directions, which serve to compensate for its better characteristics, though all may not agree that these disadvantages can be done away because we do not like them. Professor Dewey correctly observes that children in general do not like their school tasks. And he says it is no wonder, because it arises from the depravity of the system;—a touch certain to evoke a popular response. His contention is that school life has been violently divorced from the social or family life of the child, and that universal education has to do mainly with children who have little or no distinctively intellectual interest. He regards school life as properly the continuation of family life; he believes that both the things learned in school and the methods of learning them should approximate as closely as possible the actual life of our age outside the schools. This means that children should learn things concretely and from experience, as we say. They should engage in socially useful activities whose purpose is plain to them, such as various kinds of woodwork, basketry, weaving, cooking, and the like; and thus the life of the school should simulate that of the industrialised world. The children's spontaneous activity is thus directed unobtrusively and naturally into useful channels; it is also socialised, so that children learn at first hand the interdependence of human beings and the necessity of co-operation. Such activities, giving scope as they do to children's active natures, arouse and keep alive their interest, so that they like what they are doing and consequently learn far more than they otherwise would. Opportunities thus as it were spontaneously arise for bringing home to children in ways they can understand the need for writing, reading, arithmetic, so that although hard work is involved children nevertheless come to learn these things of their own volition. Similarly the activities of weaving, for example, open up opportunities for instruction in social and industrial history and in geography, in such fashion that the children not only acquire facts but understand their meaning. So, also, metal work opens up opportunities for teaching the history of science and of technology and their principles. The difficulties of these activities also afford adequate training in discipline and persistence.

This perhaps sufficiently illustrates the work of the schools which Professor Dewey advocates, though it should also be said that he regards it as a mistake to divide children rigidly into grades. As far as it is possible he would like to see children of different ages mingling together naturally in their school work, just as they do in play outside the school, and as they do in the family. He would wish to see few if any formal classes, as the word is now used. Children should do their work in small informal groups, and the school should have the appearance of, more than anything else, a busy workshop of the industrial world. In this general manner Professor Dewey would approximate the school to the activities, the viewpoint, the social contacts and interdependencies of the actual world of the present moment. The past, in the guise of historical studies, should enter in only as it relates itself naturally through the children's activities to the present; and the future should be left to take care of itself. The latter may be thought surprising, in view of the fact that the whole period of school attendance is generally regarded as a preparation for the future. Professor Dewey's view, however, is that all life from beginning to end is synonymous with growth or development—that development expresses life's essential nature. Consequently in his opinion development or growth has no end beyond itself; it *is* the end. Growth in the present moment, to be sure, does give off a by-product in the shape of greater ability to grow in the future, but this is merely what it has just been called, a by-product. It follows that both child and adult, in school and out of school, in their own appropriate ways, are engaged in the same enterprise. Both are growing, and one no more truly than the other. One, also, as much as the other is growing in the present moment, which is the only absolute reality; and, growth being its own end, we have no right to set one period above the other. Education, growth, life, are synonymous terms, and education thus is life itself, and is its own end.

On this showing it is not easy to see what becomes of progress. Professor Dewey makes a great show of belief in progress, and rests his advocacy of educational change on its contribution thereto. But he subjects the notion of progress to an ordeal of 'explanation' from which it emerges as 'readjustment.' And readjustment is the process of growth. But since growth is, if I may put it so, just as truly growth at whatever stage of life, and consequently one must also say at whatever stage of civilisation, the question of values, or qualitative difference, of course does not enter in; it no longer has any meaning. If the adult says that on his scale of values the child does not amount to much, the child can retort with equal truth that on its scale of values the adult does not amount to much. It is 'fifty-fifty.' The individual's readjustment to a new circumstance means that a problem is solved, but no value inheres in the solution; the value resides solely in the experience, in the process of solution or readjustment itself. And the solution of one problem merely brings another, hitherto unknown, into the individual's view, where it demands from him new readjustment. It is like an endless chain, and if the chain is not a circle it might as well be, for all the links are of equal strength, of equal value. This, I may say, as far as it goes seems to me an accurate statement of the dilemma of earthly life, or of the individual's physical and social existence. But Professor Dewey does not regard it as a dilemma; he rests in it with complacency and euphemistically terms it the opportunity for growth. Mere 'growth,' however, as an end in itself is not 'growth' at all; it is barren, vacuous, intolerable; it is flatly contradictory to our essential selves; it robs us of all our human values and gives us nothing in their place but empty words.

We have, after all, got caught in one of Professor Dewey's vaguer complexities, but I must leave the reader to wrestle with it further if he cares to; for it is not difficult to understand the progress which Professor Dewey thinks his new kind of school will insure. It is—for Professor Dewey evidently believes that consistency may be bought at too high a price—progress in the ordinary sense of the word. As has been said, Professor Dewey criticises present-day schools on the ground that they are not closely related to the actualities of life in an industrial democracy. He believes that in attending chiefly to children's intellectual development the schools do an unprofitable thing for the great majority, and that they do even this in the wrong way. He claims for the new type of school which he advocates that it will effectively socialise the growing child, that it will lead the child naturally into the activities of industrial society, and that it will bring home the importance of activities which are socially useful, and likewise the need of co-operation in face of the complex interdependencies of contemporary life. This new kind of school, in other words, will centre its training in the types of social life amidst which the child is actually growing up, and will seek to draw out through the child's own concrete experiences possible ways of improving the structure of industrial society. At the same time the new kind of school will be able to count on the child's own interest in its activities, so that the rudiments of knowledge which do filter in by the way will be effective;—that is, the intellectual training given by the 'schools of to-morrow' will be of better quality than that given by orthodox schools of to-day. Such education "will reconcile liberal nurture with training in social serviceableness, with ability to share efficiently and happily in occupations which are productive. And such an education will of itself tend to do away with the evils of the existing economic situation."[6]

Here, then, is the progress which Professor Dewey claims that his type of school will promote. But he believes, too, that it will do more than this. For, in giving all children whatsoever the same kind of training, it will in his opinion force children to see for themselves the evils in those somewhat uncertain but none the less real class-distinctions which at present mar our democracy. These distinctions are both social and intellectual and, as regards the latter, Professor Dewey rightly points out that industrial society is itself tend-

[6] *Democracy and Education*, p. 304.

ing to obliterate them. "Academic and scholastic, instead of being titles of honour," as once they were, "are becoming terms of reproach."[7] The 'schools of to-morrow' will hasten this tendency and will extend it to social class-distinctions as well. The minds of all alike will be subdued to the matter in which they work; the values of industrialism will reign in undisputed supremacy; "an education which should unify the disposition of the members of society would do much to unify society itself."[8]

It seems to me that, granting it would work as he asserts it would, we must all agree with Professor Dewey that education of the type which he proposes would be, for the majority of children, a great improvement upon that which they now receive. Professor Dewey has happily and effectively diagnosed many evils in our public-school system, and has described a type of elementary education which is undoubtedly in close contact with the actualities of child nature. Certainly this training, if carried out as he describes it, whether it would eventually work any miracle in the disposition of society as a whole or not, would produce better results in the majority of cases than do our present schools, and would so far promote social progress. But before we subscribe to Professor Dewey's proposals even in this moderate fashion it is a necessary duty to ask whether or not they are really practicable. This is a question with which apparently Professor Dewey does not concern himself, perhaps because a few

[7] *The School and Society*, p. 40.
[8] *Democracy and Education*, p. 305.

schools—notably the University Elementary School in Chicago of which he was a presiding genius—have achieved satisfactory results in experimenting with his methods. But, as we have been told, a swallow does not make a summer. An occasional success is no answer to this question. Types of education not nearly so well-considered as Professor Dewey's have time and again 'succeeded' in specially favourable circumstances—and have proved nothing whatever about what is practicable in a system of universal education. The same thing is true of Professor Dewey's experimental school in Chicago and of other similar schools elsewhere; such schools have picked and specially trained teachers who are conscious that large issues depend upon their work, and these teachers equally have picked pupils to train—pupils drawn from exceptional families whose parents are interested in educational experiments and are able to pay liberally for their support in tuition fees.

But with public schools the situation is necessarily very different. They must take all comers, they cannot choose their pupils. They can scarcely choose their teachers; and even in periods of industrial depression, when the supply somewhat increases, so many are needed that public-school teachers by and large can in the nature of things be but little, if at all, above average human capacity. Under actual present conditions, indeed, this is a liberal estimate. Professor Dewey's type of school, however, would require for its success very exceptional teachers—teachers with unusual tact, patience, and skill, who had had the benefit of special and exacting training and who had readily at their command a remarkable fund of information. And where such teachers are to be found in unlimited numbers Professor Dewey does not tell us, nor can anyone else. Moreover, his type of school would require a great many more teachers than are at present employed, because it is essential to his system that the pupils be supervised and taught in small groups. Some people will have an easy answer to this difficulty; they will say we can get the teachers needed by spending more of the public money. It is, however, to be feared that this is no answer at all; not only because—as few seem to realise—there are limits to the supply of public money, limits to the extent to which the industrious and the capable can be squeezed to subsidise the needy, but also because of the very number of teachers that would be needed. That number would be so great that even with extraordinary and altogether unlikely expenditure they would have to be merely average people.

This is an elementary difficulty, but one whose importance cannot be exaggerated. For it is one which of itself would appear to render Professor Dewey's type of school little better than a visionary proposal. It has to be remembered that very exceptional teachers are not merely desirable for this type of school—they are necessary. This should be plain at least to anyone who knows the problems of teaching at first hand. The average teacher could accomplish nothing definitely constructive with Professor Dewey's methods. The pupils, no doubt, would in any case enjoy themselves, and would acquire a little skill in various kinds of manual work. But more than this it would be impossible to count on—and this is not enough. The schools of to-day, with their various evils and shortcomings, do not do what we should like, but they do accomplish far more than this. And so far they are better schools than those we are asked to substitute for them. It may be useful to glance at an analogous case: of two inventions one is pronounced 'practical,' the other not. Both equally meet widespread, permanent needs, but it is found impossible to manufacture the one cheaply in large numbers—and we have to get along without it. Professor Dewey's type of school would appear to be like one of these 'unpractical' inventions, constructed without sufficient thought for all factors of the situation which it is designed to meet. Striking confirmation of this conclusion has been furnished by the *General Account of the Gary Schools* issued by the General Education Board. As is probably well known, the schools of Gary, Indiana, partially, though by no means completely, exemplify the kind of school which Professor Dewey advocates. The authors of the book just mentioned took part in a prolonged investigation of the results attained in those schools. These gentlemen, Mr. Abraham Flexner and Mr. Frank P. Bachman, are in whole-hearted sympathy with the theories of such writers as Professor Dewey; they accept them uncritically and even, it may be thought, naïvely. "The theory of which Gary is an exemplification," they say, "is derived from the facts and necessities of modern life." And they claim all for it that they can. But, spite of their obvious reluctance and dislike for the task, they are forced to the conclusion that at present the theory

EDUCATION AND PROGRESS

does not work in practice. In their report they condemn the actual performance of every branch of the work at Gary, and they point out that in some directions the new régime not only does no good, but "must do the pupils positive damage."

Similar testimony has come from many less striking sources. Disillusioned parents, and disillusioned teachers also, have begun to conclude that the victims of 'progressive' education enjoy their experience thoroughly but, unfortunately, do not learn anything in particular, or do not learn the right things. This is a sufficiently grave condemnation, brought about through trial and experience, of proposals which promise so much; yet if one takes a long view—not the short-sighted or immediate view which Professor Dewey praises and himself aims to take—of this new type of education, one perforce discovers another difficulty inherent in it. This can be stated in a sentence: Professor Dewey makes no provision for the training of leaders. No one will dispute our continuing need of them; but a capable and disinterested leader is a sheer impossibility unless he be a capable and disinterested critic of existing conditions. About Professor Dewey's whole plan, however, there is the taint of a deliberate propaganda. His plan, were it successful, would not only deprive criticism of the *status quo* of all influence, it would render such criticism itself impossible. This plan is conceived for the great majority. The small minority of those who have unusual intellectual capacity are to be thrown in with the rest, with no means provided for giving them the special early foundation essential for their own kind of later achievement. And Professor Dewey advocates this consciously, regarding it as one of the merits of his plan. His idea is that in subduing all alike to the industrial plane, in inculcating early in life a narrow, short-sighted, materialised ideal of 'service,' the new type of education will tend to increase the unity of society. This of course within limits is a good thing; but in pursuing this immediate good Professor Dewey is forced to stifle all excellence where it does exist, and so to sacrifice a far larger good—upon any long view—which he apparently quite forgets. He does in fact all that he humanly can to make impossible the development of true leadership. And he does this because his gaze is deliberately narrowed down to the existing social condition of the majority at the present moment. For him the present moment is the only reality, and this has led him into proposing a kind of education which in the long run could insure only retrogression, not progress.

I do not seek to imply, in coming to this conclusion, that our present system of education needs no improvement. I believe it to be, as it is, good in spots; a few schools do their work really well, a far greater number do not. Probably there are feasible ways by which the general level may be somewhat raised in the course of time. Yet unevenness of the kind which now exists is always to be expected, since everything depends, and always must depend, very largely upon the individual teacher. I have only attempted to suggest that it is a mistake to found large hopes of social progress upon revolutionary changes in a system of universal education; such hopes are bound in the end to be frustrated, while in the meantime great harm can be done through ill-considered experimentation. And not only is it true that universal education is no royal road to social progress, but the maintenance of such a system, even in its present unsatisfactory form, has hitherto taxed to the utmost our resources and capacities. That system has been, and is, in constant danger of breaking down at one point or another; and it is the part of wisdom, at least at the present time, for us rather to attempt to consolidate it in order that its very existence may be less precarious, than for us to lose our way in testing narrowly designed projects which are likely to negate the good things we do now accomplish.

And in point of fact one of our gravest educational problems at present concerns the colleges rather than the elementary schools upon which revolutionary social reformers naturally tend to concentrate their attention. This is not our only grave educational problem, but it is one whose ultimate issues are of the highest importance, and at the same time one which will serve to illustrate the general truth that at present all our efforts are needed for the consolidation of our actual achievements in education, rather than for the pursuit of novel and apparently larger, but merely speculative and perhaps illusory gains. Hence I propose here to indicate the nature of this problem concerning American collegiate education; and I may say briefly at the outset that it has to do primarily, not with the weakest nor with the mediocre in intellectual capacity amongst college students, but with the intellectually best.

It is generally recognised, I should suppose, that universal education by no means implies collegiate training for everybody. There are some, it is true enough, who have therefore demanded the abolition of colleges, on the ground that they are tainted with an un-American quality of special privilege. Others, more moderate, have contented themselves with pointing out that the ideal of equalitarianism, if it cannot kill can at least scotch the colleges, so that they are no longer looked up to as once they were, and so that their professors are come to be regarded by real men and women with thinly concealed pity. Such foolish, because fanciful, equalitarianism is, however, a serious menace only to those who believe in it. But the related purely quantitative ideal, of which Americans are fond, and which is fostered by universal education, is a different thing. Professor George Santayana has recently told a story which shows the difference. "The President of Harvard College," he says, "seeing me once by chance soon after the beginning of a term, inquired how my classes were getting on; and when I replied that I thought they were getting on well, that my men seemed to be keen and intelligent, he stopped me as if I was about to waste his time. 'I meant,' said he, '*what is the number* of students in your classes.'"[9] Americans have not only tended to measure the success of their colleges, as they have measured the success of everything else, in terms of mere quantity, but the colleges themselves have acquiesced in this mercantile standard. They have competed with each other, and by no means always scru-

[9] *Character and Opinion in the United States*, p. 186.

EDUCATION AND PROGRESS

pulously, simply for numbers. They have competed with each other in costly physical equipment. And, taking their lead from that remarkable president of Harvard who employed Professor Santayana and who was chiefly responsible for the free-elective system, they have competed with each other in the mere number of courses which they have given—in the number of unrelated units of credit which might procure their degrees.

During the period of expansion in which this competition was at its height apparently everybody was happy. American colleges were like Nebraska corn—one could actually see them grow, and hear them too, for that matter. But at the same time collegiate education itself was deteriorating year by year. Most seem to realise this by now, so that it is hardly necessary to dwell upon the fact. The causes were mainly three. The free-elective system was a shattering blow which, in robbing the college course of coherency, robbed it of meaning, whether right or wrong. It was an astonishing gesture of despair in the face of rapidly accumulating knowledge; though, like most novelties, it was for a time hailed as indubitably a great step in educational progress. That time was short; it soon became plain that the step was really a backward one. As Professor J. W. Hudson has said in a recent book: "Students have been enabled to specialise; but as a matter of fact most of them omit to do so in any effective way. True, they now are educated in terms of their interests. But what sorts of interests? How are their interests motived? Why do college students choose one course rather than another? It is likely to be for such a casual reason as that the course is popular; or because it has the reputation of being easy; or because the student likes the professor who offers it; or because his friends are in it; or because it comes in the morning instead of in the afternoon; or because he needs a three-hour course, and this is the only one that he can conveniently take. In other words, his motives are not the motives that belong to veritable life; they are interests hardly worth recognising."[10] No one who knows the facts can deny the truth of this indictment. The free-elective system put a premium upon laziness and aimlessness, upon the mere dissipation of energy, upon extra-curricular activities or 'college life,' as it is called, and upon the use of the college as a pre-vocational school. It induced finally a line of defence such as this: "Of any two subjects, efficiently taught for the same length of time, one is about as good as another and deserves equal recognition in a scheme of examinations."[11] Patently, this is little else than absurd, but it has had many echoes, because, probably, it has been felt that the free-elective system was an ineluctable reality, yet no other defence of it could be discerned. Now, however, the system is beginning to disappear. A few colleges, for one reason or another, never yielded entirely, and in recent years they have been praised for their strength. Harvard, moreover, under wiser guidance, has itself begun in tentative fashion to abandon the system.

A second cause of deterioration has lain in the fact

[10] *The College and New America*, pp. 60-61.
[11] Dean Le B. R. Briggs, Harvard, *Annual Report*, 1901-02, p. 96.

EDUCATION AND PROGRESS

that the colleges, unwisely clamouring for more students, got them, and got more than they could properly take care of. This has proved an exceedingly bad business. It has meant, of course, inadequate teaching and inadequate supervision of students' work. And this has been coupled with a distinctly lower average of intellectual capacity and interest amongst the students—the inevitable accompaniment of larger numbers. First to attract students and then to satisfy them once they had come, curricula have been diversified almost beyond description, and in ways it has been impossible to justify on any ground save that of practical expediency. Some colleges have become in some of their courses frankly technical or vocational schools, or pre-vocational schools—mere preparatory stages to the law or medical school. For this the distinctive character of the college, that which gives it meaning and justifies its separate existence, has been sacrificed. And from this combination of causes the general level of collegiate work has been lowered. The attention of students has naturally tended more and more to centre upon just getting through, upon piling up somehow or other the required number of credits; and at the same time students have been left with less direction of their work and have had thrust upon them a greater number of lectures. In despair of dealing with very large classes in any other way teachers have thus in effect attempted to do the work of their students for them;—an impossible attempt whose chief result has been to encourage laziness or the dispersal of energy. Further, the intellectually lame and halt have come more and more to dominate the academic scene. Teachers, commanded by their heads of colleges to 'pass' as many students as possible, and knowing that their positions depended at least partially upon the number of students electing their courses, have been compelled, naturally, to lower standards; but, more than this, they have had to centre their attention continually upon the weaker brethren, goading the listless and the lazy, doling out alms to the mentally needy, and generally adapting everything said and done to the worse elements in their classes. And this, I must add, is a moderate statement of the situation. Some colleges have adopted one expedient or another for lessening the evil; more, however, have attempted nothing at all; and in no college known to me has there been devised, thus far, any really effective method of coping with it.

A third cause of deterioration has lain in the absence of efficacious care for students' life outside of their classes. Police regulations there have been, with the college dean acting as magistrate, inflicting penalties one moment for over-cutting and the next moment for gambling or unduly riotous behaviour; and in some colleges, chiefly hitherto those attended by women, disciplinary authority has been handed over to the students themselves. This, however, is not just what I mean. I have in mind the fact that the majority of our colleges have narrowly conceived the term 'academic life' to signify, barring grave misdemeanours, the classroom existence of their students. Incoming herds of raw youth have been turned loose to shift for themselves in boarding-houses. The Eastern college of older growth has generally had some dormitories situated on its campus, and these have continued to be used—by the socially negligible. But even in these colleges prevailingly no attempt has been made to build more dormitories as the number of the students has increased; though this statement has to be qualified so far as women are concerned, conventional standards, to which colleges have of necessity bowed, having demanded for them a 'protected' life. However, by and large the country over, college students have shifted for themselves, have organised their real life to suit themselves, have defensively combined—often in secret or semi-secret societies—to perpetuate their rawness, their aimlessness, their unintelligence, and, in general, the unregenerated social and intellectual condition of the standardised American 'home-town.' The defence which has been built up, it is generally admitted, is strong, so that there is a sharp line of cleavage between students' 'real' life and their academic life. Nor this alone, for 'real' life reigns practically untroubled save when collegiate studies have a direct economic bearing. The result is that our college students are amazingly impervious, if not to information, at least to intellectual growth. This trouble, too, has not arisen simply because colleges have not had the money with which to build dormitories. Money frequently could have been found, and the more easily because dormitories, unlike the remainder of the college's physical equipment, can be made to yield as large an income as any other safe investment. Mere dormitory building, besides, as has been shown in the cases of the few colleges which have attempted to house all of their students in dormitories, though a step in the right direction, does not go to the root of the difficulty. And this difficulty, apparent to everyone by this time, was seemingly not discerned at all until experience forced it into view.

These causes of deterioration have, of course, in practice worked in combination with each other and with other lesser causes. And steps are now being taken in many of our better colleges to relieve them, though real changes for the better are tentative and slow. Nothing is more certain than that, if they are ever to be done away, heroic and protracted work will be necessary. No help will come from prophets of social progress; large, spectacular promises, indeed, are fundamentally alien to the spirit which alone can bring about improvement. For improvement will have to come, not in terms of what we might be, but in terms of what we are; it will have to come through men who have their eyes fixed, not upon some private vision of earthly felicity, but upon human nature as we find it—wretchedly mixed of good and evil, wayward, half-instinctive, groping for leadership and direction. Above all, as it seems to me at least, improvement can come only as a result of the initial recognition that society is far from the possibility of any simple or sudden regeneration, and that indeed there is real danger at the present time lest we should lose what degree of civilisation we have attained, and should lose it partially through our failure to make the largest use of such human excellence as does now exist from generation to generation.

Approached in this spirit, the improvement of collegiate education can the more easily be seen to depend upon acceptance of two simple enough ideas. These are, in the first place, that colleges exist for the sake of continuing the *general* education of men and women, and that, in the second place, since they are the final stage of general education, they exist primarily for the sake of the intellectually best in each generation. To some these truths will appear to be self-evident; yet anyone who knows the extent to which educational 'experts' in America, reinforced by such philosophers as Professor John Dewey, have sought to undermine them will hardly be hopeful of their general acceptance. And these educational 'experts,' some of them working in ways which could hardly stand the light of day, have obtained a remarkable hold upon the machinery of American education which, we may be sure, they will not easily relax. Their position they have used both to spread the notion that a general education is, briefly, an impossibility, and also to bring secondary and higher education into conformity with this notion. The fallacy in their argument against general education is not hard to see; it has recently been stated in a simple form by Professor John Burnet of St. Andrews, whom I cannot do better than quote. Professor Burnet says: "Psychologically the American theory bases itself on a denial of the old 'faculty psychology.' You cannot train the Memory or the Will or any other supposed faculty because these are merely hypostatised abstractions. . . . We should naturally expect the next step in the argument to be that, since this is so, we must assume some principle of unity in us which co-ordinates the different senses and 'faculties,' and that the aim of education should be to train this so that it can do its work of judgement and comparison efficiently. . . . It would seem, in fact, that the denial of the 'faculty psychology' should lead naturally to a keen sense of the importance of general education, but, on the contrary, we find that the comparatively limited number of faculties recognised by the old-fashioned psychology is replaced by a whole host of specific 'functions' or sub-faculties, if we may call them so. There are many memories and so on which are quite independent of one another. . . . Nothing is really gained by speaking of functions instead of faculties. No one who knew what he was talking about ever meant more by faculty ($\delta\acute{v}\nu\alpha\mu\iota\varsigma$) than the possibility of a function ($\acute{\epsilon}\nu\acute{\epsilon}\rho\gamma\epsilon\iota\alpha$), and a function has no independent existence any more than a faculty. It must be a function of something, and that something is best called the soul. It seems to me, then, that the psychology on which the new doctrine is based is open to the very same objections as the old faculty psychology, and in an even higher degree."[12] And Professor Burnet goes on also, in a passage unfortunately quite too long to quote, to point out the unsoundness of the experimental basis of this theory.

But, though the American 'experts' may be conclusively answered, they are not thereby estopped. And they have so succeeded in entangling their theory with unrelated political and social considerations that they have, as they know well enough, a powerful ground of appeal to prejudice and the emotions. Such an appeal,

[12] *Higher Education and the War*, pp. 41-43.

EDUCATION AND PROGRESS

moreover, they make both in their writings and in the instruction which they force upon intending schoolteachers. An example may be quoted from a little book by Mr. Abraham Flexner. "The modern college," says Mr. Flexner, "is impartial, catholic, democratic. Its concern is the whole field; its responsibility and duty to society at large, not to a certain section thereof. It embraces therefore all types of intellectual capacity, all the characteristic processes and activities of social expression and growth: science, industry, trade, laws, institutions are its objects not less worthily than art, literature, philosophy. It makes no question of precedence among them; amid conditions where all are badly needed, it holds it idle to indulge arbitrary preferences; wasteful and disturbing to interfere needlessly with the natural outlet of the youth's energy, by a sort of academic 'protective tariff' that tempts or drives him into an uncongenial expression. The list of things socially, hence educationally, worth while thus extends indefinitely: truth, beauty, yes; but equally, comfort, health, wholesome food, well-governed towns with pure water and clean streets. . . . Education is no longer a formal discipline, but rather a concrete device to facilitate the assertion of individual capacity in terms of rational activities. . . . The college has come down from the mountain; it dwells among men."[13] Such uncritical and indeed in part unmeaning utterances in the name of collegiate education imply, if one is to speak frankly, either well-nigh hopeless confusion of mind or an appeal to the assumed prejudices and emotions of the

[13] *The American College: A Criticism*, pp. 35-38.

reader. And that their author has been elevated to a responsible post in a powerful educational foundation is perhaps an index of the difficulty at present standing in the way of necessary reform.

The college should indeed 'dwell' amongst men; but this does not mean that an intellectual 'democracy' comparable to political democracy is therefore other than plain nonsense; it does not mean that the college is for everybody; it does not mean that the college should be indiscriminately confused with the trade school or the technical training establishment or any other vocational institution, or that the college should become a clearing-house for useful information. It does mean that the college is responsible to society—which, it might be thought, we had always known—and that its responsibility consists in the exercise, as faithful as may be, of its own distinctive function, a function as definitely its own as that of the medical school or the agricultural school. A man is something more than a carpenter, or a printer, or a lawyer, or a politician, or a teacher; and as he is something more than his trade or his profession so is he also something more than his social contacts, be they however numerous and intimate. He is these and something more which not merely co-ordinates them but also gives them all of their meaning and worth. One's trade or profession and social relations have meaning and worth for others too, but what needs remembering here is that these are strictly means to the individual's end of life, and that apart from this they have no significance whatever. A few there are who will term this a truism, and they will be right; but, perhaps in every age, certainly in this age, it is needful to recall this anciently known truth. No 'new knowledge' has invalidated it or will invalidate it; but new knowledge or the semblance of new knowledge, in combination with cloudy thinking, appears to have blinded many men to its import. Its import in education is that there is an education or up-bringing of man as a man and a citizen, distinct and different from his training as a blacksmith, or engineer, or architect, or whatever. And the distinctive function of the college is to take those who are capable of it through the final stage of such general or liberal or humanistic education —call it whichever you will—as a necessary preparation for the best life of the individual and for responsible, intelligent, mature leadership in each generation.

It should also be recognised, as apparently it is coming to be recognised in America, that this final period of general education is a necessary preliminary to the specialised training for the more exacting professions, such as engineering, collegiate teaching, law, medicine. But the benefits of this recognition will be thrown away if the professional schools, through the rigidity of their requirements for entrance, attempt to turn the colleges into mere pre-vocational schools, as some of them are in effect doing. For the sake of a smaller immediate convenience they thus throw away the larger permanent good which alike justifies the existence of the college and the demand that the members of these professions undergo the longer period of training. For the sake of throwing off upon the colleges a part of their own task they are seemingly content to produce professional men and women of smaller calibre and lesser possibilities of future development than they otherwise would; it is penny-wisdom.

Clearly, then, the American college, if it is to be true to its best possibilities, should devote itself to the general or liberalising education of men and women, and, since it is the final stage of such education, its primary obligation should be to the intellectually best in each generation. There have been signs in recent years of a partial reawakening to these truths, and tentative changes looking towards their embodiment in practice; there is indeed reason for hope that our colleges may be on the way to regaining their rightful place in American life. The way, however, is long. In the first place, since the colleges have a duty to all who are able to enter them, they will never fulfil their primary duty to their best students until they adopt some efficacious means of distinguishing them from the majority. This can best be done by the establishment of a distinction between 'pass' and 'honour' candidates for the bachelor's degree. For each of these classes of students a somewhat different course of study should be provided and somewhat different examinations; and the colleges' teachers should not devote the greater portion of their time and effort—as now they almost universally do—to their worse students, but to their best ones. The first aim of any self-respecting collegiate faculty should be proper care for its 'honour' candidates and the maintenance of really high standards of work for them. No one, of course, should be forced to become an 'honour' candidate; nor, on the other hand, should anyone be allowed to become one who had not attained a predetermined minimum rating as the result of, say, his first year of collegiate work. Some thoroughgoing measure of this kind is a fundamental necessity; it is the only feasible means of relieving the intolerable confusion in collegiate work now caused by the indiscriminate mixing together of all kinds of students in the same classes.

In the second place the free-elective system must be much further 'modified' than it has yet been. What is needed is that students should elect subjects or 'schools' rather than single brief courses of arbitrarily limited scope. Such a subject or 'school,' once elected, should require, say, half of the student's time during his second year of collegiate work and all of his time during his two final years. Only in this manner can the work of the college again become coherent; only in this manner can it have the distinctive meaning which is a necessity if it is to remain, during a student's later life, a possession of any real value to him. Subjects allowed for election, moreover, should be carefully restricted, in order that every student might be bound to occupy himself with a subject of fundamental importance. This, it should be admitted, would throw some studies which now occupy a place in the undergraduate curriculum into the vocational or professional school, or into the field of postgraduate work; the change, however, would be a clear gain for both teachers and students. And along with this change in the choice of studies should go a change in the system of examinations. Students should be examined upon the work of the last three years of their college course taken as a connected whole.

A final comprehensive examination of this sort should be necessary before any student obtains his degree; it would be an indispensable aid in insuring, what the system of brief courses taken as separate units quite fails to do, that every student according to the measure of his capacity would, by the time of his graduation, really know something which would remain a permanent possession.

Further, the number of students accepted by colleges should be limited to the maximum who might receive a real measure of individual oversight and stimulus. A few of the best Eastern colleges have long restricted their numbers, and quite recently there have been additions to the list; but it is not easy to see how the colleges connected with Western state universities can ever do this. It is one of the many serious disadvantages from which those amorphous institutions suffer. And in addition, along with restriction in numbers should go a radical change in teaching methods. Individual attention for students is inconsistent with large classes; but the good which results from individual attention will only be secured in full measure when we finally act upon the truth we all know—that a student's work cannot be done for him. The teacher's office, most of all in higher education, is properly confined to suggestion, to stimulus, to general oversight. Our students at present are over-lectured, are compelled to spend quite too much of their time in mere class-attendance, and the responsibilities which should be theirs are in despair assumed by their instructors. Many instructors are well aware that this is an impossible situation, but they are irretrievably caught in the meshes of a settled and organised routine. And the result is that now students learn the fundamentally important lessons of independence, initiative, responsible action, and ability to master situations only through their own so-called extra-curricular activities. We may be glad that they still learn such lessons at all; but it has to be remembered that the present condition has the inevitable disadvantage of leaving students, in their later lives, helpless in face of precisely those needs which colleges primarily exist to care for. In other words, the connexions in which such lessons are learned have their own fundamental importance. At the same time, the competence and, often enough, the brilliancy with which students carry through those activities for which now they are themselves responsible should be an indication of what may be expected when they are made equally responsible for their academic work.

Closely connected with the restriction of numbers is the residential problem. It is comparatively easy, however unusual it may be, for the small college of two hundred or two hundred and fifty students resolutely to remain small. But it is not so easy for such an institution intensively to develop its resources; it tends, in America at any rate, simply to be lost sight of. And there are other advantages, almost unspeakably great, in a considerably larger community. On the other hand, it is only a partial and most unsatisfactory solution of the problem of numbers for a college to resolve to limit its students to two thousand, or even one thousand. Amongst a promiscuous mass of a thousand people the individual is lost sight of with fatal ease. Competent observers have said, indeed, that if a group is to be larger than about two hundred and fifty it really does not matter how many it contains; in different words, it is no longer a group but a crowd. Consequently the advantages sought through limited numbers simply cannot be gained if a large institution virtuously determines that it cannot safely grow further in mere size. There is, however, a comparatively simple solution of this dilemma which should appeal equally to colleges at present both small and large, and it is an extraordinary thing that it should not actually have been tried in America. Both the unfortunate experiences of the American colleges and the singular success of Oxford and Cambridge point to the English solution of this problem as the only satisfactory one.

This solution is, in a word, the organisation of students into small groups, of preferably about two hundred, each group being a unit or 'family' with its own corporate traditions and residential establishment, and with its own academic and social life. With such an arrangement the great advantages both of small groups and of a large community devoted to the cause of learning appear at their best and fullest; and, practically speaking, it is thus possible adequately to care for any number of students. If we should become as willing to learn from the English in this matter as we have been willing to learn in adopting from them a beautiful collegiate architecture, there might follow a corresponding inward improvement—no longer a merely external one—in the character of our colleges. And nothing can

EDUCATION AND PROGRESS

be argued, I may add, from the failure of President Wilson to carry through such a plan as this at Princeton some sixteen or seventeen years ago. As is now generally known, the plan at that time was never discussed on its merits; the failure was caused simply by the manner in which the proposed experiment was announced—a manner which unconsciously implied a brusque disregard of certain sentimental loyalties cherished by a portion of the Princeton alumni. It was, not only for Princeton, but for American education, a decided misfortune that thus the issue should have been, through a mere accident, turned quite away from its real point and confused beyond recognition.

It should, finally, be remembered in any consideration of such a change as this that it would benefit not only the academic work of college students but would, even more, transform the social experience which is a fundamental part of collegiate education. American colleges in largely neglecting this problem have not, as I have said, thereby banished it. They have merely closed their eyes to troubles which none the less have approached and grown. And those troubles will never be relieved until collegiate life is made an integral—not a divided—experience.

These are necessary changes, not to insure 'progress' in the usual sense of the word, but simply to counteract the deterioration from which American colleges have been suffering for a generation. Put into effect, they would merely consolidate past achievements of proved worth. Yet such changes as these, it may easily be believed, are not likely to come quickly;—the path of constructive change is one both slow and tortuous. Moreover, supposing these changes actually made, they would fulfil no large promises—they would not bring us peace and plenty. They would only aid the colleges to perform their own distinctive function. The colleges would then be better able than now they are to insure to us capable leadership, social, political, intellectual, perhaps even religious. And this surely is not unimportant, though it is a far smaller thing than the righting of all our wrongs.

I have chosen here to discuss collegiate education, as being in some respects the most immediately important problem in the educational realm, but the lesson of what has been done and undone and of what is now needed in the American college is one that has its application in other fields of education as well. And it may thus serve to illustrate the general truth that at present all our efforts are needed for the consolidation of our actual achievements in education, rather than for the pursuit of novelties. Certainly we should not allow ourselves to reject good suggestions because they are new; but new suggestions, perhaps in proportion as they seem to promise extraordinary results, should not carry us off our feet into headlong, blindly hopeful action.

IV

SCIENCE AND HISTORY

NO one who has watched the course of history during the last generation can have felt doubt of its tendency. Those of us who read Buckle's first volume when it appeared in 1857, and almost immediately afterwards, in 1859, read *The Origin of Species* and felt the violent impulse which Darwin gave to the study of natural laws, never doubted that historians would follow until they had exhausted every possible hypothesis to create a science of history." Thus wrote Henry Adams in 1894 to the American Historical Association, of which he was then president. Whatever effect this communication may have had upon the minds of those to whom it was addressed, the problem of a science of history became the preoccupation of Adams's own later years. Conscious of its perhaps insuperable difficulties, he yet gave to it increasing thought; it led him to researches in mediæval history and to a remarkable knowledge of contemporary science; and it led him to the writing of three books which have become famous, making his name familiar to hundreds who before had known him only vaguely, if indeed at all, as a distinguished historian of the United States during the presidencies of Jefferson and Madison. The three books were *Mont-Saint-Michel and Chartres*, privately printed in 1904, *The Education of Henry Adams*, privately printed in substantially its present form in 1907, and *A Letter to American Teachers of History*, privately printed in 1910;—these were later given to the public in new editions in 1913, 1918, and 1919, respectively.

It would be easy to dwell upon the varied excellences of these books, though, just because of some of their excellences, it would not be easy to draw any satisfactory picture of them for those who have not read them; one cannot help feeling, indeed, that two of them at least have made for themselves a solid place in literature. My present purpose, however, is merely to review in summary fashion the latest two of these books with the object of showing, in this manner, the condition of modern exact science as regards its interpretation of human nature. For, whatever may be thought of *Mont-Saint-Michel and Chartres* and the *Education* simply as illustrations of a theory of history, Henry Adams's survey of modern science from the historian's viewpoint—found in the *Education* and the *Letter to Teachers*—is something that was badly needed and that is, at present at any rate, of great value. It is admittedly accurate; and some index of its value may consequently be got if one reflects that, as Adams says, 'science now lies in a plane where scarcely one or two hundred minds in the world can follow its mathematical processes.' Moreover, its present value is the greater because scientists are not given to popularising their own work, and indeed under modern conditions of specialisation they are scarcely fitted to do so. But the consequence is that the vast majority of men still obtain their notions of science from the great populariser of the nineteenth century, such as Tyndall and Huxley, or from altogether lesser men of more recent times. And the lesser men sometimes do not have the capacity or the intelligence, even if they have the wish, to report correctly their facts; in addition they generally—whether from the desire to tell their audience what it likes or for some better reason—manage so to censor their accounts as to report nothing inconsistent with a glowing optimism. Hence Henry Adams, incidentally to his primary aim, performed a true public service in giving to the world a review of modern science at once candid, clear, unequivocal, and accurate.

The *Letter to Teachers* was published in a volume which owes its existence to the unlooked-for popularity of the *Education*. This volume, *The Degradation of the Democratic Dogma,* contains, in addition, two short essays by Adams and a long introduction—*The Heritage of Henry Adams*—by his younger brother, Mr. Brooks Adams. This introduction is chiefly an account of their grandfather, John Quincy Adams. It is, as its author seems to have known, in some respects not a creditable piece of work, for it is confused in aim and betrays many signs of hurried writing. I do not, however, wish to complain, for its author was evidently right in believing that the character of the elder Adams illuminates that of his grandson and, besides, the life of John Quincy Adams has an intrinsic interest for anyone who regards history as a record of the upward progress of the race. There is reason, consequently, for taking some notice here of the elder Adams's life.

John Quincy Adams is pictured to us as literally "a martyr to his belief in God, education, and science." He was, we are told, "an idealistic philosopher who sought with absolute disinterestedness to put the Union upon a plane of civilisation which would have averted the Civil War." In other words, his policy, carried to fulfilment, would early have banished human slavery from the country and would have brought to it permanent peace, secured by a high degree of general enlightenment. George Washington had not had perhaps such far-reaching aims, but he had seen clearly certain tasks which lay before a successful administrator of the new nation. John Quincy Adams saw also, as had Washington, that if the thirteen colonies were to be made into one nation they would have to be united by bonds more tangibly real to the average man than any written constitution, and that, further, if the vast territories to the west were to be united with the colonies rather than with the alien territories to north and south they would have to be so united in the same way as the colonies themselves. In both cases, that is, a network of highways and waterways must be built to cement together these various portions of the incipient nation. In addition Adams saw that these avenues of communication should converge upon the new 'city' of Washington. Thus Virginia and Maryland would be-

SCIENCE AND HISTORY

come central in the nation's commercial operations and would be encouraged to utilise their coal and iron, so that these states would in a short time become free industrial communities instead of slave-holding agricultural areas. Moreover, alike for the development and for the administration for national ends of the country's untold wealth in public lands, both Washington and John Quincy Adams felt it to be necessary for the national government in every way to encourage education and, in particular, to foster the growth of the exact sciences.

In taking up this general design of Washington's, John Quincy Adams is said to have felt certain that he was acting as both statesman and Christian—according to his understanding of the latter term—"on the theory that man is a reasoning animal and that there is a God . . . whom man can intelligently serve and with whom he can covenant." And it was his sincere conviction "that such a being thinks according to certain fixed laws, which we call scientific laws; that these laws may be discovered by human intelligence and when discovered may be adapted to human uses. And if so discovered, adapted, and practiced they must lead men certainly to an approach to perfection, and more especially to the elimination of war and slavery."

This golden dream, so unmistakably a product of the early nineteenth century, does not make his grandfather out to be obviously similar to the Henry Adams who wrote the *Education* and the *Letter to Teachers*. However, he was similar enough to Henry Adams as a young man and indeed until the time, in 1870, when from a gallery of the Senate the younger Adams heard the names of the members of Grant's new cabinet. And the emotions which Henry Adams felt upon hearing that news and upon observing later, through the actions of that administration, the level which American democracy had then attained, were similar enough in content if not in intensity to the grieved astonishment which pursued John Quincy Adams throughout his later life. For through his later life the elder Adams had to learn time and again how impossible it was to carry into practice any of his aims for the upward progress of this nation.

In 1828 he was defeated by General Jackson in his candidacy for his second term of the presidency. In his eyes this defeat was nothing less than a successful conspiracy of the powers of evil. He felt, though he did not actually say so even to himself, that in effect God had betrayed him, and he was no longer able to anticipate confidently "ages upon ages of continual progressive improvement, physical, moral, political, in the condition of the whole people of this Union." What, however, he still could do in the remainder of his life to forward his general plan he did; and such possible effort lay chiefly in the direction of encouraging the development of the exact sciences, pure and applied. He was himself a man of high attainments in physical science. His *Report on Weights and Measures,* made by him as Secretary of State and sent to the Congress in 1821, has been described as an "able and extraordinary" performance in the face of great difficulties. This report, indeed, has become a classical document in the annals of metrology both for its accuracy and for its complete and philosophic treatment of the subject. Adams's varied efforts to encourage the exact sciences cannot, of course, be recounted here. It is possible to mention only one—the journey to Cincinnati which he undertook in 1843, when he was an old man, to make an address at the laying of the corner-stone of an observatory which was being erected at that remote spot. He then wrote in his diary: "My task is to turn this transient gust of enthusiasm for the science of astronomy at Cincinnati into a permanent and persevering national pursuit, which may extend the bounds of human knowledge, and make my country instrumental in elevating the character and improving the condition of man upon earth." It was this journey, undertaken for this purpose, which—Mr. Brooks Adams says—was the beginning of his grandfather's death; for though John Quincy Adams remained alive yet some five years, the hardships of this journey permanently broke his health.

Mr. Brooks Adams's comment upon this episode is that, while it gave no discernible impetus to the progress of science, the political influence of the journey was immense. Everywhere John Quincy Adams met astonishing ovations, which witnessed to the reality and depth of anti-slavery sentiment throughout the North and West. Yet this effect of his journey was one which Adams had neither considered nor aimed at. This sardonic yet truthful comment is typical of Mr. Brooks Adams's narration of his grandfather's mistakes in estimating the relations of cause to effect. As Mr. Brooks Adams says, one of the most famous and successful applications of science to a bountiful gift of God was Eli Whitney's invention, in 1792, of the cotton-gin; it made American cotton serviceable and cheap to the whole human race. This was precisely one of those forward steps in the control of nature which, on John Quincy Adams's principles, should have advanced humanity towards perfection. Yet its actual result was the propagation of slavery. It converted Maryland and Virginia from potentially industrial states into enormous slave-breeding farms from which were exported 40,000 negroes annually to the South. And there in turn the demand was further accentuated by the interdiction of the African slave-trade, which also, on John Quincy Adams's principles, had been an advance towards perfection. The South, numerically weaker than the North, was, however, cemented together by this common vested interest; and consequently in 1828 it succeeded in defeating John Quincy Adams and in gaining control through General Jackson of national affairs.

Thenceforward two other famous and successful applications of physical science were likewise turned into instruments for the defeat of Adams's aims. Canals and railroads raised the value of public lands to the West by making them accessible, as John Quincy Adams had foreseen. But the policy of the South threw these vast instruments of wealth and also the wealth itself—that is, the public lands—into the hands, not of wise administrators, but of irresponsible private adventurers. And such was the humanising effect of applied science here that "the thirst of a tiger for blood" was the fittest symbol John Quincy Adams could think of for the rapacity which he saw aroused on every hand.

Thus John Quincy Adams "had laboured all his life to bring the democratic principle of equality into such a relation with science and education that it would yield itself into becoming, or being formed into, an efficient instrument for collective administration." But this was striving, Mr. Brooks Adams says, to reconcile a fundamental contradiction in human nature. For education in actual fact "stimulated the desire for wealth, and the desire for wealth reacted on applied science," so that the latter was really encouraged in America not for John Quincy Adams's purposes at all. It was indeed neglected and ridiculed so long as those were the only purposes in view. It was later encouraged only for the sake of personal gain and of the sense of personal power, under the illusion that "man's progress in mental energy is measured by his capture of physical forces" without relation to the ultimate results of the newly attained power. The consequence was that John Quincy Adams, as far as he succeeded at all, "in fact stimulated an education of waste, and what he sought for was an education of conservation. But an education of conservation was contrary to the instinct of greed which dominated the democratic mind, and impelled it to insist on the pillage of the public by the private man."

It is clear, I think, that John Quincy Adams was one of the more restrained of the early nineteenth-century believers in human perfectibility, or the concept of social progress. It is evident enough now that even had he been able to carry out precisely all of his aims, the results which he looked for would not have followed. In this he was largely the victim of the ideas of his age; but it is worth noticing that, unlike some others of his time and later, he did what he could according to his lights without demanding that we should first abandon the good things which civilisation has already brought to man. The elder Adams was in fact not only a man of large ideas, but also one of incisive mind. In both respects his personality sheds light on the characteristics of Henry Adams. John Quincy Adams united with his strong political bent not merely an interest in the exact sciences, but in addition, as we have seen, genuine scientific capacity. It was characteristic of his type of mind, too, that he should view humanity, not in terms of individuals, but in masses or groups and in terms of material circumstance, and that he should regard moral development as the consequence of economic well-being. Henry Adams grew up as it were in the shadow of his grandfather's ideas. As he matured, his own ideas in his later life became sufficiently different, in many respects, from his grandfather's, but throughout his life his mind remained strikingly like John Quincy Adams's in all its prominent qualities, save that Henry Adams lacked his grandfather's intensity of conviction.

It is consequently true that for a complete understanding of Henry Adams one needs some knowledge of his grandfather. Whether Mr. Brooks Adams has gone the right way about furnishing this knowledge is another question. He has not spared strong colours in painting his picture, but he has painted with his eye, so

SCIENCE AND HISTORY

to say, upon two models at once. For he has used his grandfather's life also as an illustration of his own theory of history. In so doing it does not appear, however, that he has falsified the facts relating to the qualities of his grandfather's mind and character, which are all that we have been concerned with. And Mr. Brooks Adams's theory of history itself deserves brief attention, because it is to a certain extent bound up with Henry Adams's later views.

Mr. Brooks Adams says that his grandfather "fell a victim to that fallacy which underlies the whole theory of modern democracy—that it is possible by education to stimulate the selfish instinct of competition which demands that each man should strive to better himself at the cost of his neighbour, so as to coincide with the moral principle that all should labour for the common good." Mr. Adams's way of putting it at least serves to accentuate the fallacy. He regards the early years of our democracy as a crucial test of it, which showed—as he thinks our subsequent history has also—that "democracy in America has conspicuously and decisively failed, in the collective administration of the common public property. Granting thus much," he says, "it becomes simply a question of relative inefficiency, or degradation of type, culminating in the exhaustion of resources by waste; unless the democratic man can supernaturally raise himself to some level more nearly approaching perfection than that on which he stands. For it has become self-evident that the democrat cannot change himself from a competitive animal by talking about it, or by pretending to be already or to be about to become other than he is—the victim of infinite conflicting forces."¹ In using the word supernatural Mr. Adams of course means to indicate that he considers such a rise an impossibility. He has in fact no panacea to offer; he thinks all forms of civilisation, democratic or other, equally doomed to ultimate failure. He considers the strongest and controlling human motives to be fear and greed, which, dictating moral practice, engender competition. This in turn, in proportion as it is accelerated and unchecked, leads to every known form of bestiality, crime, and violence—leads in truth inevitably to war. Further, since "man can never hope to change his physical necessities . . . his moral nature must always remain the same in essence, if not in form."² Consequently Mr. Adams concludes that man is an automatic animal, all of whose movements are by necessity along this line of least resistance which we call economic competition. To him the capital phenomenon of civilisation is the periodic acceleration of economic competition to the point where it must burst, so to say, and be followed by a new rise of the wave of competition elsewhere. The consequence is that all movements of history conclude, and must conclude, with a demonstration of "the futility of ideals."

Such doctrine can of course never be popular, but that is nothing against its possible truth, and the history of past civilisations gives little or no ground for comfort. Mr. Brooks Adams has, it may be thought, an

[1] *The Emancipation of Massachusetts,* Revised and Enlarged Ed'n, 1919, pp. 167-168.
[2] *Ibid.,* p. 154.

unfortunate literary manner; in his anxiety to convince his reader out of hand he frequently over-reaches himself and, in consequence, merely makes his reader feel that he is being bullied into agreement. The result is that through its author's very excess of zeal his theory of history has probably failed to make the serious impression which in fact it should. It has behind it, at all events, a considerable weight of evidence, and it is in singular agreement with historic Christian doctrine, as well as with the doctrine of several other great religions. For of course when Mr. Brooks Adams speaks of "the futility of ideals" he means the futility of expecting earthly happiness expressed in terms of a stable civilisation which insures material well-being to all. And the fact that he is himself oblivious of any other kind of stable happiness, or blessedness, ought not to obscure the real bearing of his theory.

That theory, moreover, as it was stated in *The Law of Civilisation and Decay,* aroused the interest of Henry Adams. Henry Adams sometimes genially styled himself a Conservative Christian Anarchist, and he wrote to his brother that *The Law of Civilisation and Decay* seemed to him "the Bible of Anarchy." It may be remembered that in the 1890's people were being forcibly impressed by occasional manifestations of anarchy, which probably accounts for Henry Adams's use of the word; what he seriously meant was that he tended to agree with his brother that the movement of civilisation was really not towards collectivism, as it seemed on the surface to be, but towards disintegration. About this he pretended to be more indifferent than he

PROGRESS AND SCIENCE

was. He went on to write to his brother that the proof of such a theory "might help man to know himself and hark back to God. For after all," he continued, "man knows mighty little, and may some day learn enough of his own ignorance to fall down again and pray. Not that I care. Only, if such is God's will, and Fate and Evolution—let there be God!" Here he showed appreciation of the bearing of Mr. Brooks Adams's theory, but in such a possible outcome he was frankly not interested. Had he seen such an outcome with his own eyes he would have regarded it ironically as a curiosity —as an indication perhaps of practical wisdom shown by the mentally weak. In his later life he had occasional impulses to religious feeling, but he constitutionally distrusted them and made nothing of them. When he asked himself, as he came to do, what religion in its palmy days had meant to humanity, he found no answer. He did indeed find an answer of sorts, but it is fairest to call it no answer. What he did was to put religion on a par with the conquering hero's love of power. Remaking it in his own image, he decided that when religion had been a real force amongst men it symbolised power of economic worth. All men, he reasoned, love power and seek it, though only a few achieve it; and thus men adore or worship the manifestation of power, the more religiously the more mysterious it is. His treatment of mediæval worship of the Virgin in *Mont-Saint-Michel and Chartres* here gets its explanation. In the *Education* Adams points out that "the monthly-magazine-made American female has not a feature that would have been recognised by Adam," and he goes on to remark "that neither Diana of the Ephesians nor any of the Oriental goddesses was worshipped for her beauty. She was goddess because of her force; she was the animated dynamo; she was reproduction—the greatest and most mysterious of all energies; all she needed was to be fecund." Thus later the Virgin was worshipped as the embodiment of mysterious energy. But for us of to-day her place has been taken by the railway locomotive, the radio station, and the like, spite of the artist's complaint that the power embodied in these instruments cannot be shadowed forth in art. Adams proves the truth of this by mentioning that at the Paris Exposition in 1900 "he began to feel the forty-foot dynamos as a moral force, much as the early Christians felt the Cross." "Before the end he began to pray to this new machine, instinct teaching the natural expression of man before silent and infinite force."[3]

I have stopped to dwell upon the manner in which Adams materialised religion, dissolving it into something not recognisable by the religious, because it is characteristic of the quality of his mind. He looked at religion as it were from the outside only, and as he looked at religion so did he look at everything else—at morals, at humanity itself. He was a keen observer, and his notes on politics and society throughout the *Education* are full of interest; but he always tended, like his grandfather, to look at men in masses and in terms of material circumstance; and, also like his grandfather,

---

[3] Adams's "Prayer to the Dynamo" has been printed in *Letters to a Niece*.

he had the exclusively objective mind of the scientist. He remarks in the *Education* that he "knew no tragedy so heart-rending as introspection," and this is, as nearly as any one thing, the key to a proper understanding of the man.

Thus it was that when Mr. Brooks Adams's 'law' of the fluctuations of civilisation aroused more of his interest than at the time he cared to admit, and that when he consequently began to consider the problem for himself, he turned to the exact sciences for information and guidance. What he sought was a science of history; he complained that his brother's *Law of Civilisation and Decay* was not really scientific, and he wished at least to make the attempt to put human history on the same plane with such an exact science as, for instance, celestial mechanics. To this end he immersed himself in the literature of modern science, attaining a profound knowledge of its tendency and conclusions. He then elaborated a theory of history which is in admittedly complete accord with the general conclusions of modern science. He also sought in *Mont-Saint-Michel and Chartres* and the *Education* to give a concrete example of this theory which would amount to proof. In the latter attempt he could not succeed in satisfying himself, nor is the attempt likely to satisfy anyone else, and he was still concerned with the problem when illness and death finally put an end to his work.

The theory itself, however, weighted with the evidence of modern science, is adequately sketched in the *Education* and the *Letter to Teachers*. It may be variously phrased by saying that history is the record of the progressive degradation of vital energy, or of the development of multiplicity out of unity, or of the evolution from order to chaos. Such generalised statements are of course too abstract for any adequate appreciation of their meaning;—for that it is necessary to look more closely into Adams's books. In the first place Adams assumes, with science, that man is simply a force of nature, like the wind or lightning, only more complex. Propagandists for the encouragement of science, it is true, tell us a rather different story, claiming that science is an instrument of human progress in the sense that through it we bend nature to our will, and make her thus serve our conscious purposes. This, of course, is the popular notion of the present day, everywhere fostered by scientists, and having its obvious foundation in the innumerable practical applications of science. The fact is, indeed, that 'science' says both things, and it will become plain a little later how the apparent contradiction is resolved. Accordingly Henry Adams is within his rights both as historian and as scientist in holding that "the fiction that society educates itself, or aims at a conscious purpose, was upset by the compass and gunpowder which dragged and drove Europe at will through frightful bogs of learning." In other words, the truth is that through applied science the forces of nature capture man and bend him to do their will. As himself one force of nature man merely assimilates other natural energies and sends them out again in new directions, but he has no more control over the latter process than over the former. The reduction of the world, of society, to order is a notion that exists merely as a dream or illusive mirage in the eternally hopeful mind of man. He pushes on to new achievements in the ordering of knowledge, of society, merely to find that his apparently successful efforts have brought him face to face with new disorders, with greater chaos than any before imagined.

Not only is man simply a deluded mechanism, but the forces of nature, of which he is one, cannot be reduced to any harmony or common measure. To use Adams's own easy contradiction, "chaos is the law of nature." This means that natural phenomena cannot be reduced to any one set of formulæ, that the phenomena are of diverse kinds operating in diverse ways, and that the so-called laws of mechanics are simply convenient rules-of-thumb, of limited application. They are not 'true' in the absolute sense, the sense in which the word is generally used. This means that the universe is a congeries of forces or energies—not moving in unison towards "one far-off divine event"—but floundering foolishly, without purpose, hopelessly in eternal conflict and in consequent eternal chaos. We live, not in a universe, but in a 'multiverse' "where order is an accidental relation obnoxious to nature; artificial compulsion imposed on motion; against which every free energy of the universe revolts; and which, being merely occasional, resolves itself back into anarchy at last." The consequence for man is that he is not unlike a child's jumping-jack, hopping perilously he knows not whither nor why through a weltering chaos which too commonly overwhelms him. His dream of progress consists actually in the unearthing of new divergencies and conflicts of force; and these conflicts of energy extend to man's own expenditure of force, so that each fresh triumph of social order really brings social anarchy so much the nearer.

"Know thou this," said Edmund to the Captain in *King Lear*, "that men are as the time is." Henry Adams early in life discovered his agreement with Edmund and the Captain. His life was, in fact, one long effort to conform himself to 'the time';—generally, he thought, an unsuccessful one because things changed too rapidly for his pace. The consequence was that he had become a student of science long before he began his attempt to formulate a scientific theory of history. As he says in the words which I quoted in my first paragraph, Buckle and Darwin in 1857 and 1859 first opened men's minds to a new extension of the sphere of exact science, and laid the foundations for an inevitable attempt to make a science of human history. Adams himself had read *The Origin of Species* with eagerness and a certain enchantment, and he followed with open mind the discussions and enlargements of theory which ensued on that book. Yet Darwinism, as distinguished from Darwin's own cautious generalisations, Adams found a frail bark. He saw from the first, according to his own account, that men straightway believed in gradual, uniform evolution in accordance with beneficial natural laws rather because it was convenient than because the new theory had been proved. He became, provisionally, a Darwinian for a time, apparently because everybody else was doing it and nothing better offered; though behind the vast edifice of Sir Charles Lyell's Natural Uniformity he could discern nothing save pure inference or assumption. Ponder the evidence as he might, he could only observe "natural selection that did not select—evolution finished before it began—minute changes that refused to change anything during the whole geological record—survival of the highest order in a fauna which had no origin—uniformity under conditions which had disturbed everything else in creation"; and "to an honest-meaning though ignorant student who needed to prove Natural Selection and not assume it, such sequence brought no peace. He wished to be shown that changes in form caused evolution in force; that chemical or mechanical energy had by natural selection and minute changes, under uniform conditions, converted itself into thought. The ganoid fish [a creature which Adams seized on as an example of an uniformity not Darwinian] seemed to prove—to him—that it had selected neither new form nor new force, but that the curates were right in thinking that force could be increased in volume or raised in intensity only by help of outside force."

Adams's scepticism served him well; it made him the more ready for those revolutionary changes which have taken place in science since, say, 1890. And from the study of these he formed the conclusion which I have stated—that, since man is a natural force, the movement of human history, like the movement of the universe, consists of the progressive degradation of vital energy. This conclusion is in agreement with recent science, and Adams considered that nothing which we

SCIENCE AND HISTORY

know about the past of man contradicts it. It is generally recognised at the present time that it is illegitimate to interpret natural phenomena in terms of human purpose; but in the eye of science man himself is nothing but a natural phenomenon, and it inevitably follows that purposiveness in man also is an illusion. This makes, of course, sufficient ground for terming the universe a complex of anarchical energies. And Adams was chiefly concerned to point out this species of anarchy, which arises from the existence of rival energies in nature pulling man this way and that, blindly and against his will, whenever he can be seen to have any. The fittest generalisation, he thought, for what human history alone can tell us is that man is "a creature habitually striving to attain imaginary ideals always contrary to law." Such a conclusion, he adds, "explains much that had been most obscure, especially the persistently fiendish treatment of man by man; the perpetual effort of society to establish law, and the perpetual revolt of society against the law it has established; the perpetual building up of authority by force, and the perpetual appeal to force to overthrow it; the perpetual symbolism of a higher law, and the perpetual relapse to a lower one; the perpetual victory of the principles of freedom, and their perpetual conversion into principles of power."

Yet it is, of course, consistent with such anarchy that changes should take place in uniform ways, and hence that phenomena should be subject to constant 'laws.' And it is equally consistent with such anarchy that underlying these laws there might be some common

PROGRESS AND SCIENCE

necessity in terms of which all phenomena could be described. This is all that is needed for science's assumption of monism, and such a higher synthesis of apparent contradictions was exactly what Adams sought for. But even here he found that trouble was brewing. He quotes Lucien Poincaré as saying that "a certain anarchy reigns in the sciences of nature's domain; any venture may be risked; no law appears rigorously necessary." And none appears rigorously necessary, he found, because the several sciences have in recent years been able to develop only by proceeding on the basis of assumptions or dogmas which contradict each other. This has been true not only of different sciences, such as mathematics, physics, biology, but has been true also within the field of a single science, such as physics. Here the laws of the Conservation of Energy, asserting that nothing can be added and nothing lost in the sum of energy, and of Dissipation, asserting that nothing can be added but that Intensity is always lost, are found equally useful and consequently 'true.' Yet these laws obviously contradict each other unless we pretend that energy of lowered intensity, no longer capable of performing work, is still energy unimpaired, and unless we also pretend that the universe is like a tightly stoppered glass bottle from which nothing can possibly escape. As regards the second of these pretences, no one can either prove or deny it; it may be so, but there is nothing to incline one to belief except the convenience of physical science.

In the face of such difficulties as this Henry Adams was candid enough to say that the assumption of

SCIENCE AND HISTORY

fundamental unity, or monism, was dictated only by convenience and that it might be, indeed, "the most deceptive of all the innumerable illusions of mind." But simplicity and unity, he thought, "are primary instincts in man, and have an attraction on the mind akin to that of gravitation on matter. The idea of unity survives the idea of God or of Universe; it is innate and intuitive." He also called attention to the dictum of Henri Poincaré, who said that physicists use the formula of monism "only because all science would become impossible if they were not allowed to assume simple hypotheses." These may be susceptible neither of proof nor of refutation, yet they are regarded as true because they are unquestionably convenient. The monistic hypothesis being in this manner accepted, Adams found that in all the sciences in recent years the law of the dissipation of energy has increasingly proved a convenience. In all of them it has come to be either tacitly or openly applied to phenomena. It has been found "so simple and so natural as to satisfy every want." In other words, no other formula at present so nearly accounts for all observable phenomena; and consequently its acceptance as an unifying hypothesis is virtually forced upon us.

As was said, the law of dissipation means that energy is, in performing work, always falling from a higher to a lower level of intensity; and the intensity thus lost is irreplaceable. Work can be accomplished only by a fall in tension; and thus every material change in the universe is the result of a dissipation and levelling of intensities, so that from an original condition of high intensity the sum of energy in the universe constantly tends towards a stable equilibrium where no further inequalities of intensity continue to exist. Consequently in the course of time nothing will remain but "a dead ocean of energy at its lowest possible level . . . incapable of doing any work whatever." The universe is like a clock running down. As far as can be known it has a long time yet to run; barring sheer accidents—which, however, are relatively as common in the heavens as on the earth—there is no immediate cause for worry; yet this does not alter the fact itself, that the end of the universe unescapably approaches.

Vital energy, one of whose manifestations is human energy, may or may not be at bottom identical with mechanical or physicochemical energy; this contested point is of little significance; for equally in either case it necessarily obeys the same law, just because that law is assumed to be universal in its application. And this means that organic creatures are, as Darwin showed, subject to a law of evolutionary change; but their development is from the beginning downward, not upward, so far as useful energy is concerned. It follows that man is the embodiment of the lowest known stage in the progressive degradation of vital energies. This is no paradox. Amongst organic creatures it is a necessity to regard 'the vital energy of every stem as the source of variation in the branches, and hence to admit that a branch which has lost the power of variation is an example of enfeebled energy.' 'All anthropologists agree that man is specialised beyond the hope of further variation, so that, as an energy, he must be treated as an enfeebled vitality, a weakened will, or degraded potential.' Moreover, "he cannot himself deny that his highest Will-power (or Vital Energy), whether individual or social, must have proved itself by his highest variation, which was incontrovertibly his act of transforming himself from a hypothetical eocene lemur—whatever such a creature may have been—into a man speaking an elaborately inflected language."

It is natural, of course, that we should regard conscious human reason, if nothing else, as incontrovertible proof of evolution upward rather than downward. Here, however, we are met by the certainty that reason can be nothing other than a further "phase of the energy earlier known as Instinct or Intuition." As such it is merely an enfeeblement of archaic vital energy of greatly higher intensity. 'Thought is a more or less degraded act, which comes as the result of helplessness —it is an amputated Intelligence, a truncated Will— and Instinct, not thought, is the potential of Vital Energy. The beauties of thought—shown in the intuitions of artistic genius—are simply the last traces of an instinct now wholly dead or dying.' The fact is that one of the beauties, if I may so speak, of the law of dissipation is the facility with which it accounts for consciousness and reason. And it is now generally recognised that Darwinian evolution cannot be made to account for such facts as are known about the development of organic creatures. Darwin himself, indeed, was more nearly aware than have been many of his idolatrous followers of this failure. It is recorded that he said he could never think of the eye without a cold shudder—and this because the eye, which should have been slowest in the order of evolution, in actual fact leapt to perfection from its start. "In fact, the eye of the first fish, at the beginning of geological time, was at least as good as that of his descendant still living unchanged; and the first trilobites, somewhere in Silurian ages, had eyes of twelve or fifteen thousand facets." This is sufficiently bad for the old-fashioned evolutionist, but it is only one instance amongst many which all go to prove "the universal stunting of animal life in recent times." And a sufficiently low stage of this process of degradation of vital energy causes the appearance of consciousness and reason.

Of course it is not meant to deny that there has been, as in the case of man, an evolution of organisms more and more adapted to specific modes of existence; but it is asserted that this has been at the expense of useful, unreplaceable energy. Thus the development of conscious intelligence and of civilisation in society undeniably conveys an impression of gain; 'but this is derived from an impression of Order due to the levelling of energies, and the impression of order is an illusion consequent on the dissolution of the higher Order which had supplied, by lowering its inequalities, all the useful energies that caused progress.' Thus it is that, as was said earlier in this essay, science can appear to be both the guarantor and the instrument of progress, yet at the same time must pronounce such progress to be an illusion. Science can give us temporarily a great expansion of energy and a certain rather doubtful measure of relief from pain. When it does so we have an era of 'progress'—progress which can be measured quantitatively. In the present age we have already some indication how temporary such expansion or 'progress' may prove to be; the War has shown those who are sufficiently reflective how far our expansion contained within it the seeds of its own dissolution, and, quite beyond such a phenomenon, it is known that there is the gravest reason for alarm over our rapid exhaustion of the material resources—wholly unreplaceable—upon which our industrial civilisation is based. Such progress, while it lasts, is of course real enough, yet in proportion as it is great it must be temporary; and, viewed as a new revelation of the nature of things, it is grim illusion, behind which is nothing save "absence of the power to do useful work—or what man knows in his finite sensibilities as death."

Such in briefest summary are the grounds for Adams's conclusion that any scientific human history must be constructed on the hypothesis that man's development is the record of the progressive degradation of vital energy. If, of course, this seems an impossibly revolting conception, it is open to us to use different words. The biologist has thus in recent years quietly adopted the harmless-looking word 'transformation' to replace the no longer satisfactory word evolution, with its inconvenient popular connotation of upward progress. Similarly the historian of human society may say, if he prefers, that his constructions are based on the hypothesis of change from unity to multiplicity. This would perhaps seem less offensive, without changing the realities. Those realities are that the universe presents itself to us as a complex of anarchical, or purposeless, energies; that the only intelligible or unified view of it now possible is the picture of the whole thing running down towards what we call death, or ultimately to annihilation; that man himself is an automaton, or creature of illusory purpose—a mechanism far down in the scale of embodiments of energy, existing only as an instrument of great efficiency in the expenditure of the present comparatively low supply of unreplaceable energy.

Those who wish to be confirmed in the assurance that this is the position of modern science in its interpretation of the universe and of man should read the *Letter to Teachers,* with its wealth of citations from continental authorities, for themselves. They may also turn not unprofitably to a recent book by Mr. Hugh Elliot, *Modern Science and Materialism.* This able book is—if I may say so without disrespect—a sort of Sunday-school version of the same material;—a Sunday-school version in the sense that it is a well-developed plea for acceptance of a materialistic philosophy, and that its digest of the conclusions of modern science is deliberately censored to that end. Thus, since Mr. Elliot is out to capture the allegiance of his readers for a particular purpose, his book is not so candid a performance as is Henry Adams's; some of his statements he softens or attempts to palliate, other facts he quite neglects to mention; but he is plain enough for the present purpose.

Of the universe as a whole Mr. Elliot says "that the farther we travel, the more obscure and insignificant does Man appear. And three points also emerge. . . .

Firstly, the uniformity of natural 'law' remains as absolute in these regions of infinite greatness as in our own world of human dimensions. Secondly, no sign of purpose can be detected in any part of the vast Universe. . . . Thirdly, this great new sphere of experience affords not the smallest trace of evidence for the existence of any spiritual entity. We find nothing but unimaginable tracts of space and time, in which move bodies by fixed laws towards ends which are wholly fortuitous, and have not the smallest relation to the advantage or requirements of man." Speaking of matter and energy Mr. Elliot says "that there seems to be a general tendency throughout the Universe at present towards a diminution of the intensity factor of energy, and a consequent increase of the extensity factor." Investigation of radio-action has recently shown that something analogous is taking place in matter. And Mr. Elliot goes on to point out that these transformations "tend very unmistakably towards what may be called a degradation of matter and energy. The Universe is running down; and, theoretically, at least, a time may be imagined when it will have run down altogether, becoming still and 'lifeless.' As regards energy, this fact was discovered many years ago; as regards matter the discovery is very recent." Mr. Elliot then proceeds to treat of life and consciousness. He premises that "if we wish to obtain an idea as to the fundamental facts of life, we must consider it from the point of view, not of individuals, but of species. For an individual is simply an outgrowth upon a fragment of germ-plasm. It is a highly perishable excrescence, which protects and subserves the continuance of the germ-plasm within it—the germ-plasm being the main fact of the species itself. Unfortunately *we* are individuals, and our first outlook is naturally from the point of view of individuals. But this anthropocentric outlook has to be altered, if facts are to be seen in their correct perspective." This 'correct perspective' leads on inevitably to the conclusion that consciousness and reason are none other than specific reactions of nerve-tissue—that and nothing more. It follows that "men think, feel, and act as they do as a necessary result of their physical, and especially of their nervous conformation. . . . The organism is a machine, whose function is that of energy-transformation. A stimulus set up upon the surface works internal changes, which issue in action. That is to say, energy absorbed from without is transformed into other kinds of energy according to the common laws of physics and chemistry."

This sufficiently shows that Mr. Elliot's and Henry Adams's readings of the literature of modern science confirm each other. And the conclusions which both present to their readers show plainly enough, I think, why Henry Adams "knew no tragedy so heart-rending as introspection." To look within is merely to 'drown one's self in the reflexion of one's own thought.' It could not be otherwise when the mind is conceived as science conceives it—as simply a storage-house for natural energy. Thought is the middle stage between a human being's reception of natural energy and his subsequent expulsion of it in a new direction. There is no originative power in thought, nor, consequently, in the

SCIENCE AND HISTORY

individual; there is only the illusion of directive power. Further, since what we see in the mind is only the reflexion of external energy of various kinds, we are withdrawing ourselves from reality or truth by looking within. Only by looking outside ourselves can we approach reality.

The scientist is in the very nature of things exclusively occupied with generalisation. Not differences but resemblances are valuable to him, and the several sciences flourish in proportion as some common term can be found underlying and uniting apparently diverse phenomena. This is well enough known, but seemingly it is not often realised how clearly it follows that science can make nothing of individuality. Individuality is at the least an annoyance to the scientist, and the existence of the conscious human individual is nothing less than a scandal;—a gross anomaly in a universe otherwise amenable at least to rough generalisation. Science has always consistently attacked the pretensions of the individual, and it has many victories to its credit; it has conquered wherever human pretensions have been wittingly or unwittingly foolish. This, however, has not been enough, and as science has waxed stronger it has increased the vigour of its attacks. These attacks certainly will not cease until either science or the individual is vanquished, for neither can possibly admit the claims of the other. As Henry Adams has said, "science itself would admit its own failure if it admitted that man, the most important of all its subjects, could not be brought within its range." But science can only manage to include man within its range by absolutely denying significance to his consciousness, his reason, and his individuality. To-day science does this with conviction and confidence; man, it says, is different from the dog or the jackass only in his genial illusions. Henry Adams himself saw that man was not likely to agree. "Man," he says, "refuses to be degraded in self-esteem, of which he has never had enough to save him from bitter self-reproaches. He yearns for flattery, and he needs it. The contradiction between science and instinct is so radical that, though science should prove twenty times over, by every method of demonstration known to it, that man is a thermodynamic mechanism, instinct would reject the proof, and whenever it should be convinced, it would have to die."

This is true, though instinct is surely an inadequate word to suggest both the grounds and the force of human repulsion from this assumption of science. Science asserts, be it remembered, that man's illusions are the only things intelligible to him; this is what it comes to, for man necessarily apprehends life in terms of his conscious individuality. He cannot help it even if he would; suicide is his only escape from it. As Mr. Hugh Elliot says, "Unfortunately *we* are individuals." Consequently I wish to suggest that the real lesson to be derived from the assumptions of modern science concerns the necessary limitations of science itself. Science, in a word, inevitably negates its own claim to be the sole organ of knowledge in the very act of making it. For there can be no knowledge without the unfortunate individual; nothing can be known unless somebody knows it. Thus science depends for its very existence

SCIENCE AND HISTORY

upon the validity of thought, which in turn exists only in the persons of conscious individuals;—but science in order to establish its own claim to fundamental validity has had to deny significance to individuality and to reduce conscious thought to illusion. There could be no simpler nor more complete demonstration of the impossibilities inherent in the pretensions of modern science. It would lead us into a world inhuman, desolate, barren, where the conscious individual has no real existence whatever—yet even the bare notion or image of such a world can exist solely in the mind of that same conscious individual. Consequently if science is to maintain its claim to any validity at all as an organ of knowledge it can do so only by abandoning its pretension to supremacy. A species of 'knowledge' which can account for the individual only by attempting his destruction answers itself. In its own defence in its proper sphere science must admit that it cannot account for the individual, that it is in fact the expression of only one of the several 'faculties' or powers which unite to form him, and that its sphere of truth is accordingly restricted. Human beings in their turn can then not only admit but welcome the claims of science in its properly restricted sphere.

It is thus possible to accept the results of scientific investigation. It is only asserted that, for acceptance, these must be the actual results of actual investigation, and not mere hypotheses or—to use a plainer word—mere dogmas posited in support of science's self-confident claims to supremacy in the interpretation of life. Such results it is not only possible to accept, it is imperative that we recognise them as being, if not the final truth, at least as near the truth as we can at present get through observation and experiment. We cannot do away with them if we do not happen to like them, although we cannot, either, hypothetically extend them to convenience scientists or to soothe their vanity. If, as seems necessary in the light of present knowledge, the curve of change for the physical universe, including all physical life, must be stated in terms of the degradation of energy, we may not like it but we have nevertheless to accept it. To assume, however, that this settles the whole question of human destinies is an absurdity at once impudent and tragic. For the human individual this information may indeed be illuminating, but it is in fact, in its ultimate implications, novel rather in form than in substance, and it may certainly be to him rather helpful than disastrous. It must be remembered that it changes no fact in the life of the individual; it directly affects only the individual's purely supposititious descendants of probably some millions of years hence. Moreover, it must be remembered that this conception results from the activity of one portion only of the individual's intellect divorced from the remainder which is no less real; and accordingly in order to digest this presumed fact and estimate its meaning the individual must bring his whole intellect to bear upon it. Doing so he discovers that the scale of human values does not coincide with the quantitative measurement of vital energy; he discovers that according to the terms of this conception itself the possession of conscious reason and individuality depends upon the very enfeeblement of vital energy which he is invited to regard as a degradation. He concludes that for him degradation is progress;—and in this even a man who lives a life of mere sensation must concur, inasmuch as he would prefer a weak sensation of which he is conscious to a stronger one of which he is unconscious. The individual concludes further that this knowledge in reality only reinforces the age-old lesson that the fundamental values of life are inner, not outer; spiritual, not material; and that an unmistakable warning has been given those men who place their dependence upon material satisfactions and upon the material rewards of industrial civilisation. He concludes that those who are most disturbed by this new knowledge are precisely those who were most intoxicated with the wild promises and wild assertions of the relatively undeveloped science of a generation or two ago and of its propagandists.

Such, I believe, is the result, rather than the suicidal conclusion of Henry Adams, of any sober evaluation of the relation of modern science to human life. The justice of such a conclusion is, however, so far at present from being generally recognised that it may, finally, be not without value to inquire what type of man can accept blindly and uncritically the contemporary prestige of the exact sciences. I suppose everyone must know the common type of man who does this—nowadays the more easily because his notions of the physical and natural sciences are likely to be those which were orthodox thirty years ago or more. He is the kind of man whose beliefs are easily fixed; who, without much insight or critical talent, needs only to believe concerning the deeper meaning of life what his own little world already believes, and what consequently to his rough judgement figures as correct, in order to set free his nature for practical activities. It cannot be said that the age's answer to life's riddle is to this kind of man unimportant or indifferent; yet no injustice is done him, surely, in pointing out that he expends little time or thought upon the question, and that the stimuli to which his energies most readily and effectively respond lie within the so-called practical sphere and are largely connected with life's material, day-to-day needs. Consequently this type of man tends to accept his surroundings from age to age as he finds them. His problems arise from the attempt to satisfy his appetites under conditions already given. He becomes anxious to change those conditions only when they force upon him an undue or intolerable repression of his acquisitive nature or animal needs. Hence such a man's fundamental beliefs, though they may influence his character and happiness far more than he realises, are accepted by him from others; and he tends to scoff at any dispute about their nature or basis. He does this, it may be thought, the more in an age of science, since science itself and the values sanctioned by science are upon his own native plane of sensation. Science appears to tell him what he spontaneously thinks—that life consists mainly in the performance of deeds for which there is obvious, tangible stimulus, winning a wife, procuring subsistence, making a name, achieving power. This man, as I said, I should suppose everyone knows, and for casual purposes—so long as his interests are not interfered with—he is a good companion. It is a part of his business to fit easily into the social order. And he gives mass, weight, authority, compelling force, to any cause once it is well started. His stabilising influence is incalculable, and it is the greater pity that it works so blindly and may lend itself to harm as easily, very often, as to good.

Henry Adams, one would say offhand, belonged obviously to some less common class of men. His open-minded, vigorous scepticism, maintained throughout his life, proves him to have had a nature at once deeper and more independent than has the average man of practical affairs. Yet, despite this, Henry Adams does appear on close examination to have belonged fundamentally to the same class. And what holds for him holds for many other exceptional men who have been, as it were, hypnotised by the pretensions of science. Adams was, it is true enough, consistently and vigorously sceptical, yet after all he never carried his scepticism very far. Its restricted range he has made plain enough in his characteristic way. He says it was not his fault that the universe always seemed real to him, and that 'despite the long-continued effort of a lifetime' he perpetually concluded that not he but the appearances, not the poet but the banker, not his thought but the thing that moved it, spelled Reality. The question of fault need not be decided, but the limit imposed upon scepticism is clear. Whatever else might be questioned or decided, the viewpoint of the so-called practical man of affairs was sacred. A more thoroughgoing scepticism might in the end have brought him around to the view that both the poet and the banker are equally real; but in fact he never got so far as really to doubt the scientist's basic assumption of materialism. Though in later life he was willing speculatively to admit that monism was a convenience rather than an absolute necessity, he never seriously took one step towards the vista which this admission opened up. Moreover, he had in early life, as I have said, resolved that the current of his time was to be his current. For this there was reason. The fact is decently blurred in his narrative, but it is plain that Adams coveted power, position, at one time public office; that he yearned to meddle with the destinies of men. He sought the truth, but he sought—as he himself says—only enough for his practical purpose. That purpose was to gain prevision of the movement of society—the one kind of knowledge most necessary to the workaday wielder of power. For this he was impelled to look beneath the changing appearances of the world, but not dangerously far beneath them. He complained, and rightly, that his scepticism did in fact take him further than he intended; but it never carried him beyond materialism, or naturalism, tacitly the foundation for the viewpoint of the worldly or practical man. Adams thus was always immersed in the objective world of affairs as completely as is the average man of the street. He had a more ambitious aim and was after a bigger prize than generally urges on the latter person, but the direction of his vision was the same. In later life he grew more and more content to play the part of

SCIENCE AND HISTORY

the spectator of events, but the quality of his mind never changed; his vision was consistently outward into the world of practical activity.

That limitation of viewpoint is, I take it, characteristic alike of the scientist and of the average man who is taken in by the scientist's pretensions. Both see things and men from the outside only. About things they are right enough. But complete outwardness of vision is a fatal bar to the understanding of men. It leads in the last resort, as has been said, virtually to the denial of their existence; in plain words, the unregenerate outward view is suicidal. Henry Adams made the great discovery that 'what he valued most was Motion, and that what attracted his mind was Change'; he discovered, in other words, that the movement of the practical world feeds upon itself, growing into mere love of excitement and restless search for distraction from inner emptiness. Towards the close of his life he could only say that he was kept alive "by irritation at finding his life so thin and fruitless" and, with thinly concealed bitterness, that 'Noah's dove had not searched the earth for resting-places so carefully or with so little success' as had he. Severe, restrained, carefully based upon objective fact, the golden dreams of John Quincy Adams have yet faded into nothingness. Reared in their grandfather's own world of science, Mr. Brooks Adams has broken down in savage disillusion, and Henry Adams years before his death found the world and its works unprofitable, barren, fruitful only of ennui. And for ourselves?—elsewhere, I think, must our eyes be turned if we seek wisdom and the fulness of life.

V

WALTER PATER

IT seems already a long time since the death of Walter Pater; for much water has run under the bridge since those middle years of the eighteen-nineties when Mr. C. L. Shadwell gathered together the floating remnants of Pater's legacy, and in a manner fixed the canon of his friend's work. Pater has, too, during this time been evaluated, placed, one might almost say disposed of, by critics and scholars. His æstheticism is generally considered to be dead, and most would say well dead; yet few could deny that Pater's voice still speaks to us, though it be with altered accent, and as it were from another world.

This undoubted vitality which some have been at pains too hastily to deny him has arisen, I have come to feel, from two qualities which run through all his writings. One of these is, in a word, his fastidiousness. This is a virtue with dangers of its own, yet still a virtue so finely and consistently exemplified by Pater that his writings may long have a very considerable meaning and value for us. And we are not likely, judging by signs which all can read and very few can escape in these days, through the influence of Pater or of any other writer, to grow over-fastidious in our tastes and actions. Moreover, the other quality which has given Pater's books a peculiar meaning for the present age is curiously contradictory in its influence; and, though it is closely related to his fastidiousness and indeed forms its groundwork, it cannot be termed a virtue. This, also, is a quality, or rather principle, which has been seized upon by the majority and has been acted upon by thousands who have never directly heard of Pater. He was in fact not alone responsible for it, nor even responsible for it at all so much as simply expressive of its revival in our time. And it is this latter principle, almost alone, with which I propose here to concern myself;—using Pater, I fear, rather as an example of a general tendency than attempting anything in the nature of a rounded estimate of his work and total influence. I do this, I may say, with more than a little reluctance, yet do it nevertheless because I have come to feel that no other writer of recent years quite so well exemplifies the principle of thought and action of which I wish to treat.

The words are famous in which Pater defined the good or, as he put it, successful life. "To burn always with this hard gemlike flame, to maintain this ecstasy, is success in life";—and the flame and ecstasy are just the eagerness with which one welcomes experience of the outside world for its own sake. These words from the "Conclusion" in *The Renaissance,* with their context, give one the essence of Pater's viewpoint, maintained consistently from the beginning to the end of his career; and through pondering them alone one might come to understand well enough what was his conception of life. But in *Marius the Epicurean* he wrote out at once a fuller and a more considered statement of the same conception, and by scrutiny of the "sensations and ideas" of the young Marius one may best understand this fundamental aspect of his creator's thought and work.

Pater emphasises in this romance, as it has been called, the resemblances, more than superficial, between the age of Marcus Aurelius and the end of the nineteenth century. "That age and our own," he says, "have much in common—many difficulties and hopes"—and he warns his reader that at moments he may appear to have his own time in mind rather than that of Marius. The fact is important for any complete understanding of the book—a picture of a youth brought up carefully in his ancestral religion who, upon coming into contact with the great world, feels compelled to forsake his old religion for a form of hedonism, a materialistic sensationalism which further contact with the world illogically modifies, but in no way destroys. Pater has elsewhere noted some part of those conditions in the nineteenth century which suggested the bare framework of his 'romance.' "For one born in eighteen hundred and three," he says in his essay on Mérimée, "much was recently become incredible that had at least warmed the imagination even of the sceptical eighteenth century. . . . A great outlook had lately been cut off. After Kant's criticism of the mind, its pretensions to pass beyond the limits of individual experience seemed as dead as those of old French royalty. And Kant did but furnish its innermost theoretic force to a more general criticism, which had withdrawn from every department of action, underlying principles once thought eternal. A time of disillusion followed." Energetic souls, however, he goes on to say, attempted to recover themselves in a changed world;—"Art: the passions, above all, the ecstasy and sorrow of love: a purely empirical knowledge of nature and man: these still remained, at least for pastime, in a world of which it was no longer proposed to calculate the remoter issues."

These generalisations reflect their light upon the young Marius's questionings and search for the true way of life. We are given to understand that this youth, with all his capacity for feeling and the store that he set on sentiment, possessed also an independent intelligence. Early set free of the associations and restrictions of his country home, he found himself in the very different atmosphere of a school of rhetoric in Pisa. The town itself, in its insistent new sights and varied gayness, all in vivid contrast with the quiet monotone of his earlier years, seemed forcibly to thrust in upon him new ideals of brilliant colour, "absolutely real, with nothing less than the reality of seeing and hearing," while the old ideals of country piety grew "how vague, shadowy, problematical!" Marius soon began to suspect, "though it was a suspicion he was careful at first to put from him," that his cherished ancestral religion "might come to count with him as but one form of poetic beauty, or of the ideal, in things; as but one voice, in a world where there were many voices it would be a moral weakness not to listen to." The religious claim was still strong, but was beginning to yield to another, "proposing to him unlimited self-expansion in a world of various sunshine." The tendency was strengthened by the companionship of a school-fellow with personality of compelling charm and strength, Flavian, who never hesitated in the pursuit of "various sunshine." And Flavian gave Marius the benefit not only of his own vivid example, but also "the writings of a sprightly wit, then very busy with the pen, one Lucian." Naturally the time was not long until Marius had to come to some settlement with himself, in an attempt to determine what for him were the respective claims of his new life and his old religion. In this moment of parting ways he "instinctively recognised" that "in vigorous intelligence, after all, divinity was most likely to be found a resident." He could maintain his integrity, find his own way of life, only through "the honest action of his own untroubled, unassisted intelligence" in all fields; and this conclusion was made attractive to him by "the feeling . . . of a poetic beauty in mere clearness of thought, the actually æsthetic charm of a cold austerity of mind."

Applying, then, his unaided reason to the search for truth, or fancying that he did, Marius found it quickly enough; and found it, as had been foreordained, in the words of Aristippus of Cyrene, that pupil of Socrates who brought the sceptical inquiries of his master to a nihilistic conclusion and contrived to build upon the latter a philosophy of pleasure. Aristippus had rigidly confined his speculations about the world and life, had indeed attempted not to speculate at all about anything, but merely to interpret human life in terms of immediately known certainties. He was one of those who wished to teach men how to live, believing that all else which philosophers concerned themselves with was a species of nonsense. Moreover, for this purpose he took life, practically speaking, at its worst; he looked only outside of and around himself, and he concluded that since things and people are but doubtful shadows, never continuing a moment in one stay, knowledge about them—the truth—is impossible, knowledge being something fixed and permanent, and the search for it a mere vanity or delusion. But instead of allowing this conclusion to depress him he turned it into a "stimulus towards every kind of activity and prompted a perpetual, inextinguishable thirst after experience." It was, Pater thought, Aristippus's rich and genial nature which thus transformed his initial material—giving "the spectacle of one of the happiest temperaments coming, so to speak, to an understanding with the most depressing of theories: accepting the results of a metaphysical system which seemed to concentrate into itself all the weakening trains of thought in earlier Greek speculation, and making the best of it, turning its hard, bare truths, with wonderful tact, into precepts of grace, and delicate wisdom, and a delicate sense of honour. Given," Pater continues, "the hardest terms, supposing our days are indeed but a shadow, even so, we may well adorn and beautify, in scrupulous self-respect, our souls, and whatever our souls touch upon—

these wonderful bodies, these material dwelling-places through which the shadows pass together for a while, the very raiment we wear, our very pastimes and the intercourse of society."

Aristippus's "hard, bare truth" was of course what nowadays would be termed the 'subjectivity of knowledge.' He considered that one could never learn the truth about things because things would never remain still long enough for one to examine them. While one looked they changed from instant to instant under one's eyes, and nothing under the sun was for two seconds the same thing. But there is no need of going on; everybody knows these famous old arguments against the possibility of any knowledge of reality, or the 'thing-in-itself.' They have been wonderfully revivified and enlarged in modern times, though in essentials they have scarcely changed. The problem raised for one—alike for an Aristippus or a child of the present century—who fancies he has thus dissolved away all possibility of knowledge, is whether any kind of basis for certitude in the conduct of life can still be found. Knowledge being impossible, are we not set down in an all-pervasive fog where one man's guess, about any question, is as good as another's?—where all standards disappear and at the most one can say with Pater that "nothing is intrinsically great or small, good or evil"? So, of course, Pater's Marius concluded, yet thought he discerned an escape from universal blankness in the reflection that what any individual directly feels is his own, that, whatever it be worth, such feeling requires, at least, no proof. It is just 'there.' And this reflexion thus became the corner-stone for a theory which makes life consist wholly of 'direct sensation,' as being the one immediate and unquestionable certainty of existence.

Thus the "grace and delicate wisdom" of Aristippus and of Marius lay in the "apprehension that the little point of this present moment alone really is, between a past which has just ceased to be and a future which may never come"; and Marius appropriately resolved "to exclude regret and desire, and yield himself to the improvement of the present with an absolutely disengaged mind." "With a sense of economy, with a jealous estimate of gain and loss," he would "use life, not as the means to some problematic end, but, as far as might be, from dying hour to dying hour, an end in itself—a kind of music, all-sufficing to the duly trained ear, even as it died on the air." He would aim at every possible kind of experience. He would attempt to set all his faculties free, by "clearing the tablet of his mind" from all doctrines or theories which might set up any interference with this aim. And so would he impartially "burn with a hard, gemlike flame."

Marius was, then—as Pater more than once explicitly says—a materialist, and conceived life as exclusively an affair of the five senses, "which certainly never deceive us about themselves, about which alone we can never deceive ourselves." All things pleasurable became grist for Marius's inexhaustible mill. But Pater was of course not satisfied to stop here; taking beauty to express for himself the Epicurean or, as it was called in his century, utilitarian concept of pleasure, he attempted to answer the question, What is beautiful, or pleasant? On these principles, as is well known, one can differentiate between pleasures only in terms of quantity, not of kind or quality, and Pater did not, like John Stuart Mill, at this point give his position away. "Our one chance," he says in the "Conclusion" of *The Renaissance*, "lies in expanding that interval [of life], in getting as many pulsations as possible into the given time. Great passions may give us this quickened sense of life, ecstasy and sorrow of love, the various forms of enthusiastic activity, disinterested or otherwise, which come naturally to many of us. Only be sure it is passion—that it does yield you this fruit of a quickened, multiplied consciousness. Of such wisdom, the poetic passion, the desire of beauty, the love of art for its own sake, has most. For art comes to you proposing frankly to give nothing but the highest quality to your moments as they pass, and simply for those moments' sake."

It was well enough, as an assertion or as kindly meant advice, thus to represent the sensations derivable from the arts as making up the quantitatively pleasantest or most perfect life; but by the very terms of this creed, wherein "nothing is intrinsically great or small, good or evil," the restriction could not hold good save for Pater himself. Each individual—"ringed round by that thick wall of personality through which no real voice has ever pierced on its way to him, able only to conjecture that which may be without"—each so isolated person must prove for himself by the path of impartial experiment what sensations yield him the greatest amount of pleasure;—and we have only to look round us to see how diverse, putting it moderately, are the felt pleasures of humanity. To this fact Pater was not at all blind—he at times insisted upon it—yet he seems never quite to have taken in its consequences for his theoretic position. When later, however, he wrote *Marius the Epicurean* he had come at any rate to see that the creed of sensation perforce dissolved into nothingness both morals and religion. This he was very far from wishing. The fair orderliness, both personal and social, of which a traditional morality is the groundwork, and the observances and associations of an old religion, both meant much to Pater in his personal experience. Hence he was constrained to include them, somehow—make some place for them that would at least seem real—within the materialist's world of sensation.

In the matter of morality, Marius was led by contemplation of "the ethical charm of Cornelius," his Christian friend who in another direction had served to reinforce his materialism, to question the exclusion of moral sanctions from the creed of sensation. "The noble and resolute air, the gallantry, so to call it, which composed the outward mien and presentment of his strange friend's inflexible ethics," called into Marius's mind a suspicion of the graceless contradiction between his own 'standards' and those of traditional morality, which might make him in other men's eyes an outlaw; that is, the contradiction might rudely take from him some social pleasure, and might also defeat, socially, the impression his creed *ought* to make! Consequently, if his creed were not to figure for others as different from what it seemed to himself, he had to discover some way of forcing duty and righteousness into the Cyrenaic scheme of things. The 'way,' Marius found, lay in "the purely æsthetic beauty of the old morality." He came to see it "as an element in things, fascinating to the imagination, to good taste in its most highly developed form, through association—a system or order, as a matter of fact, in possession, not only of the larger world, but of the rare minority of *élite* intelligences; from which, therefore, least of all would the sort of Epicurean he had in view endure to become, so to speak, an outlaw." In other words, Marius would conform to the morality of his day on the ground that it would be in bad taste not to; and he would so be more comfortable in plucking Epicurean roses within the limitations of other men's standards of approval.

It is much the same with religion. Christianity gained Marius's pleased approbation—no other words quite so express it—but not his inner assent. When he was first taken to the "curious house" of Cecilia, not yet knowing that she and those about her were Christians, he was enchanted by the sound of singing, coming from he knew not where; and he felt that "it was the expression not altogether of mirth, yet of some wonderful sort of happiness—the blithe self-expansion of a joyful soul in people upon whom some all-subduing experience had wrought heroically, and who still remembered, on this bland afternoon, the hour of a great deliverance." Clinging to all that he saw there, was a quiet, astringent beauty, and in this retired, wonderfully confident new way of life Marius found a grand appeal, exactly in its atmosphere of deliverance. For "in truth, one of his most characteristic and constant traits had ever been a certain longing for escape—for some sudden, relieving interchange, across the very spaces of life, it might be, along which he had lingered most pleasantly—for a lifting, from time to time, of the actual horizon. It was," Pater goes on to explain too well, "like the necessity under which the painter finds himself, to set a window or open doorway in the background of his picture; or like a sick man's longing for northern coolness, and the whispering willow-trees, amid the breathless evergreen forests of the south." Marius was soothed by the mere sympathetic contemplation of the strange way in which other folk could be moved by this religion, as remarkable for the strength which it inspired as for the beauty with which it was clothed. He felt that the sight of it might serve for him, not quite as the cure, but probably as "the solace or anodyne of his great sorrows—of that constitutional sorrowfulness, not peculiar to him perhaps, but which had made his life certainly like one long 'disease of the spirit.' "

There is inconsistency in this insistence, for a special purpose, upon Marius's great sorrowfulness; and indeed any careful reader may perceive for himself several loose ends—contradictions not merely phraseological—in this so carefully written book, which indicate that Pater's hold upon the task he had set himself was partial and inconstant. Yet one cannot say that he was inconsistent in his treatment of morality and religion. He could not admit as valid any of the real claims of either—and he can be under no suspicion of having done so! Mrs. Humphry Ward in her *Recollections* says that while Pater, having before 1870 relinquished all belief in the Christian religion, never returned to it in the 'intellectual sense,' still, "his heart returned to it," and "he became once more endlessly interested in it, and haunted by the 'something' in it, which he thought inexplicable." Exactly so; and herein lies the difference which Mrs. Ward speaks of between the "Conclusion" in *The Renaissance* and *Marius the Epicurean;* but it should be completely evident that Pater's theoretic position remains in the later book in all respects unchanged by the perceptible—but for this purpose ineffective—beatings of his new heart. Though his mind did not remain entirely cold to his heart's call, it did remain unconvinced; and at the best Pater has shown that the 'right kind of person,' the fastidious man of "a hieratic refinement," will so feel the purely æsthetic appeal of morality and religion as not to ignore the one nor to trample down the other.[1] With the fact that both would swiftly perish from the earth under such patronage Pater does not attempt to deal. One was to become the 'right kind of person' and a patron of traditional morality and religion through the kindly offices of a purely secular culture, and yet this secular culture had come precisely to take the place of tradi-

[1] It is but fair to remind the reader that Edward Dowden in his sympathetic summary of Pater's thought has said it is 'an erroneous criticism which represents Marius as only extending a refined hedonism so as to include within it new pleasures of the moral sense or the religious temper.' The reader must judge for himself whether or not this assertion is substantiated by the explanation which follows it (*Essays Modern and Elizabethan*, pp. 17-19).

tional morality and religion. Such inconsequence may not have troubled Pater, but it must, surely, give pause to ordinary folk who try to look before and after.

The grounds of Pater's position are not very far to seek. Of course they lay, first of all, in his own temperament. This is the case, as Pater himself has rightly insisted, with each one of us; and Pater's deeply grained yet economical sensuousness, his "lust of the eye," would in any age have sealed him of the children of this world who contentedly follow the counsels of Horace, moderated and refined as those were from Horace's Epicurean teachers. Pater's affinity, too, with Ruskin, and with Morris and Rossetti, is obvious and has been much talked of. All of these men and some others of their time had in common, though with varying degrees of consciousness, a profound desire to save from impending destruction, in the swirl of nineteenth-century industrialism, the artistic and spiritual values of life. Their salutary effort was to bring men back to a sense of the inner enrichment, the pleasure and the real yet intangible good, which comes from the fair adornment of life itself and of all the instruments of life. The question why their attempts met with comparative failure is as interesting as it is complex; but it cannot be considered here save as Pater's part in it may shed light upon the whole movement.

What must be noticed is that Pater essayed to go further than the rest in linking his position with the intellectual currents of his day. It can in a sentence be written down that Pater's life-long attempt was, in substance, to save and find some valid sanction for the rewards and fruits of culture on the terms imposed by scientific naturalism. His effort was, accepting to the full the conclusions of the natural science of his time, still to provide a sure basis for the personal life of the individual particularly in its highest aspects. He betrays no sense of the difficulty of such a task, and probably felt none—for here his sensuous and fundamentally uncritical temperament made the path he inevitably chose seem also the naturally 'right' and perfect one. To many, of course, it may seem a strange, perhaps outlandish, thing thus to link Pater's name with that of Auguste Comte and with Herbert Spencer's also. Yet the relationship is clear and needs not for proof the evidence of Mr. Humphry Ward concerning the 'Comtean' quality of Pater's college lectures;[2] and the more one ponders it the more does it seem the key to any right understanding of what Pater stood for and tried to do.

How deeply impressed Pater was with the negative or restrictive aspect of Kant's criticism of the mind is made clear in a passage already quoted from his essay on Mérimée. He was but one out of very many in his century who believed, as result not only of this but of almost innumerable other opinions, 'demonstrations,' 'proofs,' that the purely empirical method which was supposed to be the one followed by natural scientists was the unique path to such tentative knowledge as mortal man may hope to attain. The great gain—or loss!—of this acclaimed method was that it seemed to clear away so much rubbish on which men had foolishly

[2] Quoted by Mr. A. C. Benson in his *Life* of Pater, p. 20.

based their lives for centuries. Not merely was historic Christianity or any other religion of moving power swept away, but much else, along with the greater part of the human mind, as most thinking persons now know. In actual practice the interplay of assumption and evidence made the new dispensation, in the hands of most men, different in its pretensions rather more than in its reality from the older, now abandoned methods of inquiry. In actual practice the new gospel of Evolution or of Natural Uniformity was scarcely less dogmatic than less inhuman gospels of our naïve forefathers had been. But all men except a few village curates seemed in that day too busy, and too enchanted, with the mere surface of their novel wisdom to perceive its underlying ambiguities and assumptions. All forward-looking spirits were ready to believe anything these benefactors of the race might say, whether in explanation of the 'new truth' or in praise of themselves, as when Renan in his *Life of Jesus* wrote: "By our extreme scruple in employing means of conviction, by our absolute sincerity and our disinterested love of the pure idea, we have created (all of us who have devoted our lives to science) a new ideal of morality." This new thing along with the rest the wholly virtuous scientist would provide. Pater, fascinated, believed that already the world had been 'proved' to be a self-sufficient mechanism, where chance evidences of intelligence should be smiled at by the enlightened. "The 'positive' method . . . makes very little account," he says in his essay on Coleridge, "of marks of intelligence in nature: in its wider view of phenomena, it sees that those instances are a minority, and may rank as happy coincidences: it absorbs them in the larger conception of universal mechanical law." In any age, Pater says in the same essay, "the clearest minds abandon themselves to" the time-spirit—to the newest notions, apparently, that they may find at hand; and to him the vision of "universal mechanical law" seemed "like the harmony of musical notes, wrought out in and through the series of their mutations." A beautiful conception, no doubt; yet to a reflective man the beauty might seem hardly skin-deep, for the conception means also that we are parts of an entirely predetermined world, deluded if we think ourselves other than helpless mechanisms.

It is more than doubtful whether Pater ever saw this, or at any rate felt its meaning, because it was of course the 'mutations' themselves—not their orderly relationships—which enchanted him. This he everywhere emphasised. And settling himself—if I may be pardoned the contradiction—in the ceaseless ebb and flow of inconstant appearances, with all else cleared away by the sciences, he preached in the creed of sensation, with his own addition of an æsthetic twist, the only 'way of life' possible on such premises. "Here at least," he says, "is a vision, a theory, $\theta\epsilon\omega\rho\acute{\iota}\alpha$, which reposes on no basis of unverified hypothesis, which makes no call upon a future after all somewhat problematic; as it would be unaffected by any discovery of an Empedocles (improving on the old story of Prometheus) as to what has really been the origin, and course of development, of man's actually attained faculties and that seemingly divine particle of reason or spirit in him." This 'vision,' too, reinforces "the deep original materialism or earthliness of human nature itself, bound so intimately to the sensuous world."

And Pater's 'vision,' elaborated with such grace and refinement of phrase as has rarely been achieved in English, thrives amongst a great and apparently increasing number of people to-day. The æsthetic turn which he strove to give it has disappeared. But I have endeavoured to point out how fragile, in theory no less than in fact, was the link which Pater took great pains to forge between the materialist creed of sensation and his own personal application of the creed. Setting up the higher life of the individual, moral, religious, poetic, as of the greatest æsthetic charm was a superior sort of ornamentation but could not be made an integral part of the Epicurean way of life; for any classification of pleasures could hold good only for the person who himself made it. Consequently, while, amongst the many, pleasures are reckoned differently as to worth, sensationalism itself—the essence of Pater's 'vision'—flourishes as the only credible gospel of the modern age.

The reasons are fairly simple. It is probable that most people who accept the scientific hypothesis of a mechanical world as a verified explanation of its real nature never reflect that on such terms their 'choosing' any 'way of life' whatever is equally a delusion. Even those, however, who are conscious of the meaning of this hypothesis have on their hands, so to say, a belief so at variance with their natures that in practice they *act* from day to day as if they were not mere predetermined mechanisms, but purposive individuals upon

PROGRESS AND SCIENCE

the character of whose deeds hung real issues. Yet almost none regards the notion of a mechanical world as simply an hypothesis useful in some sciences, useless in others, unproved in all, and, if accepted uncritically and without reservation, disastrously contradictory of immediately known facts of human nature. Some there are, it is true, who argue plausibly and carefully against the unreserved acceptance of this hateful hypothesis, but very little weight seems, with the many, to attach to their effort. Even, however, if numerous people were convinced by the arguments of some contemporary philosophers, they would be convinced only of the possibility of a mild theism—and people do not act on such possibilities. They act alone on what they take to be certainties. And they believe readily in their half-perceptions of scientific 'truth' because of the seemingly irrefragable proof offered by the practical triumphs of the exact sciences. The modern uses of steam and electricity, the phonograph, the automobile, the aëroplane —these countless new things which are revolutionising the earth—seem overwhelming evidence that the assumptions of the exact sciences are at long last rock-bottom truth. These assumptions, moreover, in the eyes of most, exclude everything for which men in other ages have lived except immediate sensations grasped from dying moment to dying moment—except these and the pursuit, on the part of a smaller number, of power in the shape of great wealth. And while to some these exclusions make life an empty mockery, to many others they come as a grateful release. With comprehensible joy the 'natural man' welcomes pronouncements which make his inclinations respectable—a creed which both positively and negatively makes over the world in his own image, "reinforcing the deep original materialism or earthliness of human nature itself, bound so intimately to the sensuous world." This is the creed to which, probably, the vulgar man in any age most easily takes. And in an age secular and equalitarian, where the tyranny of the masses is keenly felt, the cheering message of 'do-as-you-please-and-don't-care-a-damn' is bound to appear. The crowd would like nothing better, and at the same moment the high priests of the age, its men of science, providentially seem to give the message official sanction and the weight of their authority.

Other gospels are much talked of. Recently we have had altogether remarkable examples of the way in which patriotism may fire whole nations; but the emptiness of patriotism as a permanent way of life and its efficacy for only a brief period of great emergency were at the same time proved with equal clearness. And no one can seriously doubt that, however much fine talk we hear of hopeful substitutes for an out-of-date morality and an out-of-date religion, the hopeful substitute actually in use amongst a very great number of us is the materialist creed of sensation. Proof lies everywhere around us. It is to be found in every aspect of the daily life of the nations. It is vividly reflected in our newspapers, our periodicals, our novels, our amusements. From great wealth of material a single illustration may be cited, but one the more striking in that the author of *Saint's Progress*, Mr. John Galsworthy, is generally supposed to represent, as far as family and nurture and fastidious high-mindedness go, the best our age can do. Readers of this gentleman's books pride themselves upon having 'the best.' They feel, too, that their author improves as well as amuses them, since he is widely known as a moralist. Well, there is nothing to complain of in the plot of this recent novel. What there is in it to the present purpose lies entirely in Mr. Galsworthy's presentation of the heroine, Noel Pierson, and the clergyman, her father. The poor clergyman is pictured as stupidly not believing in life, while his daughter engagingly does. There is no need of summarising the story to make the point clear; I shall simply quote the meditations of Noel upon receiving a letter from her 'saintly' father—a letter in which he expresses the wish that she should not marry a man, James Fort, who has, or has just had, a cousin of Noel's (Leila) for mistress: "He wanted *her* to pass the time—not to live, not to enjoy! To pass the time. What else had he been doing himself, all these years, ever since she could remember, ever since her mother died, but just passing the time? Passing the time because he did not believe in this life; not living at all, just preparing for the life he did believe in. Denying everything that was exciting and nice, so that when he died he might pass pure and saintly to his other world. He could not believe Captain Fort a good man, because he had not passed the time, and resisted Leila; and Leila was gone! And now it was a sin for him to love some one else; he must pass the time again. 'Daddy doesn't believe in life,' she thought . . . 'Daddy's a saint; but I don't want to be a saint, and pass the time. He doesn't mind making people unhappy, because the more they're repressed, the saintlier they'll be.' "

And there you obviously are! The words themselves say just how real is the higher life, as it was once called, either to Noel or, as one cannot help suspecting, to her creator, Mr. Galsworthy. To live the higher life—as Mr. Galsworthy seems plainly to show in his portraiture of the Reverend Edward Pierson—is simply not to live at all, is just to "pass the time." This writer, if one may judge from *Saint's Progress,* does not realise that there can be other than a purely negative side to the life of a man of principles. To live means to enjoy—in this case to indulge one's sexual appetite irresponsibly, which is manfully taking the bull by the horns. For, of course, on such terms there can be no other Epicurean roses that are not worth plucking.

Indeed, where the materialist creed of sensation leads is not doubtful, nor is its ending-place a new discovery. Long ago Plutarch remarked that a man had better be a pig than an Epicurean; that, in other words, a healthy pig approaches the Cyrenaic ideal more closely than can a being endowed with human faculties. For man unfortunately, even with the firmest intentions, cannot escape some occasional thoughts of past and future, of death and its pain and mystery, of 'real good and real evil,' and the like. This, as no one can deny, is still true; yet I do not mean by implication to commend asceticism. For better as well as for worse we are in and of this present world, here and now, and we are not ourselves unless we make the most of it. But I do mean that there is more in human nature than the sensationalist or his bosom-friend, the populariser of the exact sciences, perceives, and that the stream of man's experience turns sooner or later to ashes in his mouth unless he directs his life of sensation to some end beyond itself. And I do mean that there is in human nature the capacity to judge of ends. The Dauphin of France says, after the battle near Angiers in *King John:*

> There's nothing in this world can make me joy:
> Life is as tedious as a twice-told tale
> Vexing the dull ear of a drowsy man;
> And bitter shame hath spoil'd the sweet world's taste,
> That it yields nought but shame and bitterness.

So it ever was and ever must be with the man who abandons himself to the stream of outward experience, even though for a space all may seem to go marvellously well with him. This gospel, indeed, is a gospel of the despair of life, no matter how cunningly a Pater or an Aristippus of rich and genial temperament may disguise the fact. And thoughtful materialists do not rest their case on its "exciting and nice" aspects, but on its supposed ineluctable truth no matter how tragically inhuman it be. No man of sense, moreover, can deny the substantial truth of the descriptive formulæ of the exact sciences in their own sphere. And none should wish to. But the personal world of the individual— precisely that world in which the sensationalist does take refuge after a fashion—is a different sphere which exact science does not and cannot know. The inner world of his own being is an immediate reality which no living man can doubt in his activity from day to day; yet science can subsist only by framing hypotheses which disregard or deny this world. The significance of the fact is plain, and cannot long remain obscured as now it seems to be. Its meaning can be none other than that man, as far as he is conscious of himself, is different, not in degree merely, but in kind, from all phenomena of the natural world. This striking, central fact of human nature is of momentous import, and it is a fact certain and incontrovertible. The sensationalist is at one with wiser men when he tells us that only in proportion as man makes the utmost of the material of his own inner world does he really live, is he fully a man. But there is more within us than sensations. We give as much to our perceptions as we take from them; and we live lives perilously at variance with our real selves if we do not follow this primary truth to the discovery, as far as may be, of the meaning and substance and weight of our inner selves. Even the young Marius was aware of a "loyal conscience, . . . deciding, judging himself and every one else, with a wonderful sort of authority"; he had intuitions, too, of "a fierce opposition of real good and real evil around him." These things were without meaning and absurd according to his own philosophy, yet Pater was betrayed into speaking of them just because they are our unique heritage as human beings and are immediately known by all of us, the more clearly as we let them speak. Nor only this; for in that 'other world' of the individual's inner self lies—in the 'particle of spirit' in him not 'seemingly' but truly divine—his only secure direction through life's perplexed paths;—the only certain guide even for the proudest of men, to save them from ultimate emptiness and disillusion in the wreck of earthly hopes.

Walter Pater at any rate did feel the unique quality of the individual. And if he felt this rather than saw its meaning, it still entered to good purpose into the character of all his work. It saved him from any attempt to elaborate a rigid philosophical system; it kept his presentment of his thinking ever literary or concrete in form, rather than abstract. And I cannot end without saying any word about this and other great excellences which colour all his writing. I have been concerned only to examine afresh Pater's interpretation of life; about this I have felt bound to speak plainly. Yet incidentally his books are full of the rare charm and rightness of an altogether distinguished mind. Such excellences can hardly palliate or excuse Pater's central weakness; but the humanity of the man, the unobtrusiveness of his scholarship, his scrupulous, never-failing good taste with its perfection of manner, his gift—amounting to genius—for the precise expression of his meaning, his lessons of comeliness and grace so needed by the age—these things and more tinge one's judgement with profound regret.

VI

CONCLUSION

DEATH arrives gracious only to such as sit in darkness, or lie heavy burdened with grief and irons; to the poor Christian, that sits bound in the galley; to despairful widows, pensive prisoners, and deposed kings; to them whose fortune runs back, and whose spirit mutinies—unto such death is a redeemer, and the grave a place for retiredness and rest." So wrote someone, possibly Francis Bacon, in the early years of the seventeenth century. Many at that time would have agreed with the writer, though many too would have disagreed. The time, even though so late, was still one of transition from the mediæval to the characteristically modern point of view. That change in viewpoint may be phrased in many ways, all true and illuminating, yet few approaches to perception of its import are more interesting than this one of the prevalent attitude towards death. In the modern age Carlyle, far from typical in some respects, nevertheless says, "Frightful to all men is Death"; and as we all, or nearly all, figure death as something wholly evil in nature, so do we concentre our attention upon the good things of this present life. The belief in personal immortality is not entirely dead, but it is—or has been until very recently—moribund, and is openly scoffed at by those who profess to be and are believed to be the most enlightened and representative of modern men. Its decay has given room for growing confidence in the goodness of earthly life in its own right, and for humanitarianism or meliorism which would bid us believe the time near when life will be quite perfectly happy for all men alike. The distinctively modern idea, most would agree, is that we may fashion our lives to what ends we will, and the institutions also through which we give partial expression to them; so that we may succeed as far as we please in the way, as we say, of complete self-realisation.

It has not, however, always been so. The writer whom I quoted in the beginning also remarks, "I have often thought upon death, and find it the least of all evils." And to like effect, later in the seventeenth century, Sir Thomas Browne could say, "Certainly there is no happiness within this circle of flesh, nor is it in the optics of these eyes to behold felicity"; and he adds, "I have so abject a conceit of this common way of existence, this retaining to the Sun and Elements, I cannot think this is to be a man, or to live according to the dignity of humanity; in expectation of a better I can with patience embrace this life, yet in my best meditations do often defy death; I honour any man that contemns it." This, it should be remembered, was written almost in our own day; the *Religio Medici* was

CONCLUSION

published within three years of the founding of that 'college' which a little later, in 1660, became the Royal Society. And in fact anyone who at all knows the mediæval age knows how profoundly different was then the general attitude towards death. Life then was regarded as but the inevitably miserable preparatory stage in the soul's vast journey to eternal happiness or woe. Effort then was directed, with an intensity hard now to realise, upon the achievement of good things which are not of this life, which indeed bespeak deliberate contempt for this life and all its necessities. This is such a change as can hardly be exaggerated; it cuts boldly across the whole texture of life and leaves not one of its values unaltered. It is but too easy nowadays to point the finger of derision at that benighted time, at holy monk and uncouth hermit, at pious ladies and martyred saints. Yet even hermits and saints should have their due from us, and, if they were not wholly right, we may begin to see that they cannot either have been wholly wrong.

In saying this I do not have reference simply to the fact that there are evils worse than death. Few even in our day would attempt to deny this, though such evils are from us generally more remote—barring periods of bitter warfare—than they have been, frequently, in other ages. Nor do I refer simply to the fact that whatever else modern science can do, it cannot, after all, greatly prolong life nor banish death; at the most we can attempt first to have our fling; we may shut our ears to words of gloomy warning and attempt so fully to enjoy ourselves as to forget, for a space, death's approach;—yet whatever we do we cannot banish that intruding figure, which will soon enough make an end of full meals and gay dances and joy-riding and all the variegated pride of life. Nor, even, do I have reference to the fact—for a fact it is—that personal immortality has always been precisely what it is now, a real possibility in which we may believe or disbelieve at our own peril. No one has ever proved the existence of personal immortality, and it is safe to suppose that no one, at any rate using canons of proof now recognised, ever will; but on the other hand the man of science, whatever certainty he naturally *feels* of its non-existence, is equally unable to prove that. In fact, this whole question is, like many other things the number of which nowadays we tend to forget, beyond the pale of final proof or disproof; it remains a matter of personal faith. Here too there are, of course, blind faiths which properly lead to the fools' paradise, but this may not be one of them. If in other ages people have tended to be too credulous, too easy of belief in immortality, we in our time may be too incredulous. In a day when quantitative measurements reign supreme, and when it is thought that truth lies in the reduction of all things to their physical bases or conditions, it may well be that we have blinded ourselves simply to the difficulties of not believing in personal immortality.

However, in suggesting that hermit and saint cannot have been wholly wrong in their attitude towards life and death I had not primarily in mind the possibilities of eternal reward or punishment, nor do I propose here to argue that momentous question. Neither had I pri-

CONCLUSION

marily in mind other aspects of the attitude towards death which appear to have been largely neglected in the modern point of view. I wished rather to direct attention to the positive foundations which support the prevalent modern view that earthly life is a good thing in virtue of its opportunities for self-satisfaction or self-realisation. This view labours under the initial difficulty that it converts an unescapable necessity into an immitigable evil. But positively it rests upon the belief in progress, the truth of which is supposed to be guaranteed by the exact sciences. The preceding essays in this book of course do not explore this foundation either completely or systematically. Such a task has been for several reasons impossible; yet it appears to be a fair assumption that further exploration would reveal essentially the same arguments and inferences which have here been set forth. And if this be so, progress is at the best an ambiguous term, and the popular idea of it very far from a proved reality; the latter is indeed what I have elsewhere called it, and what Professor J. B. Bury in his recent book, *The Idea of Progress,* also terms it —a sheer dogma.

Not only is the modern idea of progress unproved; it is becoming plain that the real foundation for its popular acceptance, if not also for the supposedly scientific support of it, was simply the era of great material expansion through applied science which roughly coincided with the nineteenth century. Science some years ago became doubtful in its support, and more recently scientists have in increasing numbers come out in flat denial of the notion of an universal progress which is in the nature of things. Nor is this all. Practical experience during the last hundred and fifty years, culminating in the War and its settlement, has shown the extraordinary difficulties and extreme limitations of any sort of progress worth the name, and has shown too its dependence upon sources of wealth which are rapidly being exhausted. Moreover, through all programmes of social progress there runs a fundamental contradiction which cannot be exorcised. Briefly it is this: the writers on social progress bring it out, either explicitly or implicitly, that the Earthly Paradise of their dreams ultimately depends upon the diffused spirit of what they call social service. As Mr. Walter N. Polakov puts it in a review of Herr Rathenau's *New Society* in the *New Republic*, we must "unite the productive and creative forces—workers by hand and by brain—upon a constructive programme animated with the human spirit to *give* and *serve* instead of the animal craving to *take* and *hold*." This of course sounds well, but when one attempts to get beneath such a generality one encounters difficulties. It means an equalitarian order in which, as Herr Walter Rathenau himself candidly says, "there will be *only* poor, only very poor people." But what will induce these poor people, one wonders, to expend themselves freely and whole-heartedly in the service of others? One thing, which is ambiguously termed the improvement of the common lot. In plainer words, the poor will embark upon the unselfish service of society in the expectation that others will similarly serve them. All will work for each other and no one for himself in order that all may be materially a little better

CONCLUSION

off. This is the contradiction which the social reformer cannot escape; he has to work for the material betterment of the majority, yet he finds that he cannot even plausibly hope for it, much less assure it, unless somehow he can bring the majority to what may be called a spiritual view of life—one which transcends the aim of material betterment. To ask me to live a life of self-sacrifice may be a comprehensible thing, and the life itself may be noble; but it all depends upon the reason, the sanction which is to incite me to such heroism. And for social progress I find that I am asked to sacrifice my comfort and freedom, and all effort for comfort and freedom, in order that others may provide me with comfort and freedom. I am asked to sacrifice myself for an end which can be conceived only in terms of material self-satisfaction.

This is indeed a vision of a wholly impossible order of things. Anyone who has ever learned by experience the conditions of sociability will be aided in seeing the reason; for a group of people who come together just for the sake of being sociable invariably make a complete failure of their effort. Sociability, they sooner or later perceive, is only a by-product, it cannot be aimed at directly. It comes into being, if at all, unconsciously when people are drawn together through some common interest or background, whether that be an interest in stamp-collecting, or the love of dancing, or the love of philosophy. Very little reflexion in fact is needed to see how inevitably the demand that we should sacrifice ourselves for others always comes practically to mean that others should be sacrificing themselves for us—

and are not. The consequent indignation against those who are not giving us our due is familiar enough, and leads to organisation for the purpose of holding them up for it. This may be right enough in the given circumstances—but it should at least be seen for what it is, and it should be clearly realised that no Earthly Paradise, no perfect ordering of society, will ever result from the ambiguous cry for social service.

Another difficulty from which the idea of social progress suffers is that such progress is ostensibly for the sake of the individual—it has of course no meaning whatever unless this be so; yet the only progress actually conceivable is, beyond definite limits far short of perfection, at the expense of the individual. The beehive and the ant-hill remain the instructive and only examples of the perfectly ordered animal society. Yet such development would be the mockery of humanity. It would mean the submergence or denial of all our distinctively human traits;—the conversion of the conscious individual who is properly an end in himself into a mere instrument of a pervasive tyranny which, professing the common welfare, in reality would subserve nobody's welfare. It would subserve nobody's welfare because all alike would be mere instruments in the machinery of a society which would have become its own end. This puts the cart before the horse with a vengeance. There are no social relations—if the phrase is to have any meaning at all—which are not personal; and personal relations always are means to an end beyond themselves, an end which induces the individual to engage in them but which is his own end. This is

CONCLUSION

equally true whether the individual acts selfishly or altruistically; yet the neglect of this truth is productive of much confused thinking in which the necessary limitations of political action are lost sight of. For it follows plainly enough that the state is properly a means to the ends of the individuals who compose it; and when the state attempts to be something more it means that a piece of machinery which is in and for itself of no value or significance is attempting to thwart and impoverish our lives. Furthermore, the state can in any case control only the external acts of the individual, and only those properly in so far as they may be prejudicial to the welfare of others. Its influence is thus inevitably partial and negative. The efforts of social reformers to do their work through the state are consequently similar to such a confusion, for instance, between the thought or emotion of the sonnet and its technical form, as would lead one to attempt to change its nature through alteration of the latter.[1] Expression might thus be directed into a new channel, but obviously it would not be silenced nor would its nature be changed in any essential respect.

We are bound to conclude that there is at present no valid ground for belief that life will ever be easy and pleasant for the vast majority of mankind. What John Stuart Mill said years ago is still true—mechanical inventions have not lightened the day's toil of a single human being. There is no reason to suppose that they ever will. There is likewise no reason for supposing that either political action or education can bring about

[1] I owe this comparison to Professor F. J. Teggart, who uses it in his essay, *The Processes of History*.

gion express a part of human nature which we can only neglect or deny at the risk—in truth, more than that, with the certainty—of neglecting or denying ourselves. And hence it is that any interpretation of human nature must be grossly inadequate which does not candidly admit all spheres of human experience into its purview. If poetry and religion are full of error, and even are never free from the fresh possibility of error, as their critics delight to show, in this they are no way different from science itself. And that which they seek humanly and fallibly to express is real; it is of the essence of our being, and this needs no recondite or tortuous method of proof—for to discern it we have only to look within ourselves and impartially to appraise what we immediately know ourselves to be.

Moreover, although our knowledge of what, for convenience' sake, I have called the inner world is conditioned by our experience of the outer world of nature and society, still, it is not in the end wholly limited by such experience. Just as through science we have learned that there are aspects of the outer world which we cannot directly apprehend, because of the limitations of our senses, so, once it has been opened up to us, we at least learn that the same thing is true of the inner world. And while thus we march darkly, we yet are not doubtful of the issue. For enough is plain to make us realise that although in one sense our two worlds supplement each other, they are at many points deeply opposed; and their meeting-ground in human life is a battle-field. We know those, of course, who take life to be—shall I say?—an amusement park; it ap-

CONCLUSION

pears indeed as if they have always been the majority, and our age is not the only one in which they have been encouraged by popular philosophies. But humanity has ever given its respect, its admiration, even its worship, to men of different stamp—to men who have inflexibly said and in their actions have shown that life is fundamentally a struggle, and a struggle, moreover, which is never won, yet which is not always lost. And the field of this struggle is within the individual, whose fight is not against his fellows but against himself. This is the true vocation of man; this is the activity through which, and through which alone, his essential nature, distinguishing him unalterably from the beast, shines out and becomes living reality.

Here, then, is the sufficient reason why modern notions of progress, with their pseudo-scientific sanction, can be repudiated with no trace of pessimism. Those notions of progress, spite of their fine show of solicitude for the welfare of humanity, really fall beside the mark and lead our hopes astray from the true calling of man. Beginning in humanitarianism, those ideas lead inevitably to denial of the inherent value of the individual, giving him instead only an instrumental value. This is, in the present connexion, an ambiguous, if not indeed a meaningless, phrase; and its ambiguity is the greater because the individual is given an instrumental value merely as the means to an end which has no real existence in its own right. Modern notions of progress, in other words, have encouraged men to concentrate their attention upon material satisfactions and comforts, and at the same time have placed the goal of progress in the welfare of society considered as an end in itself. We have seen that society cannot be so considered without self-contradictions which involve the immolation of fundamental human values; and we have seen that the chase after material satisfactions is circular, having no goal and no possibility of fulfilment. Progress indeed there may be for the individual, but it has no real existence outside of him, and lies in his increase of self-knowledge, of self-mastery, of character.

Christians, at any rate, have always known that they could not serve both God and Mammon. They have yet always attempted to do it, and they have always failed. The fruit of their effort has always been the implicit denial of their better selves for the sake of immediately good things. But soon or late those same good things have turned to dust and ashes in their mouths. We are in and of this world of changing appearances; to it we owe the best that is in us as well as the worst, and we know that good things have their price as well as evil. This, whatever it mean, is the nature of things; only by full experience of earthly life can we come to know ourselves truly and fully—knowledge for which we often enough pay a bitter tribute, but which, so far as we do attain it, is worth its price. Hermit and saint of the mediæval age, as no one now needs to be told, were grievously wrong in their denial of bodily claims; were blind in their failure to realise that through our physical bodies alone we may climb within sight of the better world, our truer home. But if hermit and saint were not wholly right, neither were they wholly wrong. Discovery of ancient error should not lead us simply into

PROGRESS AND SCIENCE

changes in the essential conditions of life. In both spheres much remains undone which may be practicable, yet feasible improvements must at the best fall far short of what everyone would like. Such improvements, moreover, come slowly; their path is tortuous; and at any time the forces of sheer impatience, or perversity, or fanaticism may undo in a few moments the hard achievements of a century. Henry Adams in his striking way likened the mind of a sane man to "an acrobat, with a dwarf on his back, crossing a chasm on a slack-rope, and commonly breaking his neck." Unless we wilfully prefer the reckless over-confidence of ignorance we shall do well to remember that civilisation has ever been a not dissimilar achievement. Amidst even our severest discontents with the nature of things, our anger against fortune, our monotonous and racking toil, we shall do well to act reflectively and deliberately; we shall do well to respect what imperfect order, imperfect justice, imperfect liberty we actually have secured through bitter struggle; we shall do well to remember that in any case nothing which we can accomplish will change for us the essential conditions of life.

This is a view no more pessimistic than it is novel; it is merely, if such a word must be used, realistic. If, however, it should strike anyone as pessimistic, this beyond doubt will be due to the grossly inadequate interpretation of human nature which issues from the exact sciences and which, through their ascendancy, has imposed itself largely upon the popular mind. The scientific view of reality is, in appearance and in its first steps at any rate, easy to comprehend. The scien-

CONCLUSION

tist seems to view his world in the common-sense fashion of the average man, and accordingly, for this reason as well as for others which I have mentioned, science tends easily to fix men's attention and to engage their assent. The scientist claims that he alone is devoted to the cause of understanding the Real, and the proof of his claim rests in the practical uses to which scientific knowledge is put. It should be remembered, however, that science is concerned exclusively with what may be called the mechanism of events—how things work. Modern science tells us not why a stone falls to the ground, but how. What gravitation is no man knows, but science can tell us its varied effects, and can discern the operation of gravity in phenomena which to the unlearned appear to have no connexion with each other. Thus science, framing hypotheses and testing them by experiment, detects similarities beneath apparent differences and, grouping these similarities, formulates so-called laws of nature. A law of nature is simply a generalised statement, the result of a process of abstraction. Consequently when the scientist observes two apparently different processes of change his interest is to determine whether or not, by subtracting and discarding the differences, an underlying similarity can be found. So far as it can be found we have science; where it cannot, no science is possible. Hence differences, while they may be troublesome enough, are in the strict sense of the word negligible to science, and where they cover over a similarity they become insignificant. Thus it is that the scientist, beginning with a great show of devotion to the Real, ends by concerning himself exclusively with abstractions of one definitely limited kind. Abstractions of one definitely limited kind —because only those abstractions which are the fruit of quantitative measurement can yield themselves to the scientist's method of precise observation and experiment.

Abstractions, of course, are not unreal, but abstractions which can be quantitatively measured are not the only real or valid abstractions and, moreover, the Real as we know it at first hand is never abstract. It is, as we say, concrete; similarities are invariably mixed with differences, and the latter are no less real and full of meaning than the former. This should make it possible to grasp the inadequacy of the scientific interpretation of human nature. For the scientist views humanity from the outside only, just as he necessarily views the rest of the natural world; and he discards those differences which make real people individuals, noticing only the common substratum—those respects in which people are invariably alike—for only thus can the scientist say anything at all about humanity. That something can be said indicates, of course, that we are all imperfectly individualised; but it by no means indicates what the scientist assumes for his own convenience—that our imperfect individualities are of no significance. Similarly the scientist views humanity merely as a variety of organic growth, seizing upon and emphasising those aspects of the human being which can be correlated with the characteristics of other animate beings. These are to the scientist our significant characteristics, those which unite us to the animal kingdom. The result

CONCLUSION

is that through science we have learned much about ourselves which otherwise could never have been definitely known. Yet, while I do not wish to depreciate this knowledge, it remains true that all of it is from the distinctively human point of view insignificant. The necessities of science compel it to look for the essential nature of anything in its origins, but this contradicts the equally useful and valid principle that the essential nature of anything is to be found only in its full development. The distinguishing characteristics of man, in other words, are not those which link him to other animals, but precisely those which differentiate him from them.

The point is that science neglects and necessarily must neglect these distinguishing characteristics, and also neglects those which distinguish men from each other; yet it is just these characteristics which alone suffice for an adequate interpretation of human nature. The result is, as we have seen, that science tends to reduce itself to absurdity in an impossible denial of human nature, and that humanity, accepting the limitations of the scientific viewpoint, can do no other than develop a sensationalistic philosophy which is better suited to the apparent nature of animals than to that of men. The guess may be hazarded that many men have been blind to the intolerable nature of this difficulty simply because of the large promises which science has seemed to make in the direction of unending social progress and the ultimate mastery of all the external and material hardships of life. Science has given us innumerable profitable things to do, and there has been correspondingly little time for thought. However, as the illusory nature of modern ideas of progress becomes more plain, through the changed conclusions of science and through hard experience, it is to be expected that men will become more and more aware of the tragical impoverishment of life to which the prevalent scientific point of view has subjected them. And their consequent dissatisfaction will open the way to a candid recognition that there are other avenues of real and valid knowledge besides the one afforded by the exact sciences.

This is not the place to begin any detailed discussion of the implications of such a recognition, nor of the other avenues of knowledge. My object has been simply to suggest how deeply their general recognition is at present needed, and to indicate that it is, as I think, bound to come. It is at least necessary, however, to point out that spheres of human experience which do not yield themselves to quantitative measurement may be as truly avenues of real and valid knowledge as that field of experience which gives its subject-matter to the exact sciences. For some, at least, the way to realisation of this has come most simply through the facts of human self-consciousness and individuality. Both are imperfect, partial, fluctuant; both are in the nature of insecure achievements, and vary in their degree from one man to another—vary also in the same man from year to year. Yet both are not the less real for all this, and all people possess some quantum of both in virtue of their mere humanity. And both, there is every reason to believe, are not shared with us by any other animals.

CONCLUSION

They are not the only qualities which mark us definitely off from other animals, but they are amongst the most significant. The fact of self-consciousness enables us to have a kind of knowledge of ourselves which we can have of nothing external to us; a knowledge which needs to be criticised, sifted, guarded from delusion like all other knowledge so far as in us lies, yet which has the impress of an intimate and profound certainty. This certainty can be felt rather than expressed, but it is the one key to that self-knowledge whose achievement is wisdom. At the least it serves to make men barely aware of their imperfect individuality. By virtue of it every man comes to learn that he is not wholly merged in his surroundings, that there is that within him, most truly himself, which his fellows can never fully know, which is his sole and incommunicable possession and is most precious, because it gives his own life—whatever it be in the eyes of others—an inherent and unique value. None of us is perfectly individualised, many of us most imperfectly;—there is no more equality here than there is in our intellectual capacities, and this mystery is ultimate and insoluble. But at any rate we are all alike in that the best of us, hardly less than the worst, are imperfect creatures and conscious of our imperfection. In goodness, in nobility, in unselfishness, in understanding, we all fail, and we know that our failure is shameful.

This too is elementary self-knowledge, but its issues are profound. The consciousness of imperfection is at once an immediate inner certainty and a fact daily made objectively real to all men. It comes, we may say, from two worlds, with each of which men are in contact. The stimulus, the means whereby we are made aware of imperfection, comes from the outer world of sensible objects, the world of nature and of society; but contact with the outer world alone is not sufficient, it is only half the process. Such contact makes us aware of standards or criteria of order and value existing within us, through which indeed the external world alone becomes intelligible to us. Yet these criteria of order and value have nothing exactly correspondent to them in the outer world. That world always comes short, in one way or another, of their perfection. It is never up to the mark. This is true absolutely, but it is specially notable that it is true of all our actions. Everyone knows this at first hand, and forgets it—if he can really forget it at all—only for brief spaces, either from its very familiarity or through the anodyne of distractions. Some men, indeed, endeavour to persuade themselves, in obedience to a narrow theory or from worse motives, that the consciousness of imperfection is a species of illusion. It is to be doubted, however, whether such men even to their own minds have ever succeeded, or whether—had they seen all the implications of their effort—they could have wished to succeed; since upon this quality of human nature depends the possibility of scientific knowledge as well as of other knowledge issuing from other spheres of human experience.

And the only credible explanation of the consciousness of imperfection and of perfection coexisting in the mind of the individual is that we are, as I said, actually in contact with two different worlds which are to us equally real. The outer world is the stimulus whereby we become aware of the inner world, in terms of which again we interpret the outer world. We thus occupy, as it were, a mediate position between the two, partaking of the nature of both. We are finite, but conscious of our finitude; transient, but conscious of our transiency. We know, moreover—it is ineradicably a part of our nature to know—that so far as we do not live up to our criteria of right, of justice, of apprehension, of beauty, we are failures. Such failures indeed we unescapably are—who can deny it? Yet we know too that so far as, spite of failure in achievement, we do at least indefectibly love the right, love justice, love beauty, strive for keenness of apprehension and of insight, we are not wholly failures. And in this knowledge there is a great hope, incapable in the last analysis of expression, perhaps only to be symbolised darkly, yet a sufficient reward of life.

We speak conveniently of the love of justice and of goodness and the like, yet we should remember that strictly there can be no such thing; for anything into which the emotions truly enter is of necessity personal, individual, and we can love only personal manifestations of justice or of goodness. We can indeed come to see justice itself through and beyond such concrete and partial manifestations of it, but not through any process of mere abstraction has anyone ever come to love justice or goodness or beauty. We are, indeed, here in that sphere of human experience which poetry and religion express in their characteristic ways. These are not the ways of science, yet poetry and the other arts and reli-

CONCLUSION

new error equally deep. For plainly only he who realises that there is a portion of his being which differs from and even opposes itself to his mortal constitution and its surrounding world—only that man has become in the full sense of the word human and has freed his whole nature for the tasks and problems of life.

INDEX

Accident, 59 ff.
Adams, Brooks, 157 ff.
Adams, Henry, 155 ff., 228.
Adams, John Quincy, 157 ff.
Aristippus, 198-200, 201, 216.
Augustine, S., 31.
Aurelius, Marcus, 196.

Bachman, F. P., 132-133.
Bacon, 2, 5, 8, 11, 12, 27, 219.
Balfour, Sir A. J., 102.
Benson, A. C., 208.
Briggs, Le B. R., 138.
Browne, Sir Thomas, 220.
Buckle, H. T., 155, 173.
Burnet, J., 143-144.
Bury, J. B., 1, 59-60, 223.

Capitalism, 64-65, 73.
Carlyle, 219.
Cole, G. D. H., 62 ff., 86, 116.
Coleridge, 209.
Comte, Auguste, 58, 208.
Condillac, 46.
Condorcet, 14.
Conklin, E. G., 51 ff., 87 ff., 119-120, 121.
Co-operation, 15 ff., 24-25, 30, 35 ff.

Darwin, 13, 14, 15, 155, 173, 174, 178, 179-180.
Death, 219 ff.
Democracy, 165.
Descartes, 6-7, 8, 34.
Dewey, John, 100, 121 ff., 143.
Diderot, 11, 13.
Dowden, Edward, 206.

Education, 102 ff.
Elliot, Hugh, 182-184, 186.
Empedocles, 210.
Encyclopædists, The, 11, 46.
Epicureanism, 196-197, 198 ff.
Evolution, 13 ff., 50 ff., 62, 87, 88, 89, 91-92, 155, 173-174, 178, 179-180, 209.

Flexner, Abraham, 132-133, 145-146.
Follett, M. P., 77 ff., 98, 100.
Fourier, 69.

Galsworthy, John, 213-215.
Godwin, William, 69, 113.
Grant, U. S., 160.
Guild Socialism, 64 ff.

Helvétius, 46.

241

INDEX

History, 21 ff., 155, 170 ff.
Hobbes, 27-28, 33.
Horace, 207.
Hudson, J. W., 137-138.
Huxley, 157.

Individuality, 185 ff., 216-217, 232.
Industrial Revolution, 8-11.
Inge, Dean, 1, 75.
Intelligence Tests, 119-120.

Jackson, Andrew, 160, 162.
Johnson, Dr., 41.

Kant, 3, 43, 196-197, 208.
King John, 216.
King Lear, 173.

Lamarck, 13.
Leibnitz, 7, 19.
Libby, W., 4.
Locke, 46.
Lucian, 198.
Lyell, 13, 15, 174.

Marvin, F. S., 3-44.
Marx, Karl, 60-61.
Mérimée, 196, 208.
Mill, J. S., 57-58, 202, 227.
Morgan, Alexander, 103.
Morris, W., 207.

Napoleon, 59-60.
Natural Selection, 174.
Newton, 6, 7.

Owen, Robert, 69, 113.

Pardoner, Chaucer's, 36.

Pater, Walter, 194 ff.
Patriotism, 71, 213.
Perfectibility, Human, 11 ff., 45 ff., 159, 160, 162, 163.
Plutarch, 215.
Poincaré, Henri, 177.
Poincaré, Lucien, 176.
Polakov, W. N., 224.
Prospero, 97.

Rathenau, W., 224.
Religion, 22 ff., 40, 50, 88, 168-169, 203, 204-206, 235.
Renan, 209.
Renouvier, 59.
Rivière, Mercier de la, 48.
Rossetti, D. G., 207.
Rousseau, 46-47.
Royal Society, 6, 7, 221.
Ruskin, 207.
Russell, Bertrand, 74, 76-77.
Russia, 29, 49, 63.

Saint-Pierre, Abbé de, 45-46.
Santayana, George, 136.
Sarton, M. George, 4.
Science, 1 ff., 58, 90, 155, 156, 157, 163, 170 ff., 207 ff., 223, 228 ff.
Scott, J. W., 60-61, 74.
Self-Interest, 40.
Shadwell, C. L., 194.
Spencer, Herbert, 50, 53, 208.
Sympathy, 38 ff.

Tawney, R. H., 74, 86.
Taylor, F. W., 119.
Teggart, F. J., 227.
Todd, A. J., 102, 103, 121.
Tyndall, 157.

INDEX

Vivisection, 38.
Voltaire, 46.

Ward, Humphry, 208.
Ward, Mrs. Humphry, 206.

Washington, George, 158, 159.
Wells, H. G., 3, 53, 90, 103, 104 ff.
Whichcote, Benjamin, 27.
Whitney, Eli, 162.
Wilson, Woodrow, 153.

PRINTED IN THE UNITED STATES OF AMERICA